JOHN COLET AND THE PLATONIC TRADITION

JOHN COLET
and the Platonic Tradition

By LELAND MILES

London
GEORGE ALLEN & UNWIN LTD

PRINTED IN GREAT BRITAIN
BY PHOTOLITHO
BY UNWIN BROTHERS LIMITED
WOKING AND LONDON

For ROY BATTENHOUSE

with affection and admiration

PREFACE

This is the first of a projected series of three volumes examining the relation of the Platonic Tradition to the Oxford Reformers: John Colet, St. Thomas More, and Erasmus. The contemporary fame of the latter two figures might lead the reader to assume that the author regards this volume as the least important of the three. By no means is this the case. John Colet (1466-1519) held the crucial post of Dean of St. Paul's Cathedral in London from 1504 until his death. During this time he was the acknowledged and affectionately respected leader of the Oxford Circle. The youthful More saw in him "the director of my life." And to Colet's welcome to England Erasmus glowingly replied: "I certainly rejoice . . . at being praised by you, the object of all praises. If you, Colet, can love such a man, and deem him worthy of your acquaintance, then set Erasmus down as your own."

PREFACE

If therefore we can crystallize the role of Greek philosophy in Colet, we will have taken an important step in solving certain vexed problems of the English Reformation, particularly the problems of the precise relation of the Oxford group to one another, and to the Protestant revolt. Equally important, such crystallization should provide a more precise knowledge of the way in which Colet (and English humanists in general) served as the channel through which Florentine Platonism became a pervasive force in the works of Sidney, Spenser, Donne, Milton, and other literary figures of the English Renaissance. Hence this volume will I hope prove valuable not only to students of philosophy, theology, and history, but to students of English literature as well.

I

For those who are frankly vague about John Colet, a few biographical facts might be in order. (For further details, consult the still indispensable *Life* (Bell, 1887) by J. H. Lupton.) Colet was the oldest son of a large upper-class family, his father, Sir Henry, having twice been lord mayor of London. In 1483 John went to Oxford, as did the sons of most wealthy knights; and his announcement soon thereafter that he desired to enter the ministry was a then-routine procedure for ambitious young men. According to the contemporary practice of pluralities—which Colet was later to reject—many benefices were conferred on him, even though his studies forbade his performing parish duties. Among these livings were the rectory of St. Mary Dennington in Suffolk and the Prebendary of Botevant at York.

After taking his master's degree (1490), Colet continued his study of mathematics and scholastic philosophy, but also began to devote time to classical literature (especially Ci-

cero) and to an exploration of Plato and Plotinus in Latin
translation. In 1493 he set out on a trip to France and Italy.
Studying briefly at several foreign universities, he picked up
a knowledge of civil and canon law. During the trip he also
became attracted to and began to read in such pre-scholastic
church fathers as Origen and Ambrose. Tradition has it that
Colet met his prototype, the fiery Savonarola, at this time.
After two years abroad, he began his journey home, stopping
off in Paris, where he met the French historian Gaguinus,
through whom he first heard of Erasmus.

By late 1496 Colet was back in England, his head full of
notions for reform gathered from the Greek Fathers, and his
heart afire with that love of personal liberty and free enquiry
that comes to most men who study the writings of early
Greece. It was only a matter of where and when he would
explode. This was determined when he took up residence at
Oxford and delivered voluntary public lectures in Latin on
St. Paul's Epistle to the Romans (1496-7). Audiences grew
larger and increasingly enthusiastic about Colet's new "historical approach" to Scripture, with its quoting of the Florentine Platonists Ficino and Mirandola rather than the old
schoolmen; and his listeners no doubt enjoyed the excitement
aroused by the young preacher's bold condemnation of
Church corruption. The lectures on Romans were followed
by an equally volatile series on First Corinthians. Erasmus
was an enthusiastic auditor, and the two became fast friends.

Then came the great opportunity. In 1504, a scant six or
seven years after his ordination to the priesthood, Colet (now
a doctor of divinity) was appointed Dean of St. Paul's Cathedral by King Henry VII. Undaunted by the prestige of his
position, the new Dean continued to wear a plain black robe,

was starkly frugal in domestic arrangements, and broke with custom by preaching frequently and in English from the cathedral pulpit. One of his most admiring listeners was a promising young lawyer named Thomas More.

About 1507 Colet inherited a vast fortune from his father, and decided to use it for establishing a free grammar school devoted to such humanistic principles as the importance of moral instruction for the young, and the value of classical language and literature. The result was the founding of St. Paul's School for Boys (1509), where 153 lads, picked with no regard for race, class, or geographical origin, were led into the realm of learning by the gentle William Lily, whom Colet picked as first headmaster. Under Lily, St. Paul's became the first school in England to teach Greek regularly as a recognized part of the curriculum.

For his new school Colet drew up rules of conduct, an English version of the Creed and other prayers, and a Latin grammar which became a mainstay of English elementary education for 200 years. In all, the Dean expended the equivalent of $250,000 on the project, including an endowment fund which gave St. Paul's masters and chaplains the highest faculty salaries then paid in England. Moreover, Colet deviated from long tradition by appointing the Mercers Company rather than an ecclesiastical group as the school's governing body. St. Paul's School thus became the first example of non-clerical management in English education.

Modern readers will be enheartened to know that in our Hydrogen Age Colet's School for Boys continues to flourish, though now moved to Hammersmith. Over the ensuing 450 years the student body has leaped to 650, but Colet's original concept of 153 *free* students is still sacredly preserved. The liberal entrance requirements are still in effect: thus the modern St. Paul's admits students of all colors hailing from Europe, Asia, and America as well as from Britain. Classics majors are no longer a monopoly, but they still outnumber the newer history and science majors. The school boasts such distinguished alumni as Pepys, Chesterton, Milton, Marlborough, and Jowett—not to mention such notorious graduates as Judge Jeffries and Major Andre! The most recent alumnus of note is no doubt Field Marshall Montgomery, who used the school as his permanent headquarters throughout World War II. On June 5, 1944, General Dwight Eisenhower, accompanied by Montgomery and King George, strode into the Lecture Theatre at St. Paul's School to give the allied staff their final briefing for the Normandy invasion.

In 1512, three years after the founding of Colet's school, King Henry VIII ordered a convocation of bishops at St. Paul's Cathedral to plan "the extirpation of the Lollard heresy." Archbishop Warham appointed Colet to deliver what we would today call the keynote address. The assembled bishops, fully expecting to hear a violent tirade against heretics, were thrown into consternation when they heard instead a wrathful condemnation of their own wickedness. Senile Fitz-James, Bishop of London, accused Colet of heresy. Warham had no sooner dismissed these charges than Colet was embroiled in a new controversy: he openly denounced the war-policy of Henry VIII, a monarch who was not accustomed to being contradicted. Henry gruffly sent for the Dean, but when they met face to face, Colet's dazzling personality won the day. The two discussed the possibilities of justifying war, and while they came to no agreement, they parted on the best of terms. The king is even reputed to have bellowed: "Let every man have his own doctor . . . ; but this is the doctor for me!" At any rate, Henry was impressed enough to make Colet a royal chaplain.

At Westminster Abbey in 1515 Colet performed his last notable public function: a sermon for Wolsey's installation as cardinal. With characteristic vigor, he warned the prelate against worldly ambition—a warning which, had it been heeded, might have changed the course of the English Reformation. When we reflect on such examples of Colet's astonishing honesty and courage, we can better appreciate More's anguish when told of Colet's death in 1519: "For generations," exclaimed Sir Thomas, "we have not had among us any one man more learned or holy."

Here then was a great non-conformist, a man who refused to be cowed by formidable opposition, a man who insisted on principle regardless of the consequences to himself. He might not have been the most systematic thinker in English intellectual history; but in his writings, his school, and his reform activities, he made contributions which are still discernible and operative in English literature, philosophy, and education—not to mention the English Church. In gratitude for such services, we might well emulate the stone children who still stand beside a black-carved Colet on the green campus of St. Paul's School, gazing up at the staunch old Dean with perpetual admiration and affection.

II

Any study of the relation of John Colet to pagan thought faces a difficult semantic problem, because there are at least three interrelated philosophies comprising what in this book is called the Platonic Tradition. These are (1) the initial Platonism of the *Dialogues,* itself involving alterations from

Plato's earlier to his later thought; (2) the emanationist
Neoplatonism of such figures as Plotinus (205-270) and the
pseudo-Dionysius (c. 490-550)—a largely unconscious dis-
tortion of Plato (especially of the *Timaeus* and certain portions of the *Republic*) resulting from a misunderstanding and
in some instances from the unavailability of Platonic manuscripts; and (3) the Florentine Platonism espoused by such
15th century Italians as Marsilio Ficino and Pico della
Mirandola.

This last named philosophy was largely Neoplatonic; but
there was also a substantial undercurrent of original Platonism resulting from Ficino's rediscovery and translation of
the *Dialogues*. In addition, Florentine Platonism, unlike its
antecedent types, was frankly beholden to Aristotle, Augustine, Aquinas, Arabic philosophy, and the Cabala—as well as
being extraordinarily preoccupied with theories of love and
beauty, analogies between romantic and divine love, specula-
tions on the role of love in the mystical ascent to God, and
other notions inspired ultimately by Plato's *Symposium*. All
of this was in turn combined, in Ficino and Mirandola, with
the new Renaissance emphasis on the dignity of man.

The distinction between Platonism and Neoplatonism was
not recognized until the 19th century (see the *Oxford English Dictionary*, 6:90) ; and the distinction between these two
and Florentine Platonism is of even more recent origin. From
Augustine through the Renaissance and beyond, figures like
Plotinus, Dionysius, and the Florentines were successively
but erroneously regarded as accurate interpreters of Plato.
Thus Augustine referred to Plotinus and his school as
"Platonists." Ficino followed suit by exalting Dionysius as

"the supreme Platonist," and further declared in his *Enneads* translation that Plotinus should be read as Plato speaking in the person of his pupil—indeed, as if Plato should say, "This is my beloved son, hear ye him" (W. Dress, *Die Mystik des M. Ficino,* p. 5). Similarly, Colet hailed Ficino as "the Platonist Marsilio," despite the fact that the Florentine's *Theologia Platonica* is so far removed from original Platonism that it goes wholly unmentioned in Professor Solmsen's authoritative work on the theology of the *Dialogues!*

In this book the term Platonism and its cognates are generally used in their narrowest sense, in contradistinction to Neoplatonism. These will in turn sometimes be differentiated from Florentine Platonism, though obviously Platonic and Neoplatonic elements in Ficino and Mirandola will be so labeled. "Platonism" and related terms will always appear in quotes when used in the older loose or broad sense, to mean Neoplatonism (or Florentine Platonism), or to mean these plus the *Dialogues* collectively. The outstanding and unavoidable example here is of course quotations from medieval or Renaissance writers.

Such distinctions can of course be overemphasized. Indeed, Chapters 2 through 6 of this book will document extensively Professor Kristeller's observation, in *The Classics and Renaissance Thought,* pages 48-49, that "there has been a tendency to exaggerate the differences between Plato and later Platonists, and to overlook certain genuine features in Plato's thought that ... served as a starting point for his earlier interpreters." Yet the procedure of radical analysis demands that where possible and reasonable we should seek to assign, with some degree of precision, the basic responsibility for those of Colet's ideas which can be traced to such various works as Plato's *Phaedrus*, Plotinus's *Enneads*, and Ficino's *De Amore*.

III

It is impossible to pay ample tribute to all who have helped in the preparation of this book. Chief among these has been Professor Roy Battenhouse of Indiana University, who made invaluable bibliographical suggestions, supplied strategic books and other material, and frequently conferred with the author in person and through correspondence on research problems. The dedication of this book is scarcely sufficient repayment for such painstaking aid. Gratitude must also be acknowledged to Professor Sears Jayne of the University of Virginia, for so generously sharing the secrets of his soon-to-be published manuscript, *John Colet and Marsilio Ficino* (Oxford: Clarendon Press, ca. 1961), in which he reveals the significance of his newly discovered Colet-Ficino correspondence and marginalia.

Professor Jayne's discoveries, by the way, symbolize a modern Colet revival which began perhaps with the British scholar E. W. Hunt's *Dean Colet and His Theology* in 1956. A more recent example of this reawakened interest in Colet is the research of P. Bernard O'Kelly at Ohio State University. Professor O'Kelly has just completed *John Colet's Enarratio in Primam S. Pauli Epistolam ad Corinthios: A New Edition of the Text, with Translation, Notes, and Introduction* (Harvard Ph. D. Thesis, June 1960). Because of its importance this work has been included in the bibliography, though it was regrettably not available for the preparation of the present volume.

Among others to whom appreciation must be expressed are Mr. Walter Mann, Assistant Librarian of Hanover Col-

lege, who durin₅ the past ten years has diligently secured
some 150 titles, including 60 books, through Inter-Library
Loan. I am also indebted to Professor Brand Blanshard of
the Yale philosophy faculty, for so generously bringing this
volume to the attention of the Open Court Company; to Dr.
R. L. James, now headmaster of Harrow, who in 1953 (as
headmaster of St. Paul's) provided me with many intimate
details concerning Colet's School for Boys; to my wife Virginia, who typed portions of the final draft; to Hardin Craig
of the University of Missouri, who first set me to work on
the Oxford Reformers; to The Rev. John Gordon Rowe, for
permission to use his unpublished translation of Colet's
Treatise on the Sacraments; and to Father Raymond Boehm
and Father Edwin Cuffe (Ph. D., Benedictine Order), who
helped me better to understand certain nuances of Catholic
theology. I especially appreciate the care and diligence with
which Dr. Eugene Freeman, Editor-in-chief of the Open
Court Publishing Company, has aided me in preparing the
final manuscript for the printers.

Certain groups have also aided in the writing of this book.
The Hanover College Research Committee made two grants,
one for study in England during a 1955 sabbatical leave.
The Danforth Foundation provided a scholarship for study
at Union Theological Seminary during the summer of 1956.
Finally, a 1959 Lilly Fellowship awarded by the Indiana
University School of Letters provided the proper free time,
office space, and atmosphere in which the manuscript could
be completed.

IV

This book moves into largely unexplored territory. So far
as any study of the Platonic Tradition in Colet is concerned,

there are only the scattered remarks in Seebohm's *Oxford Reformers* (1887) and in Lupton's introductions to his invaluable translations of Colet's works; two doubtful pages in W. R. Inge's *Platonic Tradition in English Religious Thought* (1925); and three German works: Friedrich Dannenberg's *Das Erbe Platons in England* (1932); Kurt Schröder's "Platonismus in der Englischen Renaissance," *Palaestra* 83 (1920); and Ernest Cassirer's *Die Platonische Renaissance in England* (1932), recently translated by James Pettegrove (1953). These works are valuable but limited. For example, Schröder devotes only 13 of 153 pages to Colet, and even these are confined to Neoplatonic influences on Colet's *Letters to Radulphus* and *Lectures on Corinthians*. Cassirer makes further observations on Colet's relation to Origen and Augustine, and his treatment of grace and love. A fourth German work, Lina Beger's "Thomas Morus und Plato," *Zeitschrift f.d. gesamten Staatswissenschaften,* 35 (1879), gives passing attention to Colet. But as its title indicates, Dr. Beger's study deals primarily with our second "Fisher with Platonic Nets."

The most significant modern study of Colet's relation to pagan philosophy is undoubtedly Sears Jayne's as yet unpublished *John Colet and Marsilio Ficino.* However, this work is necessarily limited to a consideration of personal and philosophical relations between the two men, and to such textual matters as the order of composition of Colet's works. There have been a few 20th century articles on Colet, notably by Hyma, Rice, and Duhamel; but these have almost always been from the standpoint of Colet's much debated relation to humanism and scholasticism, rather than specifically to the Platonic Tradition. Apparently the only concentrated attempt to face head-on the problem of Greek thought in

Colet has been the author's own preliminary "Protestant Colet and Catholic More: A Study of Contrast in the Use of Platonism," *Anglican Theological Review,* 33 (Jan. 51), 29-42. However, the findings of this article have been modified in the light of more intensive research, particularly in this volume's final chapter, "Dean Colet and Protestant Heresy."

The net effect of the scholarship just reviewed has been, to say the least, scattered and frequently contradictory. Hence this volume seeks to coordinate for the first time all pertinent past and present scholarship on Colet, regardless of national origin. To this end certain research materials have been included which, as the bibliography and this Preface indicate, have not yet been published. Even more important, I have sought to bring to bear on Colet's treatises every major work of the Platonic Tradition, from the *Dialogues* themselves to the *Cloud of Unknowing* to Mirandola's *Oration on Man.* This has necessitated a careful background study of what might seem to the reader a disproportionate number of primary sources.

However, as Professor Kristeller has emphasized in his "Studies of the Philosophies of the Renaissance," *JHI,* 2 (Oct. 41), 449-496, "without an understanding of the historical context within which the problems of any individual thinker have been generated, . . . investigation of any document in a purely doxographical sense, that is, the purely descriptive resume of what it states, is quite blind and without significance." To this might be added my own observation in "Review of Ernest William Hunt's *Dean Colet and His Theology* (1956)," *Renaissance News,* 11 (Summer 58), 133-138: "It is doubtful if any theology can or should be considered in a vacuum, especially the theology of a man who stood at a point in history where new and old ideas interflowed."

These attitudes have at any rate been the guiding ideals in the assembling of this book. It must be left to others to decide how successfully such ideals have been followed.

L. M.

The University of Cincinnati
January 15, 1961

CONTENTS

JOHN COLET AND THE PLATONIC TRADITION

"With Platonic nets ... do you ever

fish for the highest intellects for Christ."

—*Ficino to*

Pico della Mirandola

CHAPTER I PAGAN PHILOSOPHY AND
CHRISTIAN DOCTRINE:
TWO HISTORICAL APPROACHES

I. THE CLEMENTINE APPROACH

The active alliance between Christianity and pagan philosophy was initiated many centuries before the Renaissance
revival of Greek and Roman literature. To Tertullian, who
had argued that philosophy breeds heresy and should therefore be banished from the Church, Clement of Alexandria
(150-213) vigorously replied: "Philosophy is not a goblin
who wants to run away with us, as the vulgar think."[1] To be
sure, Clement did not accept the wholesale validity of pagan
doctrine. But in his *Protrepticus* he especially cited Plato as

---

[1] *Stromata* 6:10, quoted in *ERE*, 1:314. The footnote and bibliography
forms in this book follow the author's own research text, *Guide to Writing
Term Papers* (Second Revised Edition; Dubuque: Wm. C. Brown Co., 1959).

a "Greek prophet" who, together with the Hebrew prophets, had commendably foreshadowed the Christian faith. He argued, for example, that the Ideas in Plato's *Phaedrus* are "God's thought, which... [Christians] call the Word of God."[2] Clement's conclusion was therefore that philosophy, especially Platonism, is a useful tool, provided Christians keep it in its proper place.[3]

The Alexandrine regarded pagan philosophy as particularly useful in two ways: first, as an aid in inquiring into the meaning of Christian doctrine after accepting it; second, as a help in leading philosophically inclined men to Christ. It was with this latter aim in mind that he jokingly referred to his Platonically tinged *Miscellanies* as "fish bait to catch philosophers."[4]

Clement's "Handmaid" Position

By no means was Clement the first to attempt a fusion of pagan and Christian thought. Both Justin Martyr and Maximus of Tyre had gone far in reaping the spoils of Platonic idealism for Christianity.[5] But Clement was the first to advocate the Pagan-Christian approach openly and boldly, and the first to crystallize the proper nature of that approach for later generations. As Gilson observes, "the importance of

---

[2] *Miscellanies* 5:3:16, as quoted in Paul E. More, *Religion of Plato*, p. 317. For an analysis of Clement's theology, see Charles Bigg, *Neoplatonism*, pp. 159-179.

[3] Etienne Gilson, *History of Christian Philosophy in the Middle Ages*, pp. 32-33.

[4] *Miscellanies* 7:18, as quoted in Gilson, p. 35.

[5] Like Plato, Maximus described prayer as "intercourse and conversation with the gods" rather than a selfish asking "for things not present (cf. 2 *Alcibiades* 149), and stressed imitation as the way to virtue in language almost identical to *Laws* 4:717 and 10:904, 906. See Maximus, *Philosophoumena* 35, as quoted in More, p. 38.

Clement does not lie in the few philosophical ideas which can be found scattered throughout his works, but rather in his deep and remarkably successful elucidation of the relation of philosophy to Christian faith."[6] It is with Clement, then, more than with any other figure, that we can date the birth of the theory that philosophy is the "handmaid" of religion.

The purpose of this introductory chapter is to indicate how this Clementine approach was developed by Augustine and Aquinas, rejected in favor of a new "Florentine approach" by Ficino and Mirandola, and finally revived by John Colet, leader of that Oxford circle of Christian humanists which included St. Thomas More and Erasmus.

Plotinus and St. Augustine

Clement's view that Greek teaching can lead rationally-minded men to Christ was vindicated a century later in the life story of St. Augustine (354-430). The chief barrier hindering Augustine's conversion to Christianity was his inability to conceive of God in non-corporeal terms; and he tells us that he found this difficulty resolved when he read "certain books of the Platonists"—notably Cicero's *Hortensius* and Plotinus's *Enneads* —"which Victorinus...had translated into Latin."[7] From such "Platonists"— or, as we call them today, Neoplatonists—he learned that God is "above everybody, being incorporeal" (*City of God* 8:10).

It is only natural that Augustine, out of sheer gratitude, should have considered his introduction to Plotinian thought an act of God (*Conf.* 7:9). It is equally natural that he

---

[6] Gilson, p. 35.

[7] Augustine, *Confessions* 8:2, in *Basic Writings of Saint Augustine*, ed. Whitney J. Oates, 1:111, cf. 107. See also Roy Battenhouse (ed.), *Companion to the Study of St. Augustine*, pp. 29, 158; and Raymond Klibansky, *The Continuity of the Platonic Tradition during the Middle Ages*, p. 22.

should at first have taken the position that "the Platonists with the change of a very few words and opinions would become Christians."[8] Yet his final position as set forth in the *Retractions* was that the Plotinian system must defend itself against "gross errors."[9] Even so early as the *City of God,* in fact, we find him pinpointing at least five specific heresies which Plotinus had inherited from the *Dialogues:* transmigration; mediating daemons and lesser gods; the notion of inferior gods as creators of men's bodies; the insistence on immortality of soul alone rather than resurrection; and especially the failure to teach "the Incarnation of the unchangeable Son of God, whereby we are saved, and are enabled to reach the things we believe."[10]

On the basis of such errors, Augustine was forced to conclude that Plato cannot be compared in excellence with "the truth-speaking prophets, nor to any of the apostles or martyrs of Christ, nay, not to any faithful Christian man" (*City of God* 2:14). On the other hand, he continued to maintain that the Neoplatonists "certainly" have much to "offer" (*City of God* 8:5). Among philosophers, "none come nearer to us than the Platonists." Their "gold and silver was dug out of the mines of God's providence." Such truths as they possess the Christian should therefore take away and "devote to their proper use in the preaching of the Gospel."[11] This is of course a classic statement of the Clementine approach.

---

[8] *True Religion* 7, as quoted in Cuthbert Butler, *Western Mysticism: The Teaching of Saints Augustine, Gregory, and Bernard,* p. 57.

[9] *Companion to Augustine,* p. 97.

[10] *City of God* 10:29, 12:26, See *Companion,* pp. 265-6, 292, 304-5, 340.

[11] *Christian Doctrine* 2:40:60, as quoted in *Companion,* p. 291. Cf. *City of God* 8:4, 8:9, and Klibansky, p. 23. For a more detailed treatment of the subject, consult Leland Miles, "Plotinus and St. Augustine: The Beginnings of Neoplatonic Christianity," *Hanover Forum,* 4 (Spring 58), 67-95.

Plato versus Aristotle in Aquinas

Of this approach to pagan philosophy and Christian doctrine, Thomas Aquinas (1225-1274) later remarked: "Whenever Augustine, who was imbued with the doctrines of the Platonists, found in their teaching anything consistent with the faith, he adopted it; and those things he found contrary he amended" (*Summa Theologia* 1:84:5). In point of fact, this is perhaps a more accurate statement of Aquinas's own approach than of Augustine's: The latter tended to reject outright "those things he found contrary," whereas it was St. Thomas who was the supreme "amender" of Greek thought.[12]

In common with most medieval thinkers, Aquinas was anxious to cite authorities, not least of whom was Plato. Despite his devotion to Aristotle and his frequent scolding of Aristotle's master, Aquinas respected Plato as that "most eager seeker after truth" who had rescued the world from materialistic philosophers.[13] He therefore frequently claimed Plato's support, while at the same time redefining or reinterpreting the *Dialogues* to bring them into accord with Christian orthodoxy or with his own Aristotelian system. For example, he accepted Plato's Idea of the Good, but identified it with God and denied its superiority over being. Similarly, he retained the notion of subordinate Ideas, but redefined their nature to suit his own ends. The Platonic concept of Ideas of species he labeled a patent absurdity. Nor could he accept Plato's position that Ideas are necessary to explain sensible things. In this connection he quoted approvingly the numer-

---

12 Aquinas's knowledge of Plato came indirectly through such media as Aristotle's citations of Plato's arguments. He apparently had no knowledge of the three original dialogues—the *Meno, Phaedo,* and *Timaeus*—available to him in manuscript. See R. J. Henle, *Saint Thomas and Platonism*, pp. xix-xxi.

13 Henle, pp. 313-315.

ous Aristotelian attacks on Plato, including the one that, as principles of immobility, Ideas can hardly explain the mutation of sense-phenomena. Yet, despite such objections, Aquinas accepted the Ideas as existing in God's mind, declaring that they are what God knows distinctly—a view similar to Clement's notion that the Ideas are God's thought.[14]

In Aquinas, then, the principle of adaptation is emphasized: the admitted and frequent errors of philosophy need not necessarily be rejected: they may where feasible be modified and altered, so as to make them more compatible with Christian doctrine.

II. THE FLORENTINE APPROACH

The continuity of the Clementine approach was maintained by several figures in the late 14th century mystical movement known as the Devotio Moderna. Especially notable was John Wessel Gansfort (1420-1489), who in his works frequently quoted from Plato, Aquinas, and Augustine. After his death one of his admirers wrote that "Wessel greatly admired the teaching of Plato as being more divine and nearer to Christianity" than Aristotle.[15] The desire of Gansfort to use philosophy in the service of Christian theology prompted him to master the chief elements of Greek at a time when no instruction in the language was given in North Europe. He even visited the Academy of the Florentine Platonists, but found it less attractive than "the simple men of Zwolle."[16]

It is altogether possible that Gansfort was unhappy at Florence because he found there a radically different approach to Greek thought than the Clementine approach that the

---

14 *Ibid.*, pp. 409, 412-417, 356, 359-60.

15 See Albert Hyma, *The Christian Renaissance: A History of the Devotio Moderna*, pp. 207-8.

16 *Ibid.*, pp. 200, 206.

Dutch Brother had imbibed from St. Augustine. To be sure, Ficino was in wholehearted agreement with Clement that pagan philosophy should be assigned the task of furthering orthodox religion and of bringing men back to the Christian faith.[17] By pagan philosophy Ficino meant especially the *Dialogues* plus the philosophy of such Neoplatonists as Plotinus and Dionysius, whom the Florentines regarded as accurate interpreters of Plato.

As we have noted in the Preface (q.v.), Ficino indiscriminately lumped all of these under the single heading "Platonism"—a usage equivalent in this book to "the Platonic Tradition." In his preface to the *Theologia Platonica* Marsilio accordingly stated: "I believe ... that the divine Providence has decided that the perverse minds of many persons who do not easily yield to the authority of divine law alone, should be at least satisfied by Platonic arguments that are brought to the aid of religion." And in the preface to his translation of Plotinus: "We must not think the acute and philosophical minds of men can ever be gradually allured and led toward perfect religion except by a philosophical lure."[18] In a letter to Pico della Mirandola, Ficino approvingly remarked, in a manner reminiscent of Clement: "With Platonic nets, so to speak, do you ever fish for the highest intellects for Christ."[19]

Ficino's "Sisterhood" Position

However, unlike Clement, Ficino did not hold that philosophy is inferior to Christianity, and as such must be carefully

---

[17] See Paul O. Kristeller, *The Philosophy of Marsilio Ficino*, p. 24 ff.

[18] *Ibid.*, p. 322.

[19] Quoted in Joseph Lupton (trans.), *Two Treatises on the Hierarchies of Dionysius by John Colet* (hereafter "*Hier.*"), p. xxv. Page references to Colet's *Ecclesiastical Hierarchy* or to his *Celestial Hierarchy* are from Lupton's *Hierarchies* volume.

scrutinized for doctrinal error. For Ficino Greek teaching was not a "handmaid." Rather did he argue that "Philosophy and Religion are Sisters."[20] Indeed, he even went so far as to claim that the two are identical: "If philosophy is defined by all as the love and study of truth and wisdom, and if truth and wisdom itself is God alone, consequently legitimate philosophy is nothing else than true religion, and legitimate religion is nothing else than true philosophy."[21] With very few exceptions, Ficino therefore assumed that any apparent differences between Greek and Christian doctrine are merely the result of conflicting terminology or misinterpretation; neither can disagree on any crucial matter.[22] It was this assumption which drove Ficino to the task of harmonizing and reconciling the Platonic Tradition with Christian thought. Like Abelard before him, the Florentine "sweat[ed] dreadfully ... to make Plato a Christian."[23] The sweat was manifested in two tracts showing the supposed agreement between the Mosaic and Plotinian accounts of creation, and the Socratic and Christian ethical outlook.[24]

With Clement and Augustine, Ficino held that Socrates and Plato had been "religious philosophers" who, like the Old Testament prophets, were precursors of Christianity. But Ficino went far beyond either of the earlier two thinkers in eulogizing the pagan system. From the perspective of Flor-

---

20 *Opera Omnia*, p. 853, as quoted in Kristeller, p. 322.

21 *Op. Om.*, p. 668, in Kristeller, p. 322.

22 Ficino did concede that Plato erred in not admitting creation out of nothing. Having identified Christ with the Plotinian Mind, he also refused to follow Plotinus's position that Mind is an entity separate from and inferior to the One, and insisted that on this issue the Christian truth "stands." Such anti-pagan rebukes are however extremely rare in Ficino's writings. See Paul Shorey, *Plato: Ancient and Modern*, p. 122, and Kristeller, pp. 168-9.

23 St. Bernard, *Epistles* 19:4, as quoted in Shorey, p. 85.

24 Kristeller, p. 24 ff.

entine hero-worship, the Greek philosopher became the "divine Plato," a Saint and virtually a Messiah. Ficino kept a lamp burning in his study before the image of Plato, and revived the Symposium banquets to honor the yearly anniversaries of the philosopher's birth—much, indeed, as Christians annually celebrate the birth of Christ.[25] The *Dialogues* became a reflection of the Bible, to be read and taught in church services. For, maintained Marsilio, "whoever . . . accurately reads Plato's works will learn everything"![26] This statement was especially applied to the *Parmenides*, Ficino holding that in this dialogue Plato had presented the whole of Christian theology, and that one should prepare himself to study it through fasting.[27]

For his view of the sisterhood of Christianity and pagan philosophy, Ficino claimed Augustine as model and guide.[28]

---

[25] Lupton, *Hier.*, pp. xxi, xxxii.

[26] See *Op. om.*, pp. 493, 806, 855, and 78 in Kristeller, pp. 22, 27-8, 25, and 204.

[27] See Maximillan Beck, "Plato's Problem in *Parmenides*," *Journal of the History of Ideas* (hereafter *JHI*), 7:232, n.1. Lupton, *Hier.* p. xx, having attributed such extravagance to the natural Renaissance enthusiasm at "entering an unexplored country," raises the question (p. xxv ff.) as to whether Ficino and Mirandola might have become more Christian in later life, and repented their earlier pagan excesses. The biographer Corsius records an alleged shift in Ficino from "paganism" to a "Christian outlook" about 1475, the approximate date of Ficino's becoming a priest. There does seem to be an increasing emphasis on man's need for grace in the later works of both Florentines. See for example Kristeller, pp. 245, 297; Lupton, *Hier.*, p. xxvii; and Avery Dulles, *Princeps Concordia: Pico della Mirandola and the Scholastic Tradition*, p. 150. But even in Ficino's *De Christiana Religione* (1476) written about the time of his supposed new outlook, there is an exceedingly liberal view toward other systems (*infra.*, p. 14). Moreover, even in Pico's radically humanistic early work, the *Oration on Man*, the importance of grace is recognized in a concluding prayer (Dulles, pp. 162-3). It seems doubtful that a strong case can be made for the thesis that Pico and Ficino substantially reduced their use of philosophy in their later careers.

[28] Karl Dannenfeldt, "The Rennaissance and the Pre-Classical Civilizations," *JHI* 13 (Oct 52), 438.

C

"For a long time," he says, "I have believed in the authority of Augustine . . . and decided to produce an image of Plato most similar to the Christian truth."[29] He speaks of Augustine as the "man of divine genius, who gave the truest expression to the sublimity of Plato"; and on the affinity of Plato and his later interpreters with Christian doctrine, Marsilio quotes Augustine repeatedly.[30] The paradox of this is of course that Augustine, though initially sharing Ficino's "sisterhood" view, gradually came to the quite different position that philosophy is at best a handmaid of theology. Far from holding, with Ficino, the notion of a "divine Plato," Augustine came finally to assert flatly that Plato was "neither a god nor a demigod; we would not even compare him to any of God's holy angels."[31]

Heretical Tendencies in Ficino

Ficino's un-Augustinian assumption that philosophy and Christianity always agree on essential points, and his efforts to prove this through the process of "reconciliation" and "harmonizing," sometimes resulted in a perversion of pagan thought. An excellent illustration of this is Ficino's Christianizing of Platonic transmigration. We are told that this Platonic doctrine was not intended literally; by it we must understand the different habits and functions of human life.[32] In another context, Ficino seeks to interpret Platonic transmigration as an allegorical presentation of hell, where the suffering soul has terrible dreams of beasts, as well as gen-

---

29 Paul Kristeller, "Augustine and the Early Renaissance," *Review of Religion,* 7 (1944), 354. Cf. *Philosophy of Ficino,* p. 13.

30 Klibansky, p. 42, and Kristeller, *Ficino,* p. 24 ff.

31 Marcus Dods (ed.), *The City of God by Saint Augustine,* 1:65.

32 Kristeller, *Ficino,* pp. 117-8.

erating a gaseous body which assumes the shapes of different animals.[33]

Much more often, however, Ficino's harmonizing led him into a perversion not of pagan philosophy but rather of Christian dogma—into, indeed, some of the very "errors" denounced by his supposed model, Augustine. One such error, as Lewis notes, is the readmission of "all those 'middle spirits ... betwixt th'Angelical and Human kinde' which St. Augustine is laboring to expel all through the eighth and ninth books of De Civitate Dei."[34]

Closely allied to this heresy is the notion that the angels and daemons participate in the creation of human souls. De Amore tells us that God passes down the "gifts" or parts of souls to angels, who then "hand them on to men."[35] The gifts are nicety of observation, ability to govern, conviction, clarity of sense perception, ardor of love, keenness of insight, and fecundity of observation. This notion seems obviously inspired by Timaeus 69-70, where Plato's lesser gods "received ... the immortal principle [reason] of the soul; and around this they proceeded to fashion a mortal body, ... and constructed within the body a soul of another nature which was mortal, subject to ... pleasure [and] anger."[36] By way of second thought, Ficino notes:

---

[33] Ibid., pp. 360-362.

[34] C. S. Lewis, English Literature in the Sixteenth Century, p. 11. Plato advances the notion of daemons in Symposium 202-3; Phaedo 107, 113; Republic 616; Phaedrus 240; Statesman 271, Timaeus 90 and elsewhere. See Shorey, What Plato Said, pp. 546-7. "Now you shall learn from the ... Symposium, ... Phaedrus, ... and Laws," says Ficino in De Amore, "how the daemons inhabit the middle ground between heaven and earth." Sears Jayne (ed.), Ficino's Commentary of Plato's Symposium, p. 184. Written in 1469, Ficino's commentary was sometimes entitled Liber de Amore. See Kristeller, Ficino, p. 17.

[35] Commentary on Plato's Symposium, p. 185.

[36] Cf. Timaeus 42, where God "committed to the younger gods the fash-

Doubtless, God infuses these gifts into the souls as soon as they are born from him, the soul [then] slipping down out of the milky way through Cancer into a body . . . . Hence it happens that the souls of the planets [here identified with Christian angels] . . . strengthen in our souls . . . these seven gifts which were given us in the beginning by God.[37]

It is questionable whether this qualification successfully excludes other agents as participants in the soul's creation; even if it does, the qualification has led Ficino into still another heresy, the Platonic notion of pre-existence (see *Phaedo* 73).

Heresy in Pico della Mirandola

Unfortunately, the frequent dependence of Pico della Mirandola (1463-1494) on Ficino, his older friend and master, led Pico into many of the latter's own heresies.[38] Notable among these were three heterodoxies originating in Plato's *Dialogues,* namely: the pre-existence of souls; mediating daemons (which Pico designated as the lowest order of angels) ; and plant-animal as well as star-planet souls: "God, . . . (as Plato in his *Timaeus* says) soweth and scattereth Souls, some in the Moon, others in other Planets and Stars."[39] Another possible

---

ioning of . . . mortal bodies, and desired them to furnish what was still lacking to the human soul." *Dialogues* documentation is from Benjamin Jowett (trans.), *The Dialogues of Plato* (1937), 2 vols.

[37] *Com. on Symp.,* pp. 185-6.

[38] Ficino referred to Mirandola as "in age a son, in intimacy a brother, and in affection a second self"—Lupton, *Hier.,* p. xxiv.

[39] See Edmund Gardner (ed.), T. Stanley's trans. of *A Platonic Discourse Upon Love by Pico della Mirandola,* p. 64 and *passim.* Cf. Ficino's assigning of souls to "beasts": *Op. om.,* pp. 337, 373, in Kristeller, *Ficino,* pp. 101, 109. Plato assigns souls to "trees and plants" and to animals in *Timaeus* 77 and 91, respectively. Pico's reference to star-planet souls involves an apparent misunderstanding of *Timaeus* 41, where God sows the seed of reason in pre-existent human souls, and thereafter assigns them temporarily to star-chariots so that they might perceive the created universe before birth. However, "fixed stars" are called living "animals" in *Timaeus* 40. Souls are

heresy is Mirandola's placing between the intelligible and sensible worlds "a creature of nature as perfect as possible for a creature to be," whom God creates and who "by Plato and likewise by ancient philosophers ... is called now the Son of God, now Mind, now Wisdom, and now Divine Reason."[40]

This entity, as Rigg observes, is a "fusion and confusion" of Plato's Demiurge, Plotinus's Mind, and Philo's Son of God. Pico insists that this "Son of God" is not to be confused with the uncreated Christ, but rather may be regarded as "the first and most noble angel created by God."[41] Gardner accepts this assertion at face value, but Rigg poses the possibility that Pico had really "dethroned" Christ and was "too timid to avow the fact."[42]

As authority for this indiscriminate fusion of pagan and Christian doctrine, Mirandola, like Ficino, erroneously pointed to Augustine: "Plato['s] principles are so closely related to the Christian faith that our Augustine gives immeasurable thanks to God that the books of the Platonists have come into his hands (*Conf.* 8:2)."[43] It is possible, however, that the chief inspiration for Pico's approach was Nicholas of Cusa (1401-1464), who believed in a divinely inspired

---

explicitly assigned to the sun in *Laws* 10: 899 and to "stars" in *Laws* 12: 967. "Stars" often refers in Plato, as in *Timaeus* 38, to planets as well as stars proper. Also, *Laws* 10: 896 states that World-Soul "orders and inhabits all things moving," and the planets move harmoniously (*Statesman* 269).

40 J. M. Rigg, "Introduction," Thomas More's trans. of *Giovannia Pico della Mirandola: His Life By His Nephew Giovanni Francesco Pico*, p. xxv.

41 *Ibid.*

42 See Gardner, Pico's *Discourse on Love*, p. xxi; and Rigg, p. xxv.

43 Elizabeth Forbes (trans.), Pico della Mirandola's "The Dignity of Man," in *The Renaissance Philosophy of Man*, ed. Ernest Cassirer and others, p. 252.

tradition of wisdom originating with the Hebrew Cabalists and Egyptians and extending through Plato, the Neoplatonists, and scholastic thinkers to his own time. Cusa held that "since there is but one God, there can be but one religion beneath a diversity of rites." He therefore argued that the commandments to love God and one's neighbor lie at the base of every noble system of thought.[44] This notion of a core of "evangelical philosophy" extending through all ages was inherited by both Ficino and Mirandola. In a letter of 1489 Marsilio outlined his philosophical descent as beginning with Dionysius, continuing with Boethius and Scotus among others, and concluding with Cusa. Pico himself was sufficiently enthusiastic about Nicholas that he wanted to visit Cusa's German library, famous for its numerous medieval Latin versions of Platonic and Neoplatonic writings. It is even possible that Mirandola visited Cusa in March, 1488.[45]

Florentine Harmonizing Schemes

The tolerant spirit of Cusa is evident in the Florentine identification of philosophy and religion, and is manifest in Ficino's *De Christiana Religione* 14, where "diversity in the manner of worship" is declared to be "decreed by God" and to produce "a marvelous charm throughout His universe."[46] But in Ficino this spirit confined itself very largely to an attempt to reconcile Platonism and Neoplatonism with Christianity—this no doubt as the result of (a) his translations of the *Dialogues* and the *Enneads;* and (b) his ordination to the

---

[44] Dulles, pp. 6-8.

[45] Klibansky, pp. 31, 35-36. For a detailed treatment of this point, consult Ernest Cassirer, "The Platonic Academy in Florence," in *The Platonic Renaissance in England,* trans. James Pettegrove, pp. 8-24.

[46] Cassirer, *Platonic Renaissance,* p. 15. For Pico's identification of religion and philosophy, see Dulles, pp. 154, 160.

priesthood around 1475. Mirandola, on the other hand, had far more grandiose schemes. It was his intention not only to harmonize the Platonic Tradition with Christianity, but both of these with all other religio-philosophical systems! The treatise *On Being and Unity,* for example, had as its goal the reconciliation of Plato and Aristotle.[47] Such a mammoth project of reconciliation inevitably produced what Rigg has with some justification excoriated as "the wildest possible jumble of incompatible ideas." Even more significant, it produced an official charge of heresy which clouded Pico's final years.[48]

It has been said that "no exercise of ingenuity would ever succeed in harmonizing [Pico's] theology with the Catholic or any other form of Christian faith."[49] To this C. S. Lewis has added the contention that, "though the Florentine Platonists were wholly pious in intention, their work deserves the epithet pagan more than any other movement of that age."[50] If this is too harsh a verdict, we must nonetheless concede that the trend of the Florentines "is always away from the center of Christianity."[51] It is significant to note that historically this has almost always been the case with those who assume an essential agreement between, and the equal stature

---

[47] Victor Hamm (trans.), Pico della Mirandola's *Of Being and Unity,* pp. 13, 16. Note also Cassirer, "Giovanni Pico della Mirandola," *JHI,* 3 (Apr. 42), 126-7; and Pico's letter to Mantuanus (Lupton, *Hier.,* p. xxiii): "I am busily occupied with the reconciliation of Plato and Aristotle."

[48] In 1486 Pico published 900 theses, inviting all scholars interested to a public disputation. Pope Innocent VIII suspended the projected meeting, however, and appointed a commission to examine the theses. When 13 were branded heretical, Pico counterattacked in an *Apologia.* See Kristeller's Introduction to the Forbes trans. of "Dignity of Man," in *Renaissance Philosophy of Man,* p. 217.

[49] Rigg, p. xxvii.

[50] Lewis, *English Lit. in 16th Century,* p. 11.

[51] *Ibid.,* pp. 11-13.

of, pagan philosophy and Christian doctrine. As Hamm has so shrewdly observed, "That way heresy lies."[52]

It is true enough, in theory at least, that the reconciliation of Greek thought and Christianity can as easily produce the perversion of the former for the benefit of orthodox theology, as it can produce the contrary process. But in actual practice the result has usually been (as Saitta noted of Ficino) to put pagan philosophy "in the center of reference."[53] This is demonstrated by certain heresies of Origen (185-254), and it was very definitely the case with Meister Eckhart (1260-1327), who in the best Florentine manner labeled Plato "the great Parson."[54] Two years after Eckhart's death a papal bull condemned as heretical seventeen propositions drawn from his work, many of them the result of an indiscriminate fusion of Neoplatonic and Christian ideas.[55]

III. JOHN COLET

By the time of the early Renaissance, then, two historical approaches to pagan and Christian doctrine had emerged and

---

[52] Hamm, Pico's *Of Being and Unity*, p. 6.

[53] Jayne, Ficino's *Commentary on Symposium*, p. 22. Thus Ficino adapted Mark 1:11 to Plotinus, rather than vice-versa. See Lupton, *An Exposition of St. Paul's Epistle to the Romans, Delivered as Lectures ... by John Colet*, p. xxxii. These *Lectures on Romans* 6-16 are to be distinguished from the *Exposition of Romans* 1-5. The latter work, apparently never given in lecture form, is printed in Lupton's edition of John Colet's *Letters to Radulphus on the Mosaic Account of Creation and Other Treatises*. Page references to the *Exposition of Romans* are from Lupton's *Mosaic Account* volume. See Lupton, *Mosaic Account*, p. xxxiii ff.

[54] Susana Winkworth (trans.), *The History and Life of John Tauler*, p. 82. For a summary of Origen's doctrines and earlier troubles with the Church, see *ERE* 1:315 ff. The Fifth Ecumenical Council condemned Origen for heresy.

[55] See James Clark, *Meister Eckhart*, pp. 118-9; Maurice DeWulf, *History of Medieval Philosophy*, p. 126; and Rufus Jones, *Flowering of Mysticism and the Friends of God in the 14th Century*, p. 63. On the whole question of Eckhart's Neoplatonic sources, note Clark, pp. 101-103.

been actively practiced. Both approved the use of philosophy on behalf of religion, particularly for the purpose of attracting rationally minded men. But the Clementine approach insisted that the philosophies of the Platonic Tradition must stand in the relation of handmaid to master. The numerous doctrinal errors of pagan thought must either be rejected outright or else properly modified before being incorporated into the Christian system. This was the way of Augustine and Aquinas, both of whom are generally conceded to have been scrupulously orthodox. Thus was Gilson prompted to remark, in connection with Augustine's debt to Plotinus, that "only a St. Augustine could have absorbed such a dose of Neoplatonism without harming Christianity."[56] By contrast, the Florentine approach assumed the "sisterhood" and even the identity of the two systems—an approach which resulted in a blurring of crucial distinctions, an alteration of orthodox theology in the direction of philosophy, and consequently a frequent blundering into unequivocable heresy. This was the way of the Florentines, anticipated by Origen and Eckhart.

Which of these two approaches was predominant in John Colet?[57] To start with, it is quite obvious that Colet was thoroughly familiar with the leading exponents of both the Clementine and Florentine approaches. Erasmus informs us that Colet "did not neglect to read Scotus and Aquinas ... if at any time the occasion demanded it."[58] Similarly, he read widely in Augustine, quoting him in the Oxford lectures more

---

[56] Gilson, p. 43.

[57] The standard biography of Colet is Joseph Lupton, *A Life of John Colet* (1887). Despite J. A. R. Marriott's more recent study (1933), Lupton's work is "still indispensable for many details." Consult Paul Kristeller and John Randall, "The Study of the Philosophies of the Renaissance," *JHI*, 2:449-496.

[58] Ernest Hunt, *Dean Colet and His Theology*, p. 8.

frequently than any other authority save Origen.[59] Origen himself seems to have been a special subject of study during Colet's European trip (1493-6).[60] Especially was Colet acquainted with the work of the Florentines. As we shall note in greater detail in later chapters, he is indebted to Mirandola's *Heptaplus* in the *Letters to Radulphus,* and paraphrases at length from Ficino's *Theologia Platonica* in the *Lectures on Romans.*[61] Moreover, he quotes at length from Mirandola's *Apologia,* and paraphrases from Ficino's *Dialogus inter Paulum et Animan* in his Dionysian abstracts.[62]

Colet's Personal Relation to Ficino

Colet's first-hand acquaintance with the works of the Florentines has led to much speculation that he might have visited Florence and actually heard Ficino.[63] Two modern discoveries

[59] See the statistics in Lupton, *Letters to Radulphus ... and Other Treatises,* p. xlvi ff. Also Lupton, *Life of Colet,* p. 67, n.l. In addition to frequently citing Augustine by name as in *Exposition of Romans,* p. 125, and *Lectures on Romans,* p. 36, Colet's works are permeated with allusions to Augustine's *City of God,* this title and term being one of Colet's favorite labels for the Church—see e.g. Colet's *Ecclesiastical Hierarchy,* p. 127; *Lectures on Romans,* pp. 59, 70; and Lupton, *An Exposition of St. Paul's* [*First*] *Epistle to the Corinthians*—i.e., Colet's *Lectures on Corinthians,* pp. 12, 37. Lupton was rightly puzzled by the older Erasmus's remark that "among the old authors, there was none to whom Colet was more unfavorable than Augustine." Albert Hyma, in "Erasmus and the Oxford Reformers," *Nederlandsch Archief voor Kerkgeschiendenis,* 25 (1932), 97-98, offers the satisfactory explanation that "in 1521 Erasmus was becoming more and more hostile to Augustine as Luther grew more respectful toward him." Therefore Erasmus attributed to Colet Erasmus's own latter-date estimate of Augustine.

[60] Lupton, *Life,* pp. 56-7.

[61] See *Mosaic Account,* p. 10; and *Lectures on Romans,* p. 29 ff. A probable paraphrase of Pico's *Heptaplus* also occurs at *Lec. on Rom.,* p. 27.

[62] Lupton, *Hier.,* pp. 36, 109; and *Life,* pp. 52, 249. Lupton suggests two contemporaries of Colet's—Gaguin and Ganay—who may have mediated to him an interest in Ficino. See *Hier.,* pp. xvi-xix.

[63] For example: Marriott, *Life of Colet,* p. 38; Hunt, p. 8. Colet alludes to a visit to "Italy" in his *Eccles. Hier.,* p. 138.

have however completely invalidated such speculation. The first of these was the uncovering of a letter from Colet, dated at Rome, April 1, 1493, indicating that he very probably studied at Rome rather than Florence while in Italy.[64] This probability has very recently been enhanced to the point of certainty through the discovery by Sears Jayne of Colet-Ficino correspondence, together with marginalia by Colet, in a copy of Ficino's *Epistolae* (1495) at All Soul's College, Oxford.[65] The fact that Colet knew Ficino's *Epistolae* was shown long ago when Lupton found a quotation from the work in the Dean's abstract of Dionysius's *Ecclesiastical Hierarchy*,[66] but the existence of Colet's own private copy of Ficino's work was not known until 1952, when the All Soul's volume was revealed by the French scholar, Abbe Raymond Marcel.

The young Colet's enthusiasm for the *Epistolae* must have been considerable because, sometime after returning (in 1496) to England, he apparently wrote to Ficino in extremely flattering terms. Ficino's reply refers to Colet's "devoted and eloquent letter," and indicates that Colet had affirmed himself an "admirer" and "lover" who idolized Ficino as an intellectual "sun." When Ficino modestly fended off such praise,

---

[64] Wallace Ferguson, "An Unpublished Letter of John Colet, Dean of St. Paul's," *American Historical Review*, 39 (July 34), 696-99. We also have a record of Colet's admission to an English hospice in Rome, March 1493. See Sears Jayne, *John Colet and Marsilio Ficino*, Ch. 2, n. 10. Documentation is from a preliminary version (later revised) of Professor Jayne's manuscript, which is scheduled for publication (ca. 1961) by the Clarendon Press. Documentation in these Notes will therefore probably not match the pagination of the printed book.

[65] The *Epistolae* is essentially a collection of philosophical and theological essays in the form of letters. The All Souls volume contains on its flyleaves two letters from Ficino to Colet and one from Colet to Ficino. Marginalia, totaling some 5000 words in Colet's own hand, comment on more than sixty passages in Ficino's text. For details consult Jayne, *Colet and Ficino*, pp. 1-27.

[66] Lupton, Colet's *Eccles. Hier.*, pp. 36-38.

Colet replied with further eulogy in a second epistle: "While I am reading your books, I live; *but I should live that much more if I could see you, in person, admirable and worshipful Marsilio.*"[67] It is inconceivable that Colet should have been in Florence during his European trip and not seen Ficino. Moreover, he never again returned to Italy. The All Souls volume would therefore seem to constitute conclusive evidence that (1) Colet never visited Florence; (2) Colet never met Ficino; (3) Colet was well read in Ficino's "books" and admired them.[68]

Significance of the All Souls Marginalia

Colet's *Epistolae* marginalia undeniably reveal his interest in the Platonic Tradition. For example, he notes carefully Ficino's views that Plato was one of the earliest "worshippers of the one God," and that Plato's "wisdom was so golden and so glorious that suitable words could not be found in which to expound it."[69] Again, Colet copies out not once but twice Ficino's Dionysian list of the nine ranks of angels. At another point Colet underlines Ficino's observation that "Paul and Dionysius, the wisest of the Christian theologians, said there must exist divine invisibilia corresponding to all visible things in this world."[70] Still another marginal note singles

---

[67] From letters B and C in Jayne, *Colet and Ficino*. Italics added.

[68] These conclusions seem indisputable on the basis of Jayne's intensely thorough examination of the handwriting, ink, flyleaves, and all other conceivably pertinent data surrounding the All Souls volume, esp. the interesting memorandum interlarded among Colet's flyleaf copies of his correspondence with Ficino: "Next Monday, at the usual time and place, John Colet will try to explain as best he can . . . St. Paul's first Epistle to the Corinthians." Check Colet Marginalia No. 73, and Appendix A—"The Identification of Colet's Hand," in Jayne's new study.

[69] See Jayne, *Colet and Ficino*, pp. 360, 295.

[70] Jayne, *ibid.*, App. C, No. 8.

out three of Ficino's Neoplatonic passages "for [use in lectures on] the [First] Epistle to the Corinthians."[71]

Such evidence suggests (as Heinrich Hermelink has noted) that the chief attraction for Colet in Ficino must have been the Florentine's discovery of the connection between the Platonic Tradition and the Pauline Epistles[72]—particularly since in the *Epistolae* Colet found his esteemed "Platonist" Marsilio not only discussing many passages in Paul's letters, but even constructing an imaginary dialogue in which he and Paul discussed theological issues together. To be sure, Colet had already shown an interest in Plato, Plotinus, and Paul during his student days at Oxford. But his reading of the *Epistolae* must surely have reinforced his respect for pagan philosophers, as well as opening his eyes to the provocative interrelations between Paul and pagan thinkers.

Colet would also have gained increased respect for Greek thought and an awareness of its relation to St. Paul through reading Ficino's *Theologia Platonica,* in which the Florentine had eulogized Dionysius as the greatest authority on both Plato and St. Paul. Jayne speculates that Colet read the *Theologia* (plus Pico's *Heptaplus*) around May, 1497, as preparation for his commentary on Genesis. This fact, Jayne believes, explains the contrast between the *Exposition of Romans* 1-5, which shows no interest in Greek thought, and the apparently later *Lectures on Romans* 6-11, which cites Pico and Ficino as authorities while seeking at the same time to explain Paul's meaning in terms of analogous doctrines from the Platonic Tradition.[73]

---

[71] *Ibid.,* p. 380.

[72] Heinrich Hermelink, quoted by Karl Bauer, *John Colet and Erasmus von Rotterdam,* p. 157. See Jayne, *ibid.,* p. 161.

[73] See Jayne, pp. 80-81, 161-2. Jayne maintains further that Colet again dropped his Romans project to bone up on Dionysius (whence much of

The Paradox in Colet's Attitude

Colet's youthful affection for Ficino stands in great contrast to his famous outburst of contempt for Aquinas, whose works he had also read but whom he regarded as "arrogant" and "profane."[74] One might on this basis naturally expect that Colet should have approved the Florentine approach to pagan philosophy, rather than the more conservative Clementine approach followed by St. Thomas. To one who makes such an assumption, Colet's passage on philosophers in the *Lectures on Corinthians* (delivered around 1498) provides a distinct shock:

> We ought to banquet with Christ alone, at the choice table of the Scriptures . . . . At other tables, even the books of heathen authors in which there is nothing that savours of Christ, nothing that does not savour of the Devil, . . . no Christian ought to sit, unless he chooses to be thought a guest of the Devil. . . . If we seek to feed on the wisdom of the heathens, which is devilish, not Christian, we lose the principles of our Lord. For no one takes food at their tables . . . unless from either doubting or despising the Scriptures.
>
> Now if any should say . . . that to read heathen authors is of assistance for the right understanding of Holy Writ, let them reflect whether the very fact of such reliance being placed upon them does not make them a chief obstacle to such understanding. For, in so acting, you distrust your power of understanding the Scriptures by grace alone. . . . Those books alone ought to be read, in which there is a salutary flavour of Christ. . . . Those

---

Colet's Dionysian abstracts) and on the *Epistolae*, before moving on to the Corinthians commentary and to the final phase of the Romans project, namely, *Lectures on Romans* 12-16. For details on this new suggested order for Colet's works during the "Problem Period" (1496-99), and for speculation on whether Colet knew Ficino's Romans commentary, see the forthcoming book by Professor Jayne.

[74] Hunt, p. 9.

books in which Christ is not found, are but a table of devils. Do not become readers of philosophers, companions of devils. In the choice and well-stored table of Holy Scripture all things are contained that belong to the truth.[75]

It is difficult to imagine any passage more antithetical than this to the Florentine thesis that philosophy and religion are identical. Indeed, we have here the position of Tertullian, that pagan thought is to be wholly rejected, with an echo of Peter Damiani's contention that devilish philosophy is quite distinct from divine theology.[76]

Yet it is perhaps typical of Colet that the reverse view is also present in his writings. Cassirer has rightly attributed to Colet the attitude that "he who bears the true spirit of Christ, even though he has never heard his name, deserves far more to be called a Christian" than those who profess Christianity but do not exemplify it.[77] Note as an illustration Colet's heated assertion in the *Exposition of Romans* that noble unbaptized pagans have a truer relation to God than wicked though baptized Christians.[78] Even more to the point is another passage in the same work: "The Gentiles had for their guidance philosophers who were taught by observation of nature; the Jews had prophets who were taught by the angels; and lastly we Christians have Apostles, who were *fully taught* by Jesus."[79] Colet's observation resembles Ficino's famous expression of tolerance:

We can enjoy the divine mind through various Ideas, seek it through various traces . . . , travel toward the goal by various

---

[75] *Lectures on Corinthians*, p. 110. Cf. 1 Cor. 10:20-21.

[76] Eugene Rice, Jr., "John Colet and the Annihilation of the Natural," *Harvard Theological Review*, 45:151 .

[77] Cassirer, *Platonic Renaissance*, pp. 34-5.

[78] *Exposition of Romans*, pp. 87-88. Cf. Rom. 2:25 ff.

[79] *Ibid.*, p. 70. Italics added.

paths. God so disposed the intellectual eyes and tendencies of various souls in different manners, in order that we may approach the different possessions of the manifold divine goods by different paths.[80]

The point of resemblance here between Colet and Ficino is clear: both held that in the course of human history, God had used various media through which to reveal truth. But contrary to Ficino, who concluded that therefore all creeds are at heart the same, Colet maintained that God's media of revelation were progressively superior, so that only Christians could attain the full truth—that is, be "fully taught." Thus Colet intermittently takes the position to which Augustine finally came, namely, that Greek (and Jewish) philosophy, while inferior, contain some degree of truth, and can be accepted and used wherever they are verified by, or at the least do not conflict with, Christian authority.[81]

Importance of Context in Solving the Coletian Paradox

How do we solve this paradox in Colet—these conflicting views that pagan philosophers have nothing to offer, on the one hand; and on the other, that God revealed some degree of truth even to Jews and Greeks?[82] The answer lies partly in the fact that Colet, in the anti-philosophy passages cited, was tied in some measure to the opinions of St. Paul. Paul

---

[80] *Op. om.*, p. 353, in Kristeller, p. 254.

[81] See Jayne, *Colet and Ficino*, pp. 77-78.

[82] The paradox would seem heightened by two separate statements of Erasmus, who tells us that Christ "was always in Colet's mouth, always in his heart"; and on the other hand, that "When I hear Colet I seem to be listening to Plato himself." See Hunt, p. 12, and P. S. Allen, *Erasmi Epistolae*, vol. 1, no. 118, in W. E. Campbell, *Erasmus, Tyndale, and More*, p. 32. However, it is possible that in this latter statement Erasmus was merely complimenting Colet's eloquence by referring to a humanist tradition, based on Cicero's *Orator* 19:62, that Plato was the most eloquent of all the ancients.

had made his views on Greek learning undeniably clear not only in 1 Cor. 10: 20-21, but even more explicitly in Col. 2:8 —"Beware, lest any man cheat you by philosophy . . . according to the tradition of men . . . , and not according to Christ."[83] For Paul, Greek learning—however much he might unconsciously have imbibed it—belonged to an age of ignorance which preceded the coming of the Gospel light. This is a view which he strongly expresses in Gal. 4:8-9; Eph. 2:11-13, 5: 6-8; and Col. 3:7-10.

Under these circumstances, it would have been unthinkable for the conscientious Colet, a devotee of St. Paul, to comment on Paul's attitude toward Greek culture in any way other than he did. But for this very reason we cannot help but feel that Colet's own views on Greek learning were at least in some measure warped by the context in which they were forced to appear, and that, as Lupton rather shamefacedly concedes, the Dean was in this instance "not . . . at his best."[84]

The matter of context is also important in judging Colet's oft-quoted edict for his newly-founded St. Paul's School (1509). The desired course of study, specifies Colet, should feature

> good litterature both laten and greke, good auctors suych as haue the veray Romayne eliquence joyned withe wisdome specially Cristyn auctours that wrote theyre wysdome with clene and chast laten . . . , for my entent is by thys scole specially to incresse knowlege and worshipping of god and oure lorde Crist Jesu and good Cristen lyff and maners in the Children. . . .

---

[83] Cf. Rom. 1:18-32, 1 Cor. 1: 26-28.

[84] Lupton, *Life*, p. 76. In *Lectures on Corinthians*, p. xxxii ff., Lupton seeks to minimize Colet's outburst against heathen authors by noting: (a) that such outbursts were customary even among those Church Fathers (e.g. Jerome) who elsewhere used philosophy; and (b) that Colet was here reacting with irritation against the classical excesses and mythological jargon of the Italian Renaissance.

D

[Therefore] all barbary all corruption all laten adulterate which ignorant blynde folis brought into this worlde and with the same hath distayned and poysenyd the olde laten spech . . . —that ffylthynesse and all such abusyon which . . . more ratheyr may be callid blotterature thenne litterature I vtterly abbanysh and Exclude oute of this scole and charge the Maisters that they teche . . . the chyldren in . . . Redyng . . . suych auctours that hathe with wisdom joyned the pure chaste eloquence.[85]

Hyma sees in this passage an antipathy to pagan philosophy and literature. But as Hunt points out, this is not the case at all. A careful reading of the edict clearly shows that it is an attack on the medieval scholastics, and not even on them for their ideas, but for their allegedly crude Latin style, in contrast to the eloquent style Colet wanted taught—that is, the Latin of "seint Jerome and seint Ambrose and seint Austen and many holly doctors lernyd in theyr tymes." Moreover, the expression "good litterature both laten and greke" combined with the phrase "specially Cristyn auctours" clearly implies that non-Christian authors were not to be wholly excluded from the curriculum, though they were to play a subordinate role.

Colet's Interest in and Citations from the Platonic Tradition

Surely Colet himself never excluded pagan authors from his own reading and writing. Despite his attack on Greek philosophy as "devilish" in the Corinthians lectures, the fact remains that he frequently invited Plato and Plato's later interpreters to his own Christian "table"—so much so, indeed, that Lupton can say, with much justification, that "to

---

[85] "Statutes of St. Paul's School" in Lupton, *Life of Colet,* pp. 279-280. See also Hyma, "Erasmus and the Oxford Group," *Nederlandsch,* 25:100; and Hunt, p. 3.

Colet first, more than any other Englishman after the revival of letters, we owe the introduction of Platonism into this country."[86] How ironical it is that in the Corinthians lectures themselves, where Greek culture is heatedly denounced, there is an allusion to Homer and an appeal to "The Platonists" as respected authorities![87] Moreover, in the *Lectures on Romans* Plato's *Timaeus* is quoted, and Ficino is glowingly referred to as "the Platonist Marsilius Ficinus."[88] Still more, we have the word of Erasmus that "during his younger days, in England, [Colet] . . . eagerly devoured the works of Cicero, and diligently searched into those of Plato and Plotinus"— even though these authors were not academically required.[89]

Whether the younger Colet's introduction to Plato and Plotinus came through the Ficino translations, published respectively in 1484 and 1492, is not certain.[90] Jayne, noting that *Lectures on Romans*, pages 16-17, is apparently a paraphrase of Ficino's *Plotinus* (*Enneads* 1:1), suggests that Colet not only used the Florentine's translation, but that Colet's copy might well be extant somewhere. The same might hold true for Ficino's translation of the *Dialogues*. In any event, the 4th century Chalcidian *Timaeus*, as well as the 12th century translations by Aristippus of the *Meno* and *Phaedo*, would have been available to him. So would Leonardo Bruni's Latin translations of the *Phaedrus*, *Phaedo*, *Gorgias*, *Apology*, and *Crito*, together wth Decembrio's trans-

---

86 *Lec. on Rom.*, p. xiv.

87 *Lec. on Cor.*, pp. 84, 140.

88 *Lec. on Rom.*, pp. 29, 74.

89 Lupton, *Life*, p. 43. Re: Cicero, Jayne argues in *Colet and Ficino*, p. 125, n.51, that the modified emanationism in Colet's *Letters to Radulphus* is derived not from Plotinus but from Cicero's *De Natura Deorum*, 1:15.

90 Jayne, *Colet and Ficino*, p. 39, and pp. 51-52, n.5.

lation of the first five books of the *Republic*—all given to
Oxford University by Duke Humphrey in 1439.[91] These
manuscript translations must surely have constituted the mini-
mum that Colet read from the *Dialogues* during his student
days at Oxford.

Finally, as a student of Plato, Plotinus, and Ficino, Colet
could not help but be aware of the "Platonic" element in the
pseudo-Dionysius, whom indeed Ficino had called "the supreme Platonist." Yet two of Colet's ten major works are
devoted exclusively to abstracting Dionysius's Celestial and
Earthly Hierarchies, while a third work, *The Treatise on
Sacraments,* is patterned in structure and content on Dionysius's section on sacraments in the *Ecclesiastical Hierarchy.*[92]
Even more significant, Colet apparently continued to draw
from Dionysius even after Grocyn's Dionysian lectures at St.
Paul's Cathedral (around 1500) had convinced him that the
Areopagite was not a Christian disciple of the apostle Paul.[93]
Colet's sermon at Wolsey's installation (1515), for example
—probably his last major address before his death—was built
around the Dionysian angelic orders and the Areopagite's
notion that earthly things appropriately symbolize the things
of heaven. Thus the sermon asserted, according to preserved
extracts, that a Cardinal "represents the order[s] of Seraphim, [Cherubim, and Thrones], which continually burn in

---

[91] Klibansky, pp. 27-28; and Ralph Stob, *Platonism in English Educators
and Theologians* in *Abstract of Theses,* 8 (1929-30), 335.

[92] See Lupton, *Hier.,* p. xv ff. Colet's *A Treatise on the Sacraments of the
Church* (ed. Lupton, 1867) appears in the same Ms containing his abstracts
of the Dionysian hierarchies, filling the last sixty pages of that Ms. It cites
Dionysius by name on pp. 40, 46, 47, 66, 76, 77, 85, 88, and 92 of Lupton's
edition. See also Lupton (ed.), *A Treatise on the Sacraments of the Church
by John Colet.* p. 10 ff.

[93] Note Marriott, p. 103.

the love of the glorious Trinity. . . . For these considerations a Cardinal is metely apparelled in red."[94]

Colet's Clementine Approach

Such assembled evidence indicates that Colet was not the anti-humanist proclaimed by Rice and Hyma. Neither was he the radical disciple of the Florentines suggested by Cassirer. Rather is Colet's true position on the relation of pagan to Christian doctrine strikingly crystallized by his marginalia in the All Souls *Epistolae*. In that work, Ficino had included a section entitled "Philosophy Increases Wisdom," and had concluded with a tribute to Socrates as a wise man misunderstood by ignorant contemporaries. Colet interprets the whole passage as an allegory of Christian knowledge, substituting Christ for philosophy, St. Paul for Socrates, and interpreting wisdom not as self-acquired knowledge of Ideas but as grace-acquired knowledge of God.

Again, Colet in his marginalia rejects Ficino's mythological metaphor, but accepts enthusiastically other metaphors of a less pagan nature, particularly the favorite Neoplatonic analogy of God and the sun.[95] The All Souls volume leaves little doubt that Colet emphasized Christianity rather than Greek thought, and that Christ and St. Paul were even greater heroes for him than Plato and Ficino. This is borne out also by Colet's extravagant exclamations of respect for the "admirable" Paul in the Oxford lectures: "Think what a man was he!

---

[94] Lupton, *Life*, p. 195. This would not seem to support Jayne's contention, in *Colet and Ficino*, pp. 62-63, n. 47, that Colet deserted Dionysius after the Grocyn exposé.

[95] Consult Jayne, "Colet's Christianizing of Ficino's Text," in *Colet and Ficino*, p. 86 ff., and *passim*.

godly-minded and thoughtful beyond all others . . . this great St. Paul."[96]

In the last analysis, then, Colet is seen to stand clearly between Tertullian and the radical humanism of the Florentine Academy. Hunt correctly speaks of his "Christocentric Humanism."[97] Colet was not interested in Florentine "harmonizing," for the very reason that he did not assume the essential agreement between the two systems.[98] With Augustine, he clearly recognized and repudiated such Plotinian heresies (derived from Plato) as immortality of the soul alone, and transmigration: "The absurd notions that have arisen . . . from hearing . . . philosophers . . . are to be utterly rejected by Christians," asserts the Dean; "I mean, either that souls . . . survive, but destined not to resume their bodies; or that they survive and migrate into other bodies."[99]

Such passages indicate that it was very obviously Colet's aim to make Greek thought no more than the servant of orthodox theology. If he was enthusiastic about Erasmus's Greek edition of the New Testament, this was not because it exhibited classical learning *per se,* but because in this instance a knowledge of the classics had been used in the service of Christ.[100] In his approach to the problem of pagan philosophy and Christian doctrine, we must therefore place John Colet, in intention at least, squarely within the Clementine tradition of St. Augustine. This cardinal point will be further demonstrated in the chapters which follow.

---

[96] *Lec. on Rom.,* p. 56; *Lec. on Cor.,* p. 51.

[97] Hunt, p. 10.

[98] Note Jayne, "Ficino and the Platonism of the English Renaissance," *Comparative Lit.,* 4:224.

[99] *Eccles. Hier.,* p. 139.

[100] Hunt, pp. 12, 6-8. Stimulated by his friend's accomplishment, Colet himself set out at the age of 50 to learn Greek.

CHAPTER 2
COLET ON GOD
AND CREATION

This chapter will show that the chief source of Colet's *Letters to Radulphus on the Mosaic Account of Creation* is St. Augustine, both directly and in some instances through the medium of Ficino. It is therefore not surprising that Colet, in his treatment of the Platonic and Plotinian outlooks on God and creation, should have followed Augustine's Clementine approach.[1]

---

[1] For Augustinianism in Ficino, see Kristeller's "Augustine and the Early Renaissance," *Review of Religion* 7 (May 44), 339-358; *Philosophy of Ficino*, p. 211; and *The Classics and Renaissance Thought,* p. 85. Also Cassirer, "Ficino's Place in Intellectual History,"*JHI*, 6:487. As Colet's debts to Augustine's *Confessions* 11-13, Lupton cites: (1) the assertion that Genesis is obscure; (2) the metaphor "water" for matter; (3) the notion that the opening Mosaic verses are an epitome of the whole creation afterwards re-

Platonic and Neoplatonic Concepts of God

Plato held that God is, in both nature and function, "perfectly good" (*Laws* 10:900). Indeed, it is this very goodness of God which explains "the origin and creation of the world." For God "was good, and the good can never have any jealousy of anything. And being free from jealousy, [he] desired that all things should be as like himself as they could be" (*Timaeus* 29-30). Plotinus confused this "good God" of *Timaeus* with Plato's Idea of Beauty and particularly

---

lated successively in detail (cf. *City of God* 11:33)—Lupton, *Mosaic Account,* pp. xxvii-xxviii.

Origen and Macrobius are cited by Colet (*Mosaic Account,* pp. 27, 28) as authority for the "accomodation" theory of Scriptural exegesis, and Origen (p. 11) for the notion that even angels have some degree of matter. Mirandola and Dionysius must also have influenced Colet's acceptance of the "accomodation" theory. Pico had advocated and applied the theory in his own Genesis commentary (see Jayne, *Colet and Ficino,* p. 39), and Dionysius had suggested "accomodation" in his *Heavenly Hierarchy,* trans. J. Parker, pp. 2-13.

Lupton, *Mosaic Account,* pp. xxvi-xxvii, credits Philo's *Legis Allegoriarum* and *De Mundi Opificio,* respectively, as the inspirations for Colet's rejection of literal days, and for his argument that Moses mentioned plants before stars so as not to give the impression that the stars control earth. However, Augustine also asserts that the Mosaic days must be taken "in some other way" than as literal days (see *Companion to Aug.,* p. 318, and Gilson, p. 74). Moreover, Colet's implied antipathy for astrology might just as well have been suggested by the *Disputationes in Astrologiam* of Mirandola, from whose *Heptaplus* Colet paraphrases in *Mosaic Account,* p. 10. See Lupton, pp. xxii-xxiii and 19, n.l.

Colet must also have learned a contempt for astrology from Ficino's *Epistolae.* In one passage from that work, Ficino had begun: "I have written a book against the worthless pronouncements of astrologers." Colet's marginalia paraphrases the passage thus: "The pronouncements of astrologers, based on the influence of the stars, are false and worthless and cause much erroneous thinking. For they infringe upon the providence and omnipotence of God." However, according to Jayne's suggested order of composition for Colet's works, Colet wrote his *Letters to Radulphus* prior to reading the *Epistolae.* See Jayne, *Colet and Ficino, Epistolae* fol. xcviv; cf. Colet marginalia No. 51.

with Plato's Idea of the Good.[2] Plotinus's confusion is to
some extent understandable, because *Republic* 6:508-9 describes the Good as the "author of . . . all things," and as
occupying "a place of honor yet higher" than the Ideas;
consequently, we are told, the Good "is not essence but far
exceeds essence in dignity and power." This Good is called
"the One" throughout *Parmenides* (e.g., 137-143), and at the
end of that dialogue (165-6), the possibility is raised that
the One "is not"—that is to say, is beyond being.

On this basis Plotinus asserted that God is the One-Good-
Beauty who is beyond being (*Enneads* 2:4-5).[3] Committed as
Augustine was to the Christian concept of God as the deity
who "truly is," he could not accept Plotinus's view that God
is beyond being.[4] Yet he readily followed Plotinus in calling
God "the One," and in identifying this One with the Platonic
Ideas of Beauty and the Good. Thus for Augustine God was
"Goodness, Beauty," "the highest and truest Good."[5]

Augustine's successful fusion of the Christian and Plotinian concepts of God was imitated by many medieval and
Renaissance thinkers. Aquinas, for example, identified unity
with being and goodness in the highest sense, namely, God.[6]
Ficino repeated the notion, calling God "the One Itself,"
"the Good Itself," and (especially in his later works) the

---

[2] See More, *Religion of Plato*, pp. 119-120, on this "persistent error" in
Platonic interpretation.

[3] See Thomas Whittaker, *The Neo-Platonists*, pp. 53-70, for an analysis
of the Plotinian system. The best source for Plotinian passages cited in
parentheses in the main text is the 1957 revision of Stephen Mackenna's
Enneads of Plotinus (Pantheon Press).

[4] Note Exodus 3:14—"I am that I am." Cf. Augustine's *The Nature of
Good* 19 as quoted in Butler, *Western Mysticism*, pp. 47-48; and Gilson,
History of Christian Philosophy, pp. 70-71.

[5] *City of God* 8:9; *Soliloquies* 1:3 in Butler, pp. 52-54. See also Butler,
p. 47, and DeWulf, *History of Medieval Philosophy*, 1:117.

[6] Henle, *St. Thomas and Platonism*, pp. 356-7, 409, 412-417.

"first Being," the "supreme Being."[7] Mirandola even went
so far as to devote an entire treatise to arguing that Plato,
like Aristotle and St. Thomas, regarded Being and the One
as interchangeable terms.[8]

Colet's Concept of God

Against this background, Colet's concept of the deity is what
we would expect. God is "divine beauty," "pure Goodness,"
and "the One."[9] "When St. Paul was caught up to the One,"
he was therefore united to "The Unity of Unities."[10] Sometimes these terms are applied to the entire "Trinity, its
beauty, unity, goodness."[11] More often, however, they are
applied separately to the three divine Persons. God is "very
Goodness"; "the unity, beauty, and perfection of all things."[12]
But since Christ is of one substance with God, Christ is also
"the highest good," "the first and undivided one, Jesus
Christ."[13]

For Colet God is also "very Being."[14] To be sure, he does
remark at one point in the *Letters to Radulphus* that "God
. . . is exalted far above existence."[15] The pressure toward this
unorthodoxy must have been considerable, because some of

---

[7] Sears Jayne, Ficino's *Commentary on the Symposium*, pp. 209-210, 126;
and Kristeller, *Philosophy of Ficino*, pp. 141, 165.

[8] Victor Hamm, Mirandola's *Of Being and Unity*, pp. 13-16.

[9] Colet's *Celestial Hierarchy*, p. 20; *Lectures on Romans*, p. 65; *Lectures
on Corinthians*, p. 32, cf. pp. 26, 98. Hereafter these works are referred to
as CH, LR, and LC, respectively.

[10] LC pp. 26, 131. Cf. 2 Cor. 12:2-3.

[11] CH p. 115.

[12] LC p. 18; CH p. 41; LR p. 32; and John Gordon Rowe (trans.), Colet's
Treatise on the Sacraments, hereafter Sac., p. 4.

[13] LC p. 54, CH p. 53.

[14] LC p. 18.

[15] *Mosaic Account*, hereafter MA, p. 8.

the writers whom Colet most respected advanced the idea. Ficino himself had in his early works taken such a view even to the point of arguing the matter heatedly with Mirandola.[16] Even more important, Dionysius had, with Plotinus, declared the One-Good-Beauty to be "above being" and "super-essential Essence" (*Divine Names* 1, 2; *Cel. Hier.* 4:1).[17] That Colet was amply aware of Dionysius's position is indicated by his careful paraphrase (in his Dionysian abstracts) of the Neoplatonist's negative theology.[18] But a careful scrutiny of Colet's remark in the Radulphian letters indicates that he was in this instance apparently betrayed by his euphuistic style into a remark which is, in any event, not consistent with the orthodox concept which he elsewhere expresses. We must conclude that for Colet God was essentially the merciful "Being" who through Christ "united with human nature."[19]

Especially did Colet emphasize the Neoplatonic notion of God as the Good, combining it with the Augustinian and Platonic explanation for the goodness of creation. Thus commenting on Moses' statement "And God saw that it was good," Colet exclaims: "For it is from the good that good comes; and what comes from good is good; and whatever is from God is good, for He is Goodness Itself."[20] Again, in his abstract on Dionyius' *Celestial Hierarchy*, Colet notes approvingly that "God created all things because he is good."[21] Compare this with *Timaeus* 29-30 and with Augustine's exclamation: "Thanks be to thee, O Lord, these things

---

16 See Kristeller, *Ficino*, p. 41, and Dulles, *Mirandola and the Scholastic Tradition*, p. 67.

17 Inge, *Christian Mysticism*, p. 105. Also Gilson, p. 82.

18 CH p. 13.

19 LC p. 20.

20 MA p. 15.

21 CH p. 16.

we behold, and they are severally good, and altogether are very good... By the good God good works were made" (*Confessions* 12:32 and *City of God* 11:21).

Platonic Ideas from Plotinus to Ficino

Colet also followed the lead of Augustine in incorporating the Platonic Ideas into the Christian system. Plotinus had contended that these Ideas constitute Mind, the first major emanation from the One.[22] Augustine accepted the Plotinian notion of Mind as the seat of Ideas, but identified this Mind with Christ or "the Word" (John 1:1), the second Person of the Christian trinity: "You proclaim the Father and His Son, whom you call the Father's intellect or mind" (*City of God* 10:29).[23] Having identified Ideas with Christ, Augustine could not accept the Plotinian view of Mind as an entity distinct from and inferior to the One. In effect therefore he merged Mind with the One, thus placing the Ideas within God himself. In so doing, he was anticipated not only by Clement, who argued that the Ideas are "God's thought," but also by Origen, who identified the "Word" with Mind or Ideas, and pictured these Ideas as existing in God:

> There is in God a treasure of sight much greater than the spectacle of earthly or heavenly things . . . Beyond these God treasureth . . . in Himself much greater things, which He shall manifest when "all the creatures shall be delivered from the bondage of corruption." . . . Then at last we shall . . . attain to the nature of Ideas and to the beauty of truth itself.[24]

In the Augustinian system, as in Plato and Plotinus, the

---

[22] Inge, *The Philosophy of Plotinus,* 2:44-45.

[23] See *Companion to Aug.,* pp. 304-5. Cf. 1 Cor. 1: 24—"Christ is the . . . wisdom of God."

[24] *Exhoratio ad Martyium* 13, as quoted in More, *Religion of Plato,* p. 316. The last sentence in the quotation is More's paraphrase. See also Gilson, p. 39.

unchangeable and eternal Ideas (or, as Augustine sometimes calls them, the "reasons" or "exemplars") are the intelligible patterns whereby God creates the universe: "each thing is created according to its own proper 'ratio'."[25] In highly Platonic language Augustine likens Ideas to "the plan of building" by which an "architect" builds the visible edifice.[26]

Ficino, particularly in his later works, maintained this Augustinian concept through the use of picturesque biological metaphor. He described the Ideas in God as "an embryo equal in life to Himself" and "contain[ed] within Himself," arguing further that "If . . . nature [is] full of forms . . . , God, who is the formgiver . . . , cannot be without forms." It is therefore reasonable, said Ficino, that from this embryonic pattern within Himself God "should produce outside of Himself an inferior fruit," namely the visible universe.[27]

Colet's Use of Platonic Ideas

The result of this development was to eliminate the original Platonic heresy of Ideas co-eternal with God, and to increase the majesty of God by placing the divine Forms in God's mind. This was no doubt the reason that the Augustinian-Ficinian concept of Ideas appealed to Colet. At any rate, in Colet as in Christian Neoplatonism generally, the Ideas are deemphasized through incorporation with the deity.

To be sure, there are passages which would seem to suggest an intelligible realm independent of God. Thus in Pauline language Colet argues that "the heaven and visible earth are an unfolding of the earlier and invisible world." "All things in heaven are prior to those on earth. . . . The archtype and

---

[25] Butler, p. 51.
[26] DeWulf, p. 117.
[27] Kristeller, *Ficino*, pp. 138, 246.

pattern of all things is in heaven; to that reality the work begun by God on earth will someday return to be completed."[28] But broader scrutiny indicates that for Colet the

---

[28] MA p. 13; *Sac.* p. 11. Cf. Rom. 1:20 ("The invisible things of Him from the creation of the world are clearly seen, being understood by the things that are made"), and *Exposition of Romans,* hereafter ExR, p. 52— "The Creator...manifested His invisible and intelligible things by the sensible creation." It was no doubt Ficino who showed Colet the affinity between Platonic and Pauline dualism. Thus did Colet underline from Ficino's *Epistolae* this previously cited passage: "So Paul and Dionysius...said there must exist divine invisibilia corresponding to all visible created things" —see *supra.,* p. 20.

It would be far beyond the scope of this book to delve with any detail into the controversial issue of St. Paul's secular sources. However, we know that Paul conversed with "Epicurean and Stoic philosophers" (Acts 17:18). Moreover, certain of Paul's terms, particularly Stoic "conscience" and Platonic "outer-inner man," are not found either in the Old or New Testaments. Stewart supplies convincing evidence that Paul not only "knew the main Stoic trends of thought," but even "here and there...availed himself of their ideas" and speaking techniques. To be sure, Paul expressed disapproval of secular philosophy: "Beware, lest any man cheat you by philosophy" (Col. 2:8, cf. Rom. 1: 18-32, 1 Cor. 1: 26-28). But, as Reitzenstein points out, it was not a question of conscious borrowing: it was rather "a question of the subtlest form of unconscious influence." Dodd properly emphasizes that Paul was "a writer of the Hellenistic Age, when a mixed civilization arose out of the interaction of Greek thought with that of various peoples of the Near East." In such a hybrid civilization, almost all barriers of language had vanished. Stewart notes that "everywhere the people were bilingual and all knew Greek.... The very use of the Greek tongue involved a certain infusion of the Greek spirit." By all means the Jewish and the nascent Christian religions fought for their identities against the surrounding paganism. But as Stewart observes, even "the best defenses, invincible though they may be to direct assault, are not proof against something so subtle and pervasive as an atmosphere." This is underscored by the fact (noted by Moffatt) that Paul's own teacher Gamaliel was "distinguished...by his comparatively liberal attitude to Greek culture."—On this whole problem consult C. H. Dodd, *The Epistle of Paul to the Romans,* pp. xxxi f., 36, 185; Robinson, *The Body: A Study in Pauline Theology,* pp. 9, 12; Prat, *Theology of St. Paul,* 2: 39, 49-51; Moffatt, *Paul and Paulinism,* pp. 2-3; and Stewart, *A Man in Christ,* pp. 27, 49, 54-59.

On the basis of the above and similar data, plus a careful examination of the Pauline Epistles and pertinent pagan philosophy, the conclusions of this book are as follows: (1) there are definite Platonic elements in Paul; (2)

"divine and spiritual reasons" or "naked reasons of things," which constitute this "pattern" are clearly within God himself. "All things are truly in God; aside from God there is but an imitation of Him." "God, who is . . . the fullness of all things, contained all in Himself. . . . before he had diffused them abroad."[29] Everything is therefore "after the form and pattern of God." He is "the pattern of the Order of all."[30] The frequency with which this notion is repeated in Colet's Dionysian abstracts indicates that the Areopagite was here, as in so many other instances, an important factor in Colet's thinking. Thus Colet tells us that

> there are nine orders of Angels, figures of the nine archtypes in God. . . . These Orders . . . have in God himself their models which they represent. . . . [God] is a glorious and mighty pattern to the first hierarchy. . . . After his own pattern . . . he forms, disposes, and perfects all things.[31]

Schweitzer in *The Mysticism of St. Paul* notwithstanding, these elements are not mere coincidental "analogues"; (3) Paul was unquestionably influenced by Platonism, though not in any large degree consciously; (4) this influence came chiefly through the channel of Stoicism, which retained many Platonic ideas (see Chapter 6 of this book, p. 161 ff.). Hence this book assumes that many ideas used by Colet and common to both Plato and Paul represent at the very least an ultimate Platonic influence. However, Colet's own acquaintance with the *Dialogues* would make it reasonable to assume that he was quite aware of certain Pauline-Platonic agreements, and that in such instances we therefore have a joint influence operating. In short, this book takes its stand with Professor Kristeller's eloquent plea in *The Classics and Renaissance Thought*, pp. 77: "I must leave it to the judgment of present-day theologians . . . whether they are really serving their cause by trying to eliminate from Christian theology all notions originally derived from Greek philosophy."

29 LC p. 32; *Sac.* p. 1; MA p. 16. See also Eugene Rice Jr., "John Colet and the Annihilation of the Natural," *Harvard Theol. Rev.*, 45: 159. In one of his *Epistolae* marginalia, Colet notes that the "Ideas [are] in God's mind" —this is a reference to Ficino's longer statement to the same effect.

30 CH pp. 24, 32.

31 CH pp. 24, 27, 4, 37.

Because God himself contains the "spiritual reasons," the terms previously used by Plato for the realm of Ideas are now reapplied by Colet. In the Dean's system, it is God who is "Truth," "very Wisdom," "the abode of Truth," "the light of Truth," and "the intelligible world."[32] Moreover, since Christ and the Holy Spirit are one with God, the same labels are applied to them. Jesus is "Truth itself," as well as "Wisdom" and the "Sun of Truth."[33] He is "this master of truth —himself also the very Truth."[34] There are even passages in Colet which suggest Augustine's identification of Christ or "the Word" with the Plotinian Mind. Thus of Jesus, Colet in one instance remarks: "Thou were God's mouthpiece, Word, and Incarnate Truth. . . . This wonderful Word made human, this Reason of God" (cf. *City of God* 10:29).[35]

Similarly, the Holy Spirit is the "Spirit of Truth" and as such "the exemplary cause and agent . . . of . . . the Church."[36] As Lupton has pointed out, to the four causes of Aristotle a fifth or exemplary cause was added in some medieval and Renaissance systems. If a statue were chiseled on the model of another, the latter was said to be the exemplary cause of it. Hence Colet's reference to Spirit as an "exemplary cause" further emphasizes his belief that the archtypes exist in God.[37]

Colet's Use of the "Limited-Unlimited" Concept in Plato's "Philebus"

Echoing *Timaeus* 28-29 and *Laws* 10:897, as well as Augustine, Colet describes the Creator as a "great Artificer" or

---

[32] CH pp. 41, 21; LC pp. 18, 85, 115; LR p. 82; MA p. 16. In the last cited context, "intelligible world" might also include angels.

[33] LC pp. 123, 62, 57, 126.

[34] LR p. 105.

[35] LC pp. 62, 63.

[36] CH p. 61; LC p. 141.

[37] See Lupton, LC p. 141, n.1.

Craftsman who moulds matter into the best possible imitation of the ideal "pattern" within him.[38] Elsewhere God is labeled the "Husbandman" or "Masterbuilder."[39] In this connection, Plato's *Philebus* had a special impact on Colet. In sections 23 to 27 of that dialogue, Plato used the term "Unlimited" for chaotic matter before the act of creation, "Limited" for the realm of Ideas, and "Mixed" for the physical universe which resulted when God moulded matter into an imitation of Ideas and therefore figuratively "imposed" the Limited on the Unlimited.[40]

Plotinus understandably though wrongly interpreted such language to imply emanation. He therefore retained Plato's terminology, calling indefinite shapeless matter "The Undelimited," and assigning to the Ordering Principle of Form the Platonic term "Limit."[41] Following these leads, Colet, having merged Ideas with God, calls God "the true limit" who "stays" the flux of matter, and elsewhere refers to matter as "subject to flux and mutation, save when upheld by constancy itself, even God."[42] This notion is repeated in the *Exposition of Romans:* "Law is nothing else than God ... He established all things, fixing the proper limit of each, and ordaining a beautiful order in the world."[43]

The most remarkable use of the Platonic "Limited-Unlimited" notion comes in the *Treatise on Sacraments.* Here we are told that

[38] MA pp. 10, 17.

[39] LC p. 28.

[40] See Raphael Demos, *The Philosophy of Plato*, p. 7 ff., who feels these Platonic classifications have been much neglected. Colet might have learned the Limited-Unlimited concept indirectly through Ficino's special commentary on *Philebus*, written in 1469. See Kristeller, *Ficino*, p. 17.

[41] *Enn.* 2:4:8, 10, 15.

[42] MA pp. 11, 15.

[43] ExR, p. 129. As indicated here and elsewhere, Colet's use of the Platonic

Order itself is that all-embracing principle of God, drawn forth
from the hidden mind of God, from the complete whole-height
of the Divinity, beauty itself, which is itself the word of God
. . . ; in that most excellent Order all things are disposed . . . .
Therefore the first priest is Order Itself . . . . This is the most
sacred, the eternal Son of God. That first Priest and archtype,
in whom all things have their existence, . . . is Himself all
things most truly.[44]

This passage once again stresses the Augustinian concept
of Christ or the Word as identical with Ideas. Here, however, the Word is presented as a single Form or Principle—
a concept similar to that of Nicholas of Cusa, who held that
there is only one Form, namely God or the One.[45]

Notions of Matter in Plato and Plotinus

Colet's treatment of matter is a curious blending of Platonic
and Neoplatonic with Christian ideas. Plato believed in
co-eternal matter, "upon the surface" of which God merely
"stamped" some degree of order. After some vacillation as
to the nature of this clay which God the potter needed to
create, Plato affirmed in *Timaeus* 51-52 that it was an
"invisible" substratum lacking color, solidity, and shape.
Because this chaotic matter thwarted God's desire for perfection in his creation, Plato viewed it as "antagonistic to
good" (*Theaetetus* 176) and therefore as the principle of
evil.[46]

Plotinus retained this notion of already-existing matter as
"the first evil," the principle opposed to the goodness of the

---

term "Limit" swings back and forth from (a) God who imposes the limit,
to (b) the form or limit which is imposed.

[44] *Sac.* pp. 2-3.

[45] See Henry Bett, *Nicholas of Cusa,* pp. 130-141. Cusa also describes
creation as a limitation of the unlimited—Bett, p. 133.

[46] Friedrich Solmsen, *Plato's Theology,* pp. 42, 112; Cornford, *Plato's
Cosmology,* p. 36.

One.[47] But, unlike Plato, he conceived of creation as a spontaneous overflow of the One or Fountainhead whereby God, through the intermediary stages of "Mind" (Ideas) and "General Soul," extended himself into "The Void" of shapeless matter, thus creating visible phenomena (*Enn.* 2:4:10, 11, 15). Such phenomena were therefore said to be mixtures of evil and good—that is, of matter and of forms (*Enn.* 6:7:2, 4:4:16). These forms derive from the Ideas which, having emanated from the One, themselves overflow and crystallize as individual souls. The souls, initially constituent parts of the transcendent World-Soul, then extend themselves into matter (*Enneads* 4:3:4), so that in Plotinus's words "all things are in various degrees endowed with the essence of Soul."[48]

Augustine's Adaptation of Plotinus's Theory of Creation

This scheme was unacceptable to Augustine on a number of counts. First, it violated the Christian concept of God's free creative will.[49] Second, it followed Plato in assigning souls to animals and plant-life. Indeed, *Enneads* 3:2:3 tells us that Soul descends even to inorganic phenomena.[50] Third, it denied the omnipotence of God by asserting the existence of co-eternal matter not wholly controllable by the One. Fourth and most crucial, Plotinian emanationism breached the barrier which Christianity had always established between God and creature.

Yet Augustine was attracted to the Plotinian notion of

---

[47] *Enn.* 1:8:3, 14; 2:4:16; and Inge, *Plotinus,* 1: 134.

[48] See Inge, *Plotinus,* 2: 44-45, 56; 1: 210 ff.

[49] Contrast Plotinus's view also with the Creator's words in *Timaeus* 41— "If I so will, all that is bound may be undone."

[50] Inge, *Plotinus,* 1: 209. Cf. *Timaeus* 77 on souls in "trees and plants," and *Sophist* 249 as interpreted by Demos, p. 94, which assigns some soul-element even to inanimate things.

creation as a fusion of form and matter, and to the corollary Neoplatonic concept of an ontological hierarchy. According to this hierarchy, things closest to the One, such as man and animals, partake more of being or form than do objects which are farther away, because the emanative flow from God decreases in intensity as it moves out from the Godhead (*Enn:* 5:8:1).[51] This scheme had already been suggested by Plato's increasingly irregular scale of movements in *Laws* 10:893-7; by the hierarchy of souls in *Timaeus* 77 and 91; by the notion of human souls as "derived" from World-Soul in *Philebus* 30; and by the further Platonic point that such souls were created from the same "elements," yet "not ... pure as before, but diluted to the second and third degree" (*Timaeus* 41).[52]

Approaching Plotinus from the Clementine perspective, Augustine began by insisting that "God had no need of any material he himself had not made."[53] Thus in the Augustinian scheme, God creates matter as well as form. But Augustine follows the Plotinian notion, based ultimately on *Timaeus* 51-52, that matter is "near to nothing" (*Confessions* 12:7:7), because it is *per se* invisible and unformed. God's creation of this formless matter is said to precede the bestowing of form, but only in a Plotinian casual rather than chronological sense. Form was "concreated" with matter, "because thou didst give form to its formlessness without any lapse of time. Thou madest . . . the visible form of the world from unformed matter, yet both together, so that the form followed the matter with no interval of time" (*Confessions* 13:33:48).

This view of creation pays mild deference to Plotinus by

---

[51] Inge, *Plotinus,* 1: 217.

[52] In this connection note Kristeller, *Classics and Renaissance Thought,* pp. 48-49.

[53] *Nature of Good* 27 via *Companion to Aug.,* p. 332.

continuing to describe the created world as a mixture of matter and form; but intrinsic form is of course no longer an infused divinity emanating from the One.[54] Moreover, since God is the creator even of matter, it follows that even matter must be good. Hence evil is nothing—it is merely the absence of good. This does not mean that there are not levels of goodness. In *Grace and Free Will,* using terms reminiscent of Plato's soul-hierarchy in *Timaeus* 77 and 91, Augustine distinguishes three categories of created goodness: that which is (inanimate objects); that which is and lives (plants and animals); and that which is, lives, and knows (man).[55]

Colet's Debt to Augustine's Scheme of Creation

Colet follows the main outlines of this Augustinian model. He begins by affirming the Christian doctrine of creation *ex nihilo.* "*In the beginning,* that is, in eternity, *God created the heaven* (form) *and the earth* (matter)." Actually, "matter never existed apart from form." Both were produced and fused instantaneously, so that creation was a simultaneous concreation and "general union of matter and form."[56] However, Moses realized that his followers could not comprehend such a concept. In order to convey a more readily understandable chronology of events, Moses therefore made it appear that matter had been created first, and that God had then "breathed" form or bestowed "light" upon the matter. In terms once again reminiscent of Plato's *Philebus* 23-27, where the "Limited" or Ideas is figuratively imposed on the "Unlimited" or chaotic matter, Colet writes:

By water [Moses] implies the unstable and ever-shifting nature of matter. [Cf. Augustine's *de Gen. ad literam* 4:14] For con-

---

[54] See Gilson, p. 73.
[55] Oates, *Basic Writings of St. Aug.,* p. xxii.
[56] MA p. 5.

sistence arises from form; its opposite, from matter. And it was to check and put limits on this unsettled state, that God breathed upon the inconstant matter. This is the meaning of the words: *And the Spirit of God moved upon the face of the waters.* What else is this Divine breathing, than an expression of being, and goodness, and form, and light?—words which all denote the same thing. This is what Moses calls *light.* Accordingly, . . . he continues: *And God said, Let there be light*—that is, form and definition of things.[57]

Colet's interpretation of Mosaic "light" (and elsewhere of Mosaic "dark") undoubtedly reflects Plotinus's favorite metaphor for form. "The light is the stable thing," said Plotinus; "the air flows in and out; when the air passes beyond the lit area it is dark; under the light it is lit" (*Enn.* 4:3:22). Just as form is "light," so is matter "darkness" or "dark air" (*Enn.* 2:4:5). In Ficino, the Plotinian light metaphor was used synonymously with being, form, goodness, and beauty. Thus Marsilio argues that the being of a thing resides in its form, that this form is to be identified with an object's beauty, and that "beauty is a kind of force or light shining from God."[58] This identification, with the exception of the term "beauty," is apparent in Colet's passage.

Aristotelian Rather than Neoplatonic Influence in Colet?

Following Schröder, the German scholar Dannenberg argued that the recurrence of the terms "matter" and "form" in the Radulphian letters and other of Colet's works indicated Aristotelian rather than Plotinian influence, citing as Colet's chief source Aristotle's *De Generatione et Corruptione.*[59]

---

[57] *Ibid.,* pp. 5-6.

[58] Kristeller, *Ficino,* pp. 38, 150; *Com. on Symp.,* p. 140.

[59] Friedrich Dannenberg, *Das Erbe Platons in England* (1932), pp. 56-57. In two chapters, "Der Akademische Platonismus vor und um Colet," and "Der Hohepunkt des Platonischen Humanismus in Colet," Dannenberg re-

However, these terms represent an indebtedness to Aristotle which all Neoplatonism manifests. Plato had utterly separated Forms from created phenomena, and in doing so had refused to recognize the intrinsic forms of visible objects. To Aristotle this position was ridiculous; objects must exist to some degree, he argued, and their existence is by virtue of their form or shape.[60]

Plotinus accepted Aristotle's argument and accordingly emphasized repeatedly that visible things are indeed mixtures of form and primal matter.[61] But Plotinus wished also to retain the Platonic notion of the created world as an imitation of Ideas. He did this through the theory of Emanation, by which the infused forms, as lesser degrees of goodness, are themselves imitations of transcendent Ideas and ultimately of the One-Good.[62] Thus Plotinus could argue that "Soul . . . is in labor to create after the pattern it saw in Mind, and from this desire the whole world that we know arose and took its shapes" (*Enn.* 4:7:13). To be sure, the Plotinian Creator is Soul, not Mind (corresponding to Plato's Demiurge); and the distinction is no longer between a real and unreal, but between a relatively real world and a sphere "more real than ours is" (*Enn.* 5:1:4). Yet the Platonic doctrine of imitation has nonetheless been retained.[63]

---

traced in greater detail the ground originally covered by Kurt Schröder, *Platonismus in der Englischen Renaissance* (1907, 1920).

[60] For this view Aristotle was later applauded by Aquinas. See Henle, *St. Thomas and Platonism*, pp. 315-319.

[61] *Enn.* 2:4:6, 6:7:2, Cf. 4:4:16—"One, Mind, and General Soul are "not Matter and Form [as are visible objects], but Form only."

[62] On this point note Lupton, LR p. xxvii.

[63] Attempts have been made to prove that Plotinus's thought is more properly called Aristotelian than Neoplatonic. Such was K. H. Kirchner's thesis in *Die Phil. des Plotin* (Halle, 1854), as quoted by Carl Horst in *Vorstudien zu Einer Neuuntersuchung von Plotins Aesthetik* (Marburg, 1905), pp. 18-19. See also Paul Correns, "Dominicus Gundisalvi de Unitate," *BGPM,*

Colet's Retention of Plato's "Intractable Matter"

Despite the fact that God has created matter, Colet retains the Platonic concept of intractable matter antagonistic to God's desires. "The nature of matter [is] fluid, in ceaseless flux and motion, and with difficulty kept in bounds by form; so opposed is it by its own nature to consistence and stability."[64] It is probable that Colet was disposed to this view by Ficino's *De Amore,* which asserts that "since matter is far removed from the divine artificer, the nature of man degenerates from that true Idea of man. But he becomes more like it according as the matter is better disposed, and more unlike in other matter."[65]

However, Ficino breaches orthodoxy by following the Platonic position to the letter: God does not have complete control over matter. Colet, on the other hand, in the instance cited, remains within the bounds of orthodoxy by noting that God controls matter only "with difficulty." In another context, however, he falls into the Ficinian error. "The universal brightness, or form," he says, "infused into the abyss of darkness, *is somewhat impaired, even in its purest region,* by the blackness of that darkness and matter."[66] Here is a denial, no doubt unintentional, of God's omnipotence.

Colet Seduced by Plotinian Light-Dark Metaphors

Colet sometimes seems to have been seduced by his Plotinian metaphors of "light" for form and "darkness" or "blackness"

1:1:44, where he concludes that the Emanation theory is Neoplatonic, but that back of that it rests ultimately on Aristotle. Philip Merlan in *From Platonism to Neoplatonism* (1953) comes to much the same conclusion.

[64] MA p. 10.

[65] *Com. on Symp.,* p. 172. Cf. Ficino's idea that a soul cannot always mould a body to the soul's nature, *ibid.,* pp. 132, 188.

[66] MA p. 8. Italics added.

for matter. "Darkness" has of course traditionally connoted evil. Since Plotinus regarded matter as evil, this was for him a thoroughly appropriate connotation. Under the pressure of such Plotinian metaphor, however, Colet himself sometimes seems to imply that matter is evil (even though he elsewhere inconsistently maintains that a good God created it). This Platonic and Plotinian bias toward matter is especially manifest in the Dean's intermittent restriction of "good" to the form of creation. Thus he remarks that God was pleased when he "saw this form, that it was good, in keeping with the nature of God's goodness and being."[67]

From the view of Augustine, who regarded the entire creation as good, this is a breach of orthodoxy—and indeed, it is not consistent with Colet's implied agreement with Augustine on this point elsewhere in the same work.[68] Here again it is possible that Ficino steered Colet wrong. Having identified beauty and the good, Ficino had gone on to say that form is to be identified with an object's beauty, and matter with its ugliness: "These bodies are partly beautiful, partly ugly. For in respect to their matter, which is something else than beauty, they are judged to be ugly."[69] The clear implication of this is that matter is also wicked in contrast to the good of form.

In this connection, it should also be observed that, from the standpoint of Augustinian theology, Colet makes a metaphysical error in sometimes calling matter "nothing" and "nothingness."[70] In Augustine, as well as in Dionysius and

---

[67] MA p. 6. Cf. the association of "darkness" (i.e., matter) and "evil" at MA p. 6. Also the association of "multiplicity" (of matter) with "evil" in the *Epistolae* marginalia—Jayne, *Colet and Ficino*, p. 144.

[68] See *ibid.*, p. 15.

[69] Kristeller, *Ficino*, p. 150.

[70] MA p. 11. Cf. MA p. 6—"darkness [i.e., matter], which is nothing."

Ficino, there is a distinction between nothing (i.e., evil) and no thing. "Nothing" falls entirely outside the series of created things, and Ficino therefore calls it a mere imaginary counterpole to God.[71] "Evil," says the Florentine, "has no true seat anywhere."[72] "Prime matter," on the other hand, is the lowest entity in the series of created phenomena. It is not nothing, but "no thing" or "next to nothing." Its existence is merely potential—that is to say, it exists only in so far as it is joined with form. Thus Ficino says that each thing receives from its own form its own existence, its nature.[73] This is of course a retention of the Platonic concept of matter as an invisible substratum lacking solidity or shape.

It is curious to observe that other passages in the *Letters to Radulphus* do make the correct Augustinian distinction between "evil, which itself is nothing,"[74] and matter as an unsolid indefinite "no thing": "*And the earth* (matter) *was without form, and void:* this is, without any solid and substantial existence; *and darkness was upon the face of the deep;* that is, matter was in darkness and devoid of life and being."[75] Such inconsistencies must be explained either by Colet's ignorance of the Augustinian distinction between "nothing" (evil) and "next to nothing" (matter), or else by carelessness in terminology. In either case, one cannot help but feel that we have here another example of Colet's admitted "blundering on in this perplexity."[76] Yet it might be generous to remember that on similar issues Plato himself confessed bewilderment: "If . . . amid the many opinions

---

[71] Kristeller, *Ficino*, p. 91.

[72] *Ibid.*, p. 352.

[73] *Ibid.*, p. 38.

[74] MA p. 6.

[75] *Ibid.*, p. 5; cf. p. 8, where matter is "potentiality."

[76] *Ibid.*, p. 25.

about the ... generation of the universe, we are not able to give notions which are altogether ... consistent with one another, do not be surprised" (*Timaeus* 29).

Augustinian and Thomistic Hierarchy

Colet conceived of matter and form as the chief features of a hierarchy of being derived ultimately from St. Augustine. The Augustinian hierarchy of goodness (*supra.*, p. 45), was elaborated notably by Aquinas, who observed that "all the perfections of Creatures descend in order from God who is the height of all perfection."[77] Ficino repeated the idea: "Gradation in existence cannot be known but by an approach to the highest existence, which is God.... God is for us the measure of all things."[78]

Under the joint influence of St. Thomas and Aristotle, Ficino conceived of the ontological ascent as marked by an increase of form and corresponding decrease of matter.[79] Ficino also followed Aquinas in identifying unity and rest with being, good, and form. In the Thomist system God is "the most perfect unity"; creatures possess lesser degrees of unity by virtue of intrinsic form.[80] Similarly, Ficino maintains that the higher rank of an entity involves a higher degree of unity (as opposed to plurality), culminating in the absolute unity, God. Also, since "rest is more perfect than movement," the higher something is in the scale of being, the more rest and less movement it will have.[81]

---

[77] Underhill, *Mysticism*, p. 117.

[78] Kristeller, *Ficino*, pp. 77-78, 83.

[79] *Ibid.*, p. 77.

[80] Underhill, p. 117, and Henle, pp. 356-7, 409. Unity is also associated with being and good in Dionysius—see Jayne, *Colet and Ficino*, p. 104 and p. 127, n.40.

[81] Kristeller, *Ficino*, p. 88.

The germs of these ideas were already in Plato. *Timaeus* 38 tells us, for example, that "eternity itself rests in unity," while *Laws* 10:894 emphasizes that motion, change, and process are the qualities of created things, in contrast to the immoveable unchanging Ideas.

Colet's Hierarchy of Being

All of these elements can be found in Colet's scale of being. Note this typical passage:

> Motion, sense, and corruption, arise from participation in matter. And therefore God, . . . being incorruptible, inaccessible to sense, and utterly immoveable, is altogether devoid of matter. But the remaining worlds, in proportion to their potentiality and receptivity, have an admixture of base matter.[82]

Colet's "utterly immovable" God here corresponds to the complete "rest" of Ficino and to the "unchangeable" deity of Augustine.[83] Only God possesses this complete stability. Everything else, even the angels, is characterized by some degree of matter and therefore of movement: "Of matter and form all beings consist. . . . Every object that exists—with the exception of God alone, . . . consists of the pure and impure, actual and potential, flux and permanence, ceaseless motion and rest; that is, matter and form."[84] The Platonic order of movements in *Laws* 10:893-897 and *Statesman* 269-270 seems reflected in Colet's remark that the stars and planets have the most regular movement of all sensible things.[85]

In the manner of Aquinas and Ficino, Colet also identifies unity with form: "The farther creatures are away from God,

---

[82] MA p. 10.

[83] See *Nature of Good* 19 as discussed in Butler, pp. 47-48. Cf. Colet's "unchanging God," LC p. 129.

[84] MA p. 8.

[85] *Ibid.*, p. 26.

the less simplicity and unity they have."[86] Colet's view that God is pure Form and as such lacking in the "potentiality" or "potential existence" (i.e., matter) which partly characterizes all creatures, is ultimately indebted to Aristotle through Plotinus and Aquinas's *Summa Theologia* 1:3— "Deus est purus actus, non habens aliquid de potentialitate."[87] From some measure of this potentiality Colet excludes "not even the angels."[88] Indeed, it is for this reason that he assigns the Augustinian metaphor "waters" to angels as well as men, and on this basis interprets the Mosaic statement, "Let [the] firmament . . . divide the waters from the waters."[89] This interpretation had been suggested by both Origen and Mirandola. Note in this connection Pico's *Discourse on Love:* "Matter . . . is represented by Water. . . . This being first in the Angelick Minde, Angels are many times exprest by Water, as in the Psalms, 'The Waters above the Heavens praise God continually'; so interpreted by Origen."[90]

Colet's Hierarchy of Elements

In point of fact, Colet's *Letters to Radulphus* feature five hierarchial schemes, all of them interrelated. There is first of all the basic scale of being-form-goodness-unity-rest. Second, there is an order of elements: "Ether, Fire, Air, Water, Earth. Among these . . . there is an orderly gradation of descent. . . . And in this descent, since all go on producing an

---

[86] *Ibid.*, p. 22. Cf. Colet's *Epistolae* marginalia No. 10 in Ficino's *Epistolae*—"Go from motion and multiplicity to stability and unity. . . . God [is] the greatest unity."

[87] Cf. *Contra. Gent.* 1:16, and Lupton, MA p. 8, n. 1. In LR p. 74, Colet combines Plotinus and Aristotle by referring to God as "the one First Cause."

[88] MA p. 11, cf. p. 7.

[89] *Ibid.*, p. 11.

[90] Edmund Gardner, Pico's *Discourse on Love*, p. 36.

inferior copy of their pattern, it is inevitable that there should be an ever degenerating series."[91] This notion seems indebted to *Timaeus* 31f., where, during an exposition of the four elements, Plato introduces water and air as the necessary middle terms reconciling the contrast of fire and earth.

Colet's Propagation Hierarchy

The third hierarchial scheme is that of propagating power: "The nearer in order any beings are to God, the greater and fuller is this power in them.... The nearer any are to the fountain-head [cf. Plotinus] ... the fuller they naturally are of conceptive power." For matter has

> derived ... seminal principles from the Sower and Planter, God, even as the female does after impregnation. God, who is the greatest and best, and the fullness of all things, contained all in Himself ... before he had diffused them abroad. It was inevitable, therefore, that in the bosom and embrace of so great and so fruitful a Progenitur, the female embraced, so to speak (namely Matter), should be let go from the Father of all, teeming with every kind of increase, and should bring with her the seeds of all things, called by philosophers *seminal principles*.[92]

Lupton attributes the notion of seminal principles to the Stoics, and the concept of God as a propagator of life to Dionysius, who gave the term "Life" to Plotinian emanation.[93] But the notion of form as gradually evolving seminal principles is also prominent in Augustine's thought, especially in *De. Gen. ad Litt.* 6:6-8.[94] Moreover, Colet's picturesque notion of female Matter impregnated by a divine Father

[91] MA p. 17.
[92] *Ibid.*, p. 16.
[93] Lupton, MA p. 16, ns. 1, 2.
[94] See *Companion to Aug.*, pp. 329-330.

vividly recalls *Timaeus* 50, where matter is labeled "the receptacle" or "receiving principle." Plato thereupon likens this matter to a mother, God to a father, and the resulting child to created phenomena. Colet's concept of progressive degeneracy may also be compared to the last chapter of *Timaeus*, where (says Grote) the "first stage and the least amount of degeneracy was exhibited by the formation of woman, the original type of man not having included diversity of sex. By further steps of degradation, the inferior animals were formed."[95]

Mirandola's Cosmology

The fourth hierarchical scheme is that of Mirandolan cosmology. "Let me first...divide the whole universe," says Colet,

> as is done by the Platonist Mirandola in his *Hexameron* [i.e., *Heptaplus*], into four worlds. The first of these is God himself ... ; and this I call the *divine* world. The second is the *angelic*, consisting of the bright choir of angels. The third is the *heavenly*, composed of the everlasting orbs. The fourth and last is this world inhabited by men; the whole region contained beneath the orbit of the Moon, which may be termed the earthly world."[96]

Under the influence of Dionysius's notion of analogical spheres, Pico had held that whatever is found in the sublunary sphere has its counterpart in the other two, but of a nobler character. Thus to terrestrial fire corresponds in the celestial realm the sun; in the super-celestial, the seraphic angels. Again, God above his nine orders of angels in the

---

[95] Grote, *Aristotle* 2: 173, as quoted in Lupton, MA p. 17, n. 2.

[96] MA p. 10. For an analysis of Mirandola's scheme, see Dulles, p. 17. Also Lupton, LR pp. xxxii-xxxiii, and J. M. Rigg, Introduction to *Life of Mirandola*, p. xiv.

super-celestial world is paralleled in the celestial world by the stable empyrean surrounding its nine revolving planets.[97]

This complex scheme was essentially a combination of the Dionysian angelic orders with the geocentric cosmology popularized by Plato. The *Timaeus* had pictured earth as encircled by eight spheres, the outermost being the orbit of the fixed stars. The seven planets increase in distance from earth in this order: the Moon, Sun, Venus, Mercury, Mars, Jupiter, and Saturn.[98] *Republic* 616 described this revolving system by comparison with the whorl of a spindle: the whorl (representing the outer circle of fixed stars) was presented as hollow, and as containing seven lesser ones rotating concentrically within itself. Mirandola, committed to the Dionysian system of nine angelic orders and obsessed with the Dionysian mania for balancing, added to the Platonic scheme a ninth heavenly sphere, the primum mobile, and an "empyrean" corresponding to God in the higher realm.[99]

Colet's Cosmology

Through sources quite independent of Mirandola, Colet was thoroughly familiar with the Dionysian angelic orders and with Plato's cosmology.[100] But in his *Lectures on Corinthians* he combines the two schemes in a manner almost identical to Pico's: "You may conceive of the Spiritual World," says Colet, "as consisting of nine orders of angels, ... revolving in perfect bliss within their spiritual circum-

---

[97] Rigg, pp. xiv-xvi.

[98] Cornford, *Plato's Cosmology*, pp. 75, 88.

[99] Dulles, p. 79. For an analysis of medieval and Renaissance cosmology, see Lupton, LC pp. xi ff. and 127-8, n. 1.

[100] See CH, p. 15 ff. Colet's knowledge of the *Timaeus* might have come partly through the medium of Macrobius's translation of Cicero's *Somnium Scipionis*, to which Colet refers at MA p. 28.

ference and firmament, even God."[101] These nine orders and God correspond or "answer . . . to the nine spheres" revolving within the stable empyrean, which is for the stars and planets "as it were an unchanging God." With the exception of the Sun, which Colet lists after Mercury, the order of the planets as they move out from earth is the same as Plato's.[102]

Colet insists that the angelic, heavenly, and earthly worlds were all created instantaneously: "All these things were created simultaneously. For it is unworthy of God . . . to suppose that He made first one thing, and then another, as if He could not have made all things at once."[103] However, the Dean concedes that the Mosaic "days" do signify a causal sequence, during which there was a simultaneous emanation of angels, heaven, earth, the "inhabitants" of heaven (i.e., stars and planets), fish-inhabitants of earth, and animals, in that order.[104] "This number six appears to me to denote, not so much any number and distinction of time, which had no existence in creation, as a number and order in the events themselves.[105]

Colet is here resorting to the Plotinian notion of creation as an emanation involving a logical order of causation without any sequence of time.[106] Indeed, he explicitly uses the term "emanation" on at least three occasions in the Radulphian Letters.[107] However, Aquinas himself used the term without intending or conveying the Plotinian concept. Like-

---

101 LC p. 127.

102 *Ibid.*, pp. 127-129.

103 MA p. 27.

104 *Ibid.*, pp. 22-23. "Heaven" is here used in the conventional sense.

105 *Ibid.*, p. 22.

106 On this point see Whittaker, p. 55. Cf. Philo's *De Mundi Op.*, p. 2, and Lupton, MA p. 22, n. 2.

107 MA pp. 18-19.

F

wise with Colet, there are many counter-balancing passages which make it undeniably clear that for him intrinsic form is not an overflow of God's essence, but rather an entity created by God outside of himself and out of nothing.[108]

Heretical Emanationism in Eckhart and Ficino

This is an interesting fact, because it was on this very point that so many Christian Neoplatonists went astray. Meister Eckhart, for example, conceived of creation as God's "boiling over," so that God was even in "wood and stone."[109] He maintained further that the "Ground" or deepest part of the soul is consubstantial with God: "The Ground of God and the ground of the soul are one and the same."[110]

The most striking example of unorthodoxy on this score, however, is Ficino. To be sure, the Florentine repudiated both types of pantheists: those who "have thought he [God] was a kind of World-Soul," and those who "have thought he was material."[111] But to reject pantheism is not necessarily to escape the heresy of emanationism—that is, the doctrine that God, though ultimately transcendent, makes himself immanent through extension.[112] What Ficino does is affirm Neo-

---

108 E.g., *ibid.*, p. 5.

109 James Clark, *Meister Eckhart*, pp. 37-38, 56; Underhill, p. 121.

110 Clark, p. 88; Jones, *Flowering of Mysticism*, pp. 72-75.

111 *Com. on Symp.*, p. 161.

112 See Inge's careful consideration of such terms in *Christian Mysticism*, p. 121. Much of the controversy over Ficino's orthodoxy would be eliminated if this distinction were made. Note for example Cassirer's attack on Saitta in "Ficino's Place in Intellectual History," *JHI* (Jan 45), 483-501. Dulles, pp. 70-72, seeking to defend Mirandola against admitted emanationism, argues that Christian orthodoxy has always taught some kind of divine immanence. But the Christian doctrine of Holy Spirit dwelling in Christian hearts is to be distinguished from the Neoplatonic notion of God's immanence in everything, including non-human phenomena. The Neoplatonic view is also to be distinguished from the Christian belief that the Creator's characteristics are reflected in creation.

platonic emanation while at the same time denying its involuntary nature: "The divine will, as Plato says in *Timaeus* [29], ... wills all other things, which are God Himself as being in God, and as flowing out of God are images of the divine face."[113] Again, in *Theologia Platonica* 16, we are told that the divine ray, which contains all forms, passes from God in different degrees to angels, humans, and the corporeal world, which it fills with objective forms.[114]

Any suggestion that Ficino is here, like Colet and Aquinas, using Plotinian terms without intending Plotinian concepts, is demolished by the fact that Ficino elsewhere expresses emanationism without using Plotinian metaphor. In *De Amore*, for instance, we are told that God "is everywhere, dwelling in the inner life of everything."[115] From such evidence one can only conclude, with DeWulf, that Ficino espoused emanationism without realizing its incompatibility with Christian dogma.[116]

Colet's Avoidance of the Emanation Heresy

Ficino's excessive Plotinianism is thus an excellent illustration of the way that the Florentine approach to pagan philosophy can lead to unintentional heresy. It is highly significant that Colet, with his more conservative Clementine approach, should have ignored Ficino's excesses in favor of a less frequent and more orthodox Ficinian view that "the lower parts of each higher order are somehow connected with the highest parts in the next following order."[117] Colet repeats this idea,

---

[113] Kristeller, *Ficino*, p. 144, cf. p. 266. Also *Com. on Symp.*, pp. 142, 202, 140.

[114] Kristeller, *Ficino*, p. 232.

[115] *Com. on Sym.*, p. 153.

[116] See DeWulf, p. 271.

[117] Kristeller, *Ficino*, p. 80.

noting that the "four worlds" (counting God as the first) "are linked together by a kind of interconnection and community of condition." This interconnection lies in the fact that the first two worlds (God and angels) are eternal and the fourth world (earth) sensible; the third world (heavenly) binds the whole together by being both sensible and to some extent eternal, in that it possesses "eternal time" or perpetuity, as distinguished from the finite time of earth.[118] This scheme is really a fifth Coletian hierarchy: the hierarchy of eternity-perpetuity-time.

Colet's Pauline-Platonic Association of Time with Sensibilia

Colet argues that God is invisible, hence uncreated and eternal; whereas the heavens are visible or "sensible," hence must be created and subject to some sort of time sequence. The notion that sensibility necessarily involves creation and precludes eternity seems indebted to *Timaeus* 28-29: "Was the world always in existence and without beginning? or created, and had it a beginning? Created, I reply, being visible and tangible and having a body, and therefore sensible; and all sensible things are ... created." Further, "The world [is] ... visible and ... therefore created.... But ... the patterns [are] ... eternal." The same notion is expressed in St. Paul: "The things which are seen are transient, but the things which are not seen are eternal" (2 Cor. 4:18). Allowing for a slight alteration in Plato's sentence order, this Pauline statement is anticipated almost verbatim in *Phaedo* 79: "Things ... you can ... see ... are always in a state of change ..., but the unchanging things are ... not seen."

Here obviously is another instance of joint Pauline-Platonic influence on Colet. It is probable that this combined influence

---

[118] MA pp. 10, 23.

was mediated through Ficino, who insisted that the created universe, being in movement, is necessarily bound to the attribute of time, while God and the intelligible world, alone being wholly at rest, must necessarily dwell in eternity.[119] However, in Colet's thinking there is a disconcerting illogicality: If angels (like men) are created and therefore to some degree sensible, why are they not also excluded from eternity? Yet Colet states that "God and the angelic nature are measured by eternity. Time takes its beginning with the heaven."[120]

This last sentence is almost identical with *Timaeus* 38—"Time, then, and the heaven came into being at the same instant." By "heaven" Plato meant the entire created universe (see *Timaeus* 37-38). Thus, Augustine, in approving this Timaean statement, wrote: "Without doubt *the world* was not made in time, but with time" (italics added). If however Colet took the term "heaven" in its usual and narrower sense, he might have thought of Plato as authority for assigning to the firmament a special time scheme different from that of earth. In fact, Plato himself confuses the issue by referring at one point (*Timaeus* 37) to the time of "heaven" as "eternal."

Definitions of Eternity in Plato and New Testament

In other ways too Colet's treatment of time and eternity shows Platonic influence. In *Timaeus* 37, for example, eternity is not only assigned to a sphere which wholly transcends the "world of becoming"; in addition, it is itself a sort of pseudo-Idea. Thus in Plato time is defined as a mere "moving

---

119 Kristeller, *Ficino*, p. 295.
120 *Ibid.*, p. 13.

image" or copy of eternity, in the same sense that created things are mere imitations of Ideas. From a Platonic perspective, therefore, eternity itself is beyond time, and is really timelessness. As such, it has no past or future, and Plato objects to denoting it by any other verb tense than the present (*Timaeus* 37-38).

As Cullman has noted, this "circular" concept of time and eternity as spheres utterly removed from each other differs from the early Christian "linear" concept, whereby eternity is time endlessly extended in both directions, with "time" in the narrow sense simply a limited portion of an upward sloping line. In New Testament thinking, eternity therefore refers to past, present, and future—that is to pre-creation, creation, and what Hebrews 11:10 calls the "future" Jerusalem. The "eternal" God of the New Testament is clearly he who "is, who was, and who will be" (Rev. 1:4).[121]

In the post-New Testament history of ideas, the Christian future and present seem to have been confused with Platonic eternity and time, with the result that many essentially orthodox Christian thinkers subsequently viewed the problem in the Platonic manner.[122] Augustine, for example, Platonically defined eternity as "God's today."[123] Ficino virtually translated *Timaeus* 37-38 by asserting similarly that eternity is nothing but a pure present, without past or future. Hence the only verb proper to it is "is"; it is improper to say that God or Ideas "were" or "will be." Man is therefore exhorted by the Florentine to flee the flux of time and ascend to the pure present.[124]

---

[121] Oscar Cullman, *Christ and Time,* pp. 51-58, 61-67.

[122] *Ibid.,* pp. 54-55.

[123] See Lupton, MA p. xxviii.

[124] Kristeller, *Ficino,* p. 296.

Colet's Definition of Eternity

Colet's views on the problem are ambiguous. At one point he describes eternity as "earlier than time . . . a measure of wider extent than all time." This description, which gives eternity a past and spreads it out on either side of time, sounds compatible with the New Testament concept.

But in the same passage Colet also pictures eternity as "more self-contained than even a point of time."[125] This statement would suggest that the Dean accepted the Platonic definition of eternity as a pure present, without past or future. Such acceptance is also implied in Colet's assertion the "eternity is all time united," and especially his observation that in eternity "every time is one undivided time: every day is one day."[126] Moreover, the special time of the firmament is said to be "a kind of unfolding of eternity, just as the heaven and visible world are an unfolding of the earlier and invisible world."[127] Unfortunately, the word "earlier" here confuses the issue, alluding as it does to the New Testament linear notion. In all other respects, however, the statement is an accurate expression of Plato's view that time bears the same relation to eternity that creation does to Ideas, and that therefore eternity is timelessness—that is, beyond time.

Summary

We may conclude, then, that Colet's doctrine of God and Creation is very largely an imitation of Augustine's Christianized adaptation of Plotinus, reenforced at certain strategic points by some of the more orthodox teachings of Ficino. Thus Colet accepts Plotinus's views that God is the One-

---

[125] MA p. 4.
[126] *Ibid.*, pp. 12, 6.
[127] *Ibid.*, p. 13.

Good-Beauty who creates the world from a pattern of Ideas within his own Mind, and that this creation involves an instantaneous fusion of form and matter. The Dean also makes lavish use of the Plotinian hierarchy (prominent in Ficino) of being-form-good-unity-rest; and adapts Plotinian emanation to an explanation of Mosaic days in terms of a causal rather than chronological sequence. Another interesting feature of Colet's Creation-system is his combination of the Dionysian angelic orders with Platonic cosmology in the exact manner of Mirandola's *Heptaplus*.

From Plato's *Dialogues* themselves come a number of notions which Colet finds compatible. The first of these, that God is a Master Architect who built the world because he is good, was stressed by Augustine. Another Platonic teaching, found especially in Colet's *Letters to Radalphus*, is the view (bolstered by St. Paul, Augustine, and Ficino) that the world was created not in time but *with* time, and that time is therefore necessarily associated with created sensibilia. Colet also makes surprisingly extensive use of the *Philebus* Limited-Unlimited concept, applying these terms to God (or form) and matter respectively. Further, he builds his rather odd propagation hierarchy around the mother-father impregnation imagery of *Timaeus*.

Following Augustine's Clementine approach, Colet avoids three possible heresies by denying Plotinus's contentions that (1) God is beyond being; (2) matter is co-eternal with God; (3) intrinsic forms result from an emanation of extrinsic forms which have in turn emanated from God. In so denying these Plotinian notions, Colet shows a far keener awareness of the strictures of Christian dogma than does the Florentine Ficino.

Colet does however breach orthodoxy at three points. The first of these is an intermittent association of evil with God-created matter, a position into which he apparently stumbles as the result of his fondness for the Plotinian light-dark metaphors. Under both Platonic and Plotinian pressure, he also denies in certain instances God's complete control over resistent matter, and in so doing necessarily implies that God is not omnipotent. Finally, in the Dean's ambiguous definitions of eternity we find echoes of a Platonic view not compatible with New Testament teaching. However, this third possible heterodoxy represents a minor deviation characteristic of many essentially orthodox writers.

So far as Colet's doctrine of God and Creation is concerned, we must therefore say of him what Gilson said of Augustine: It is astounding that he could absorb such a dose of pagan philosophy and still remain so much within the boundaries of Christian dogma.

The concept of man in Dean Colet can be measured only against the backdrop of the Platonic and Pauline views. In the *Dialogues,* there is a sharp ontological, psychic, and moral cleavage between soul and body. First of all, the Platonic body belongs to the lowest order of created existence, the realm of "becoming"; as such, it is automatically "inferior" to (*Laws* 5:728) and possesses less "truth" (*Republic* 9:585) than the soul. Signs of this ontological inferiority are the fact that the body was created after the soul (*Timaeus* 42, 69), and is "liable to speedy dissolution" in contrast to the soul's immortality (*Phaedo* 80-81).

Platonic Attitude toward Soul-Body

Moreover, the Platonic body exists merely "for the sake of the soul" (*Laws* 9:870); it is not part of the human per-

sonality, of the "real man" or "true self" (*Republic* 4:443).
The real man is the soul, which pre-exists the body (*Phaedo*
73, *Timaeus* 41-42) and is thereafter temporarily "encased"
(*Timaeus* 44, 87) "like an oyster in his shell" (*Phaedrus*
250). The point is reinforced by the fact that it is the soul
alone which is immortal. Evil souls transmigrate to other
bodies (*Phaedo* 81-82), while pure souls enjoy the company
of God "henceforth altogether without the body" (*Phaedo*
114), "for immortal no such union [of soul-body] can be
reasonably believed to be" (*Phaedrus* 246).

The body is not only non-essential, it is also inherently evil
(*Phaedo* 66) because it was created from disordered matter,
which opposes God's desire for perfection in his work.[1] Thus
in Plato, despite his toying in *Timaeus* 69-70 with "mortal"
parts of the soul, there is a considerable moral contrast between the "divine" soul and the rebellious "human" body
(*Phaedo* 80, 94). "Evils ... hover around this body or "mortal nature," and make it "antagonistic to good" (*Theaetetus*
176). The body is morally reprehensible not only because it
opposes the ethical guidance of soul, but because it hampers
the soul's search for knowledge. The life aim of the soul is
to escape the body in order to reach Ideas (*Phaedo* 67). But
(at least in Plato's early thought), this feat is impossible.
It follows therefore that the body is the soul's "grave"
(*Cratylus* 400), "tomb" (*Phaedrus* 250, *Gorgias* 493),
"chains" (*Phaedo* 67), and "prison" (*Phaedo* 80-83, cf.
Phaedrus 250)—metaphors which simultaneously imply
moral condemnation and the soul's non-essentiality.

Pauline Attitude toward Soul-Body

By contrast, the Pauline body is not divorced from personal-

---

[1] See *Timaeus* 30, as analyzed by Cornford, *Plato's Cosmology*, p. 36.

ity. To be sure, Paul uses the Platonic terms "outward" and "inward man," as found in *Republic* 4: 443-4 (cf. 9:589)— "Justice [is] ... concerned ... , not with the outward man but with the inward." Compare this with Rom. 2: 28-29— "He is not a Jew who is one outwardly; ... but he is a Jew who is one inwardly; ... circumcision is that of the heart, in the spirit" (cf. Eph. 2:11, 2 Cor. 5:12, 4:16). But such Platonic terminology should not mislead us into thinking that Paul conceived of the soul or "inner man" as the "true self." For Paul as for all Hebrews, man does not *have* a body for a while; he *is* a body, as well as a soul. He is "flesh-animated-by-soul, the whole conceived as a psycho-physical unity."[2] In Plato "the relation of the soul to the body is not essential to it and may be dissolved."[3] But in Paul the ultimate necessity of the body even in the afterlife is illustrated by the Apostle's emphasis on resurrection: the body which is "sown a natural body" must be "raised a spiritual body" (1 Cor. 15:44).[4]

It is true that in two isolated instances Paul compares the body to a "vessel" (2 Tim. 2:21), and to a combination garment-tent-dwelling (2 Cor. 5:1-4). The second instance is a tantalizing echo of *Phaedo* 87, where the transmigration of one soul through many bodies is allegorized by the story of "an old weaver" and his "many coats."[5] But even in his garment-figure, Paul emphasizes that the existence of soul apart from some type of body is a condition of unnatural "nakedness" (2 Cor. 5:1-4).

Nor does Paul recognize any moral discrepancy between body and soul. Baur, Holsten, Ludemann, and others who

---

[2] John Robinson, *The Body: A Study in Pauline Theology*, p. 14.

[3] Demos, *Philosophy of Plato*, pp. 304-5.

[4] Fernand Prat, *Theology of St. Paul*, 1:139-140.

[5] In *Gorgias* 493 it is the soul, not the body, which is called a "vessel."

claim such a Platonic moral dualism ignore the fact that for the Jewish Paul there could be no such phenomenon as Plato's evilly autonomous matter from which bodies are supposedly created. As for all Jews, God is for Paul the creator of all things, and all things must therefore be essentially good.[6] Pauline psychology therefore holds that soul and body are together either holy or unholy depending on whether they are in contact with Christ. The Christian is "holy in body and spirit" (1 Cor. 7:34); his body is a glorious "temple of the Holy Spirit" (1 Cor. 6:19-20) which can be "presented as a living sacrifice, holy, acceptable to God" (Rom. 12:1).

Only in the area of ontology (the hierarchy of created things) do we find an analogy between Pauline psychology and Platonic dualism. Though in Paul the body is not Platonically divorced from personality or inherently wicked, it nevertheless occupies a lower status than the soul. Were this not so, the "lowly body" (Phil. 3:21) would not need to be made more adequate before rejoining the soul in the afterlife. The chief reason for this lower status is that it is the body, rather than the soul, which gives sin its opportunity.

Paul apparently believed in unseen spirit-forces similar in nature to Plato's mediating daemons (*Symposium* 202-3 and elsewhere), but more hostile in function.[7] The chief of these "elemental spirits" (Gal. 4:9) he called " the prince of the power[s] of the air" (Eph. 2:2). For Paul this "prince" was Sin or Satan, analogous in function to Plato's "evil Soul" (*Laws* 10:897). In Paul's thinking it is this external force of Sin which is the real origin of evil, because Sin attacks the essentially good body and perverts it. Thus the ultimate enemy of the Pauline soul is not the body but the prince of

---

[6] Prat, 1:233, 2:69. Cf. James Moffatt, *Paul and Paulinism*, pp. 51-52.

[7] See 1 Cor. 1: 16-20, Rom. 8:38.

darkness who chooses the body as his instrument: "Do not let sin therefore reign in your mortal bodies" (Rom. 6:12).

Colet's Attitude toward Soul-Body

Colet's concept of the relation of soul to body is a curious and erratic mixture of the Platonic and Pauline. "We must observe," says the Dean, "that man consist[s] . . . of a soul (which St. Paul calls the inner man), and a sentient body (which may be termed, in Plotinus's words, the animal part of man)."[8] Colet here retains not only the Platonic terms "animal" and "inner man," recognizing the latter as also Pauline; but he speaks—here and in most instances elsewhere —of the inner man as the "soul," and the outer man (by implication) as the "body." The significance of this should not be overlooked. The term "soul" is used very infrequently by Paul.[9] The Apostle prefers such synonyms as mind, heart, and especially spirit.[10] Moreover, though Paul often uses the Greek term "body," an even more characteristic usage is that of "flesh."[11] Colet's preference for the terms soul and body seems obviously the result of Platonic pressure.

However, it is just as clear that Colet, with Paul, rejects Plato's notion of the soul as the real man. "Man consist[s] . . . of a soul *and* a sentient body" (italics added). To be sure,

---

8 LR p. 16.

9 By Prat's count, 2: 404, only 13 times in the whole Epistles.

10 Prat, 2:50-51, 47, 72-74.

11 The precise relation between the Pauline terms "body" and "flesh" is immensely difficult. For example, G. O. Griffith, in *St. Paul's Gospel to the Romans*, pp. 18-19, 87-89, and *passim.*, argues that Pauline "flesh" refers to desire, not to the body. However, one of the most exhaustive studies of these terms was made by Prat, who concludes, 2: 52-53, that "a synonymy between the body and the flesh exists . . . to a considerable degree." This conclusion is compatible with Paul's grammatical context. For a detailed discussion of this problem, see Ernest Burton, *Spirit, Soul, and Flesh*, pp. 50, 71, 168, 187, and *passim;* and Robinson, *The Body*, pp. 11-13.

there is Colet's isolated complaint that "we are here...
shrouded in this poor murky body."[12] However, the garment-
figure is found even in Paul (2 Cor. 5:1-4). No doubt we have
here, in both Paul and Colet, the use of Platonic language
without any intention to express the Platonic notion of psychic cleavage. At any rate, Colet's basic position that the body
is an integral part of personality is emphasized by his insistence on "complete resurrection," and his observation that
man is of a divided nature, body and soul.[13]

The "Microcosm" Idea in the Platonic Tradition

This attitude is reinforced by Colet's treatment of man as a
microcosm, or little world. As Gale once put it, Plotinus observed that "in man lies hid the seeds of all things. He is
indeed the Compend of the Universe; prefiguring the Earth
by his pulverous Masse, the Plant by Vegetation, the Brute
by Sense, the Sun and Moon by his eyes, the Heaven by the
swiftness of his motion, the Angel by his Reason."[14] Back of
this lay the *Timaeus*:

> Plato having discoursed at large of the Macrocosme, or greater
> world, he descends to the microcosme, or lesser world of men
> (*Tim.*, p. 68), where he lays down this Hypothesis, That God
> made man such an Universe as contains all other Animals, both
> mortal and immortal: i.e. Man is a singular microcosme, where-
> in is to be seen whatever lies scattered up and down in the
> greater World.[15]

However, it was the Florentines who developed the concept
into a pivotal doctrine. Mirandola worked out an especially
elaborate parallel between man and the hierarchy of being,

---

12 LR p. 26.
13 LC p. 63; CH p. 3.
14 Gale, *Court of the Gentiles* 3:9:3 in Lupton, LC p. 133, n.2.
15 *Ibid.*

arguing that man's intellect corresponds to the angels, his reason to planetary souls, his appetite to animals, his powers of nutrition and generation to plants, and his body to the elements.[16]

Colet's Imitation of Mirandola's Microcosm Scheme

It is not difficult to perceive the influence of Pico's view on Colet's statement that "Man is to such a degree a composite being, that we may consider him the child of the whole universe, corporeal and incorporeal."[17] Even closer to the Mirandolan concept is this passage: "Because that microcosm, man, is an epitome of the whole universe, resembling in his spiritual faculties the nine orders of angels; it follows that he will resemble the heaven in the more refined part of his body, and the sublunary world in the lowest part."[18]

As these quotations indicate, in both Mirandola and Colet man's body as well as his soul is compared to the universal hierarchy. Underlying such parallels is the assumption, as Mirandola put it, that "Man is composed of a body and a rational soul."[19]

Colet's Avoidance of Ficino's Heretical Microcosm Concept

This assumption stands in the greatest possible contrast to Ficino, who clearly excluded the body from human personality. Thus Ficino speaks frequently of the soul's pre-existence, and its descent into its "earthly prison" and temporary "dark dwelling." [20] Even more explicitly, he asserts that "man

---

[16] Dulles, p. 115. The Florentines distinguished between "intellect" and "reason," giving the former priority. See Kristeller, *Ficino*, pp. 366-9.

[17] MA p. 22.

[18] LC p. 133.

[19] Dulles, p. 114.

[20] *Com. on Symp.*, pp. 185-6; 158; Kristeller, *Ficino*, pp. 332, 344.

is the soul itself. . . . Everything that a man is said to do, his soul does itself; the body merely suffers it to be done; wherefore man is soul alone, and the body of man must be its instrument." He acknowledges that when we say "men" in the sense of "souls," we speak "in the Platonic fashion."[21] Any argument that Ficino was here paraphrasing rather than approving Plato is belied by the fact that, even in his later works, Ficino uses the terms man, soul, and mind interchangeably, though sometimes "mind" refers in a more restricted sense to the soul's upper portion.[22]

It is understandable, therefore, that Ficino's microcosm concept should differ radically from that of Colet and Mirandola. Since the real man is soul alone, it is the soul alone which is compared to the universal hierarchy, intellect being said to correspond to angels and the soul's lower instincts to animals.[23] It is noteworthy that Colet, with his Clementine approach to the nature of man, should have preferred the Mirandolan notion of "microcosm." In doing so, he avoided Ficino's heresies of pre-existence and the soul alone as the true self.

Colet's Heresy of the Evil Body

However, Colet was not as successful in avoiding the related Platonic heresy of the body as intrinsically evil. There can be no doubt that he understood and approved St. Paul's position

---

[21] *Com. on Symp.*, p. 157.

[22] Kristeller, *Ficino*, p. 328. Note especially Colet's *Epistolae* marginalia Nos. 33, 20, and 13 paraphrasing similar Ficinian passages: "A man is like a star wrapped in a cloud"; "God creates our souls, but the world creates our bodies"; "The soul rather than the body, is the real man" . ✝. It is significant that Colet dutifully noted such ideas, then clearly rejected them.

[23] Kristeller, *Ficino*, p. 385.

G

on this point, to wit: that the body is essentially good and is made evil only by the invading force of sin. Thus again and again Colet asserts that the Devil is

> author and father of evil. . . .. We have no enemies and opponents except sin . . . and the evil spirits that tempt to sin. . . . Evil spirits love the flesh. . . . St. Paul teaches us that we have our wrestling against the prince of the power of the air. . . . The Devils . . . strive to injure the human race. . . . delude their senses, and corrupt their affections. . . . We wrestle not, writes the Apostle, against the flesh and blood, . . . but against . . . the ruler of the darkness.[24]

In line with these assertions, Colet frequently states the Pauline view that soul and body are together holy or unholy, depending on man's relation to God. "This state of sanctity," says the Dean, exists when man is "holy alike in mind and body."[25] Again, "every righteous man, with his full individuality in Christ, may be blessed both in body and soul in glory."[26] Indeed, it would be difficult to find any more careful and succinct statement of the Pauline position than Colet's observation in the *Mystical Body* treatise: "Christ died not for the substance of our body, which is good, and will remain in the blessed, but for the sins of the body."[27]

Yet, despite such assertions, Colet frequently lapsed into Platonism when he was not tied immediately to the Pauline text. Apparently he was unable to escape the attraction of Plotinus's Platonic emphasis on matter as "the first evil."[28]

---

[24] *Sac.,* p. 12; EH pp. 73, 127; CH pp. 44, 65.

[25] LC p. 92.

[26] CH p. 137.

[27] Colet, "On Christ's Mystical Body, the Church" (hereafter MB), in Lupton, *Letters to Radulphus . . . and other Treatises,* p. 41.

[28] *Enn.* 1:8:3, 14; 2:4:16.

In any event, the association of matter with darkness and evil, already cited in the Radulphian letters, continues throughout his works. In the *Mystical Body* treatise, for instance, the "earthly world," by virtue of its "conflicting" matter, is "black and cold."[29] Thus, in contrast to Paul, Colet sometimes advances an intrinsic moral cleavage between the soul, which is devoid of matter, and the body, which is composed of matter: "The soul, ... being, as it is, *light, good,* eternal, and immortal, ... exist[s] in this finite body of ours, which is temporal, *evil, dark,* and mortal."[30] On one occasion the Dean seeks to straddle the Pauline and Platonic viewpoints. In a discussion of carnal appetite he argues: "In other cases the body appears rather as the instrument of sin; [but] in this of fornication, as the very originator and agent."[31] In other cases, he finds Platonic metaphor too attractive to resist, speaking of the "prison of the body" and noting that Christ "was willing to seem weak and foolish ... in the dark prison-house of weak human flesh."[32]

Even if we concede that Colet probably did not here mean to imply the exclusion of the body from personality, we must still reckon with the connoted moral condemnation. Likewise in the Dionysian abstracts, Colet clearly pictures the body *per se* as exerting a destructive influence on the otherwise unified and divine soul:

> Men ... are not themselves of a single and undivided nature (since there clings to their souls the heavy and wearisome mass of the body, in which the soul, degenerating from its simplicity, becomes in some degree corporeal, so as now to be unfitted and

---

[29] MB p. 31.
[30] LC p. 63. Italics added.
[31] LC p. 48.
[32] LC pp. 24, 17.

altogether unable to gaze upon the purely spiritual, and so
weakened also by admixture of the body, as to be powerless to
endure any strong light . . .).[33]

From such passages we can only conclude that there is in
Colet a considerable vacillation between the Pauline and Platonic views of the body's moral status.

Intrinsically Wicked Flesh in Pre-Colet Christian Thinkers

However, it would have been surprising if Colet had wholly
escaped the Platonic heresy of intrinsically wicked flesh, because almost all of the sources he prized highly, including
the Christian ones, espoused it. Philo had talked in Platonic
language of prison-house bodies.[34] And Ficino had spoken
harshly of man's physical nature as base, pestilence, filth, dirt,
and unwholesome.[35] Since in other contexts Ficino states that
the lower appetite of the soul for the body is a desire for a
particular good created by God, we would probably be wrong
to interpret such adjectives as deliberately intended to imply
the body's inherent wickedness.[36] On the other hand, there
can be no question that, under Platonic influence, Ficino's
contempt for the body was greater than St. Paul's; nor can
there be any question that Ficino's terms might easily have
led to misinterpretation by Colet.

The language of Augustine was also subject to misunderstanding. He clearly did not accept the view that the flesh is
per se evil. If God created the body, then "in its own kind
and degree the flesh is good" (*City of God* 14:5). It is not

---

[33] CH p. 3.

[34] Lupton, MA p. xxvi.

[35] Kristeller, *Ficino*, pp. 207, 293, 315. Cf. Colet's paraphrase of Ficino, in
the *Epistolae:* "Scorn the body."—Jayne, *Colet and Ficino*, p. 319.

[36] *Ibid.*, pp. 194, 19.

therefore the body which is a burden to the soul, but the body in consequence of being invaded by sin (*City of God* 13:16). This is of course the Pauline position. But Augustine nevertheless tended to emphasize, not the natural or originally created goodness of the body, but rather the perverted body produced by Adam's Fall. The body had not been created as a prison for man's soul, yet that is what it had become.[37] In referring to the post-Fall body, Augustine therefore uses the Platonic prison-metaphor, and speaks of the soul as exercising over the rebellious body a permanently noble act of "vital attention," similar in nature though deficient in moral power to the Platonic soul's "energy" and "watchfulness" (*Laws* 10:904; 906).

The prison-metaphor, as we have noted, implies not only moral condemnation, but also the Platonic notion, repeated by Plotinus, that the soul is the imprisoned "real man." To be sure, Augustine often expresses the Pauline view that man is neither soul nor body alone, but the two together. Yet, following Plotinus's *Enneads* 1:1:3, which in turn followed Plato's 1 *Alcibiades* 129, Augustine also inconsistently defines man as "a soul that uses a body."[38] Indeed, he even uses this definition as the basis for the Platonic argument (*Phaedo* 105-106) that the soul must be immortal, because it is in itself "life"; in surviving the body it is therefore simply continuing to be what it is. Such passages support Gilson's contention that "the Plotinian notion of man has deeply influenced the noetic of St. Augustine."[39] Considering the respect which Colet accorded Augustine, it is therefore remarkable that on these points the Dean remained as orthodox as he did.

---

[37] Gilson, p. 78.
[38] *Ibid.*, pp. 74-75.
[39] *Ibid.*

Colet's Platonic Concept of Soul as Origin of Life

Colet was also heavily indebted to Platonism for his views on the relation of biological life to body and soul. Like Plato, he accepts the soul as the immediate origin of life: "This life in the body is a combination of light and heat, poured forth ... from that inmost and highest soul."[40] Compare this with *Phaedo* 105 (cf. *Cratylus* 400)—where "whatever the soul possesses, to that she comes bearing life." Colet emphasizes that this physical life is merely a Platonic imitation of the soul's life, which also consists of light (intellect) and heat (will): "Of this older and purer life, the light and heat felt in the body ... are a later and grosser image, reproducing it roughly and coarsely, as in a poor and unfitting substance."[41]

Physical life is conveyed into the body in this manner: The "lower and obscurer part" of the soul blends with the clearer, more refined elements of the body. This blending creates "vital spirits" which, "coming midway between the exalted soul and the humble body, cause both the body to resemble the soul, and the soul to recognize the body."[42] This notion is chiefly indebted to the Florentines. Ficino emphasized a favorite Neoplatonic idea, that of an intermediary "spirit" between man's two extremes: "The soul ... is more pure, therefore, it cannot be united to this thick earthly body, ... except by a most ... light-bearing body, which we call spirit."[43] This spirit "receives the powers of the soul and transfers them into the body."[44] Mirandola, speaking of man

---

[40] LR p. 72.

[41] *Ibid.*

[42] LR p. 73. Cf. CH p. 128—"In man, between his soul and body, there intervene ... fiery spirits."

[43] Kristeller, *Ficino*, p. 372.

[44] *Com. on Symp.*, p. 189.

as a microcosm, repeated the idea, noting that, just as natural heaven and earth are connected by light, so man's soul and body are connected by "spirits."[45]

Colet's Use of Florentine "Vital Spirits"

Mirandola's concept of "spirits" seem to represent an attempt to parallel the Platonic mediating daemons. At any rate, such a parallel was apparently in Colet's mind. Having analyzed the "vital spirits" of human beings, he compares them to the Apostles, who like mediating daemons operated between God and man, and were therefore called by St. John "spirits of God."[46] In a later passage a similar analogy is made between "vital spirits" and the clergy, who are said to stand midway between "Prophets" and "Teachers." This time, however, the authority is clearly Dionysian: "This was the order I thought St. Paul wished to convey because . . . it contains . . . a resemblance to that Heavenly Hierarchy where the first orders burn and cleave to God in ceaseless contemplation; the last have regard to the lower matters here on earth . . .; whilst midway between them speed to and fro the ministering spirits."[47]

By means of intermediary "vital spirits,"

> these two principles, light and heat, emanate together in order from the highest to the lowest; and . . . they pass downwards

---

[45] See Lupton's analysis of Mirandola's *Heptaplus*, in Colet's LR pp. xxxiii-xxxiv.

[46] LR pp. 75-78. In his *Epistolae* marginalia, Colet paraphrases Ficino's attempt to reconcile the benevolent Platonic daemons with their wicked counterparts in St. Paul: "Demons in whom the spirit element is strongest . . . work for the good. On the other hand, demons in whom the bodily element predominates wreak dreadful evil on the strength and judgment of a man."—See Jayne, *Colet and Ficino*, pp. 363-4.

[47] *Ibid.*, p. 90. Cf. CH p. 128.

and become deteriorated. But wherever they are conveyed, their effort is to preserve themselves so far as they can, and to confine and keep together in unity the scattered substance that they have penetrated. It is the constant care of each higher gradation to sustain in union the next lower to which it is neighbor. There is also an anxious attention on the part of each towards the one higher than itself, that by that higher one it may itself be sustained in unity and life.[48]

This passage is an interesting blend of Plotinian emanation, Neoplatonic intrinsic form as stabilizer, and Dionysian universal love as emphasized by Ficino. In *De Amore* we are told, on the authority of Dionysius, that "Love ... [i]s an innate and uniting force that drives the higher things to care for the lower ones, the equal things to some special communion with each other, and finally induces all lower things to turn toward the better and higher ones."[49]

Plato's Tripartite Soul

Colet's views on the parts of the soul, and the soul's method of controlling the body, were also heavily tinctured with Platonism, yet at the same time essentially orthodox if measured by the standard of St. Paul. The soul of the *Dialogues* is "tripartite" (*Republic* 4: 435-443). It consists of reason, passion, and appetite. By reason is meant "the principle with which ... a man learns"; by passion, emotions like indignation, enthusiasm, anger, ambition; by appetite, primarily the gastronomical and sexual instincts. Only when this soul is properly "harmonized," with reason in control of passion and appetite, can the whole soul govern the body and steer it toward good acts (*Republic* 4:442, 443-4; 6-485).

---

[48] LR pp. 73-74.
[49] *Com. on Symp.*, p. 148, cf. p. 153.

Pauline and Platonic Psychology Compared

Since Paul himself had no precise psychological vocabulary, it is very difficult to compare his scheme with Plato's.[50] However, in Plato passion is good or bad, depending on whether it is under reason's control. In Paul, on the other hand, passion seems to be the perennial ally of reason and as such part of the soul; while appetite or desire is assigned to the body.[51] Thus, with one isolated exception (Rom. 1:24, 26), noble emotions are associated with the heart or inner man—for example, courage in 2 Cor. 4:16, and compassion in 2 Cor. 7:3, 1 Thes. 2:8, and Rom. 10:1. Conversely, "the desires of the flesh" (Gal. 5:16-17) are always pictured as perverted by sin and hence in opposition to the soul.[52]

As this implies, Paul had no specific terms for designating reason and passion separately. By all means he recognizes an emotional aspect within the soul: the Pauline soul can suffer "pain" (Rom. 9:2) and possess "joy" (Gal. 5:22-23). But this aspect is always included in the terms spirit, mind, and heart, all of which were intended to denote both intellect and noble feeling.[53]

Plato and Paul on Man's "Civil War"

This fact that Paul did not emphasize "partitions" within the soul, and did not conceive of one partition as battling against another, must be kept in mind when comparing the Platonic

---

[50] Note *Interpreter's Bible,* hereafter IB, 10: 201.

[51] See Prat, 1: 236.

[52] Plato used appetite, desire, affections, and lusts synonymously—see *Republic* 4: 439, 9: 571; *Phaedo* 81, 82, 94. KJV uses the last two exclusively. RSV often uses desire, but sometimes confuses the issue by using passion in the sense of appetite. Compare, for example, KJV and RSV on Gal. 5: 24.

[53] See Prat, 2: 50-51, 47.

and Pauline views that man is the locale of an "immortal conflict" (*Laws* 10:906) or "civil war": "I see in my members another law at war with the law of my mind, and making me captive to the law of sin which dwells in my members (Rom. 7:23).

Griffith has compared Paul's notion of a personal war to the "similar tension and conflict" in *Republic* 9:588.[54] But even this single citation poses crucial distinctions. In Plato the "war" is really two wars: first, the relatively minor "opposition" of the soul to the body (*Phaedo* 94); and second, the far more important "conflict" within the soul itself (*Republic* 4:440), on the outcome of which victory or defeat in the first war depends. It is this second battle which is allegorically described in *Republic* 9:588-590 as the attempt of the "monster" appetite and the "lion" passion to "drag about" and "devour" the "god" reason. But in Paul the "monster" is not part of the soul; he is assigned rather to the body, while the "lion" is noble and allied with reason.

Thus for Paul the human "war" is far simpler than in Plato: it is merely a battle between the unified soul (reason-passion) and the body with its desires. Moreover, the Pauline body must be "pommeled" and "subdued" (1 Cor. 9:27), not because it is Platonically evil in itself, but because it has been seized by invading sin, which thereupon "dwells" in the "members."

Although there is in Paul no concept of rival partitions within the soul, and therefore no concept of Platonic "disharmony," Paul does hold with Plato that the soul at birth is weakened to the point that it cannot control the body. In Paul's case this weakness results from Adam's original sin (Rom. 5:12-16), while in Plato it results from the shock of

---

54 Griffith, pp. 87-89.

incarnation, which "corrupts" and bewilders the reason (*Timaeus* 44, 90). For Paul this situation can be corrected only by the active aid of God, who through the Holy Spirit must infuse sanctifying grace into the human soul, so that it is strengthened with might through the Spirit in the "inner man" (Eph. 3:16 cf. Phil. 4:13, 2 Tim. 4:27). This parallels the Platonic concept that the "polluted" soul is "fascinated with the body" (*Phaedo* 81) and must therefore be purified before it can govern. But in Plato, this purification or harmony is secured chiefly by man's own efforts: through the soul's "watchfulness"; the "strong influence" of noble friends; education; philosophy; or through assimilation to the harmony of the universe (*Laws* 10:903-6, *Timaeus* 44, 90).

Colet's Psychological Scheme

In Colet the structure of the human soul is neither precisely Pauline nor Platonic. Basically, "the soul of man consists of intellect and will."[55] To this bipartite structure Colet sometimes adds "passion" or "feeling." For example, he speaks of unsanctified men's souls as containing "as many separate feelings as there are individuals, and as many wills as feelings."[56] But in the main he holds to the view that "minds and wills" are the essence of souls.[57] These two divisions, together with memory, are sometimes found in the Neoplatonic writings.[58] The will, with which Colet on most occasions

---

[55] LC p. 12.

[56] MB p. 32. Cf. the soul's "passion" and "reason," ExR p. 85.

[57] MB p. 37, cf. ExR p. 133.

[58] Eckhart, for example, assigns these three faculties to the upper half of the soul. See Clark, *Meister Eckhart*, pp. 58-59, 63. However, it is doubtful that Colet's bipartite soul owes anything to Neoplatonism. Certainly it owes little to Ficino, whose soul comprised mind (intellect), reason, and "idolum," the first faculty yearning toward God, and the third toward the body. See Kristeller, *Ficino*, pp. 366-369, 375, 392.

seems to have incorporated Plato's passion, is called "the lower and obscure part of the soul."[59] As Lupton has observed, the Coletian "charioteer" (reason) has therefore only one "steed" (will or passion) to ride, instead of the two steeds (passion and appetite) pictured in Plato's *Phaedrus* 246.[60]

Appetite is never assigned by Colet to the soul, though infrequently he conceives it to be associated with the "vital spirits" which mediate between soul and body. Thus: "In the soul itself heat and light are intelligence and will; in these middle spirits sense and desire; in the body again, they are sensible light and warmth."[61] Most often, however, appetite is clearly presented in association with the body.[62] Hence the man divorced from Christ necessarily follows "after the flesh and fleshly appetites."[63] The body has "the power of sense, appetite, and action."[64] The source of fornication "is in the remotest and lowest faculty of our body, ... the sense of touch. ... In it resides the ... appetite, and ... that carnal act. Hence it follows that the sensation of that lust deserves especially to be spoken of as in the body."[65] Sometimes Colet speaks of "brute-like" or "beast-like appetites in the body."[66] This is reminiscent of *Timaeus* 70-71, where the gods seized appetite and "bound it down like a wild animal."

---

[59] LR p. 73.

[60] Lupton, LC p. 12, n.2.

[61] LR p. 73, cf. CH p. 129.

[62] Note ExR p. 133; LC p. 122.

[63] LR p. 26.

[64] *Ibid.*, p. 62.

[65] LC p. 48.

[66] ExR p. 144; LR p. 61.

Colet on Man's "Civil War"

Especially is appetite or lust associated with the body in a remarkable passage inspired by Plato's *Republic:*

> From Adam's transgression . . . this animal part of man [i.e., the "sentient body"] . . . has borne sway in . . . the human commonwealth. After its own folly and lust it has governed all things in man, and sunk all down to misery. . . . The animal and bestial part of man . . . was committed to the inner man, and soul, to be ruled by it. . . . But after that man loosed himself from God, through . . . want of faith, and sank to the corporeal, our bestial nature . . . broke forth at once in riot and madness, and seized upon the reins of government in man. His soul it placed in miserable subjection to folly and lust, and dealt with everything after the judgment of the senses. Then did there wax strong in man a republic, as it were, wholly of the people and the commonalty, administered by the decision and decrees of sense, with no interposition of the authority of understanding and reason; a republic held in blind subjection, forced in a measure to be a slave.[67]

The allusion here is unmistakably to *Republic* 4:434-435, 441, where man is pictured as a little commonwealth, his reason, passion, and appetite corresponding respectively to the rulers, soldiers, and workers of the larger State. In Colet these latter became the usurping "people and commonalty." However, in the *Republic* the chaos of human government refers to internal disharmony, whereas in Colet's passage it is in the characteristic terms of Pauline soul versus body.

This might seem to imply that Colet, like Paul, recognized no possible internal disharmonization. Actually, however, in those places where he digresses from the Pauline text, he often speaks of the fact that the soul must be "ordered by Reason" before "the body and the sensual appetites [can]

---

[67] LR pp. 16-17, 22.

be ordered by the soul."[68] His previously cited comment on the non-believer's soul as a morass of conflicting feelings and wills is further evidence for the Dean's Platonic belief in warring factions within the soul. But for Colet this internal disorder cannot be rectified by man's efforts alone, as in Plato. It is not by reason alone, but by "Reason and Grace" that harmony is restored.[69] For whatever men "may attempt among themselves, of and by themselves, nothing but mischievous deformity can be the ultimate result."[70]

Summary

Colet's psychology is thus seen to be an amalgamation of Pauline, Platonic, and other influences. His concept of the soul as the origin of biological life, and his preference for the terms "soul" and "body" rather than the more characteristically Pauline "spirit" and "flesh," are undoubtedly the result of Platonic pressure. The presence of Plato, reenforced by Plotinus, is also evident in Colet's intermittent emphasis on the God-created body as evil—a heresy into which he might have been led by his usually infallible guide, Augustine. However, Colet does manage to reject Ficino's Platonic heresy of the soul as the "real man," and insists instead with Paul that the body is part of personality. This rejection is especially apparent in Colet's imitation of the Mirandolan microcosm concept, whereby man (body as well as soul) is compared to the universal hierarchy.

---

[68] From "A Right Fruitfull Monicion concernynge the Order of a Good Christen Mannes Lyfe," in Lupton, *Life of John Colet,* Appendix D, p. 306. Hereafter *Right Fruitful Monition* or RFM. Ficino also emphasizes the soul as "the ruler of the body" in his *Epistolae* marginalia in Jayne, *Colet and Ficino,* p. 311.

[69] RFM p. 306.

[70] MB p. 34.

In explaining how life gets from the soul to the body, Colet is apparently indebted to the Florentine notion of intermediary "vital spirits," though the context shows that the Dean was also here thinking of analogies with Platonic and Dionysian mediating daemons. The downflow of life from soul to body is described by Colet in terms of Plotinian emanation and especially in terms of the Ficinian (ultimately Dionysian) notion of a universal love which, in this case, unifies the body by encouraging its higher parts to care for the lower, and the lower parts to rely on the higher.

The Coletian psychological scheme uses the three basic Platonic faculties of reason, passion, and appetite. However, Colet follows Paul in assigning appetite to the body, rather than (as in Plato) to the soul. Unlike Paul, Colet recognizes reason and passion (or will) as Platonically separate partitions battling against each other and needing harmonization before the soul can rule the body. But in both Colet and Paul the emphasis is on Plato's secondary "war" of the soul versus body—a war which Colet elaborates via an ingenious adaptation of the *Republic's* notion that man is a "little state." In Colet the usurping body with its appetites is accordingly compared to a rebellion of Platonic workers against their proper guardians—a rebellion which (from the Dean's perspective) can be quieted only if God lends his aid to the disordered soul.

Hence in the last analysis Colet's concept of man involves a fusion of Platonic and Pauline psychology within the framework of Christian redemption: Infused grace produces internal order or harmony of soul, with reason supreme; the soul then governs the body with its appetites, steering it toward noble acts. It is to this redemptive scheme that we must now turn our attention.

CHAPTER 4 "SECOND CREATION"—
COLET'S REDEMPTIVE SCHEME

Original Sin in Colet

The starting point in Colet's redemptive system is original sin. In "Adam ... all sinned. ... As the whole tree is in the root ... ; so the entire human race was in Adam; and in him all our nature sinned unto death."[1] The result was not the absolute obliteration of free will, but the perversion of that will, so that it thereafter had a "proneness to evil."[2] From the Fall of Adam "man had ... no unclouded reason, no upright will. Whatever men did amongst themselves, was fool-

---

[1] ExR pp. 156-7.

[2] MB p. 32. Cf. "We are prone to lust" in *Epistolae* marginalia—Jayne, *Colet and Ficino*, pp. 34-5, 367.

ish and wicked."[3] In contrast to Ficino, Colet can scarcely find words adequate to describe man's present

> defiled and corrupted nature. . . . Nothing is here but iniquity, ignorance, weakness, downfall, destruction, nothing but the cold of wickedness, the darkness of folly, winter of death, nothing but . . . deformity, . . . baseness, shame. And . . . the Devil . . . strives unceasingly . . . to keep man in this unhappiness.[4]

This state of evil is also described as "a falling away from God," "a lapsing toward darkness."[5] This was a favorite view of Augustine's—that in the realm of human action, evil is a falling away from one's created good nature; a perversion of a will which has "turned aside" from God.[6] No doubt this privative view of evil had come to Colet also through Dionysius, who regarded sin as "a warping, a declension from . . . right condition; a failure, and imperfection, and impotence, and a weakness" (*Div. Names* 4: 24).

Colet on Plato's Dictum: "No Man Knowingly Seeks Evil"

Man's fall toward evil is sometimes explained by reference to one of Plato's most provocative ideas, that no man knowingly seeks evil (if by evil we mean that which brings down misery on one's own head). Colet notes that all men are bound "by one common desire; namely, of following what

---

[3] ExR p. 133.

[4] *Ibid.*, pp. 134, 130, cf. 129. Such passages contrast with Ficino's apparent denial of original sin. The Florentine maintained that souls always love God, either directly or else indirectly through love of the God-created body. Thus Ficino was not sympathetic with the Platonic-Pauline notion of soul-body conflict. See Kristeller, *Ficino*, pp. 188-94; and *Com. on Symp.*, pp. 191-2.

[5] EH p. 80, cf. p. 92.

[6] *Companion to Aug.*, pp. 29-30. Also Oates, *Basic Writings of Aug.*, p. xxv.

H

is better, and shunning what is worse, so far as they are able to do so. For he is not of sound mind, who voluntarily chooses a lesser good, if it is in his power to gain a greater. But what was good for men, or what was bad, before Christ showed us, was unknown."[7] All but the last sentence of this seems to be an almost verbatim transcription from Plato's *Meno* 77-78: "The desire of good is common to all, and one man is no better than another in that respect. ... No one desires ... evil." Some men "desire what they suppose to be goods although they are really evils."[8]

Fallen Man Excluded from Universal Love of Timaeus

By way of emphasizing man's fallen state, Colet contrasts it with the mutual love of all other creatures and even of the inanimate elements:

> Nothing can be so pleasing to God as a wise society of all things, mutually loving and beloved. This was religiously observed first of all in the great body (the animal, as Plato calls it) of the world; and all living creatures in succession, following the example, strenuously observe it also . . . in the mutual seeking for classification and society. The race of man alone deviates from this course from a deficiency of the life [i.e., infused grace] which wins and binds together, that is, wisdom and love.[9]

This notion was obviously inspired by *Timaeus* 30, though in Plato the term "animal" embraces World-Soul as well as World-Body: "The Deity . . . framed one visible animal comprehending within all other animals. . . . Out of these elements, which are in number four, the body of the world was created in the harmony of proportion, and therefore having

---

[7] LC p. 52.

[8] Cf. *Protagoras* 345, 353 ff.

[9] LR p. 74.

a spirit of friendship." With this notion Colet has combined
Dionysius's concept of universal love as mediated through
Ficino. In *De Amore,* for example, the Florentine observes
that

> There can be no doubt that all things have an innate love . . .
> that drives the higher things to care for the lower ones, the equal
> things to some special communion with each other, and finally
> induces all lower things to turn toward the better and higher
> ones. . . . So love may well be called the perpetual bond and
> juncture of the world.[10]

It is a sign of Colet's severity that man is even excluded, by
his fallen nature, from a love which characterizes birds and
rocks.

The Need for Grace

From this ignominious condition, Colet sees no rescue save
by a power beyond man. The "remedy . . . must be sought
from some external source, not from the patient himself. . . .
For evil can never be cured by evil . . . ; neither can bad men
bring themselves into order."[11] Before the time of Christ no
such remedy was available: "Forsaken . . . and unsteady, man
could not set foot down and walk in the slippery ways of this
world, without stumbling. In his actions, he was as one plant-
ing his footsteps on ice; and on this slippery path he was ever
falling."[12] But through the Atonement "the divine mercy
came to his aid, and God dragged, as if seizing it by the hand,
the miserable nature of man, darkened and squalid, to Himself."[13]

---

[10] *Com. on Symp.,* p. 148, cf. 153—"No part of the world hates another
part."

[11] MB pp. 33-34.

[12] ExR p. 135.

[13] *Sac.,* p. 14.

This "divine mercy" is grace, which Colet describes simply as that love which God, through the Holy Spirit, infuses into man, so that men love him in return: "This goodness, shed forth by a good God . . . is the power that renders the soul strong and victorious. . . . And what else is this than the grace of God and the love of God, . . . aye even (as St. Augustine will have it) the Holy Spirit of God himself?"[14] This almost fanatic emphasis on man's fallen state and imperative need for grace is in definite contrast to the infrequent mention of man's dependence in the Florentines, though in modern criticism the contrast has perhaps been exaggerated.[15]

Plotinian Emanation Adapted to Colet's Redemptive Scheme

The major feature of Colet's redemptive scheme is however not his emphasis on original sin. Rather it is an adaptation to redemption of Plotinian emanation. The Pauline notion of sanctification as a rebirth or "new creation" (2 Cor. 5:17) was much in Colet's mind: "As God created the world, so he new-created mankind. . . . He who created men could similarly re-create them."[16] But nowhere in Paul do we find Colet's Neoplatonic concept of the non-believer's soul as metaphorically chaotic evil matter into which the Holy Spirit

---

14 LR p. 65, cf. pp. 11-13; ExR pp. 53, LC p. 141. St. Augustine notwithstanding, this identification of grace with Holy Spirit is probably unorthodox, at least from a Catholic viewpoint. See this chapter, n. 31.

15 As for example Eugene Rice, "John Colet and the Annihilation of the Natural," *Harvard Theo. Rev.*, 45 (July 52), 141-2. See Chapter 1, n. 27. That Ficino did not ignore grace is indicated by the heading of one section of his *Epistolae:* "No one rises to God unless . . . God has descended to him." Also, in Ficino's imaginary "Dialogue between Paul and the Soul," Paul says: "All of our glory rests in that King of Glory alone to whom no one may voluntarily ascend, but may only be raised"—as translated by Jayne from Ficino, *Epistolae*, fol. lxxv, 105.

16 LC p. 127, ExR p. 12.

infuses stabilizing "form"—that is, grace. For the Spirit, "when it seizes on the soul of man, influences, disposes, and forms it; so that there arises a new thing by divine working, compounded of the soul itself, as the matter, and the embracing spirit, as the formative principle."[17] Just as God is the efficient cause of the original universe, so is Spirit "the Agent" who "predisposes" a human "object to the proper form":

> Man is the shapeless matter, so to speak; devoid of spiritual form, though in a fit state to be formed by the Spirit ... The Spirit ... moulds ... the rude matter ... ; that man may at length become what he is potentially able of becoming, and may be transformed according to the free pleasure of the moulding Spirit ..., even as soft wax is moulded, when drawn and worked about in the hand. ... The ... end ... of His action, is the ... introduction of form.[18]

This quotation incorporates almost verbatim certain passages from Mirandola's *Heptaplus* 1: 204.[19] Note how the Mirandolan thought contains a favorite Neoplatonic view of matter, namely, its potentiality. The corollary view, that matter is evil, also figures in Colet's concept of grace, through which God "would consumate the marriage with man, not only created from nothing, but recreated from evil. ... Evil is material for the grace of God." Thus God's mercy is even greater in re-creation:

> For there is no reason why man should not be created in the beginning; yet evil is the reason as to why man should not be re-created. Evil obstructed God more in recreation, for it did not exist in the creation; thus it would require greater power to recreate the world from evil than to create it from nothing.[20]

---

[17] LR p. 28. See Rice, *HTR*, 45: 160.

[18] LC p. 138, cf. LR p. 80.

[19] See Lupton, LC p. 138, n. 2.

[20] ExR pp. 12-13; cf. LC p. 151.

Here Colet metarphorically applies to redemption the Platonic and Plotinian concept of evil matter as intractable and resistant to God's efforts.

Holy Spirit as Platonic Architect Who Bestows Form (Grace) on Matter (Soul)

By way of emphasizing his concept of sanctification as a miniature "second creation," Colet is fond of speaking of two universes. The second of these is the "Christian universe," where "there is none that has not a round and perfect and heavenly form and figure in Christ."[21] Just as God was the "Artificer" of the first universe, so also is he, through Spirit, the Platonic "Architect" of the second.[22] Before Christ the human race was drifting on, "disorganized; without order, without form, without goodness."[23] But this "human race" was "the material, the clay for God to fashion" as he would.[24] From this chaotic and evil clay God therefore in certain cases produces Christians—that is, "men beautiful" who "excel in form and beauty."[25] "He ... arranges in beautiful order what was in shapeless disorder."[26] For the second as well as for the first creation, God is therefore (through Christ) the Platonic and Plotinian "Limit" who imposes order on the Unlimited—he is "the highest principle and limit of order" (cf. *Philebus* 23-27).[27]

---

21 LC p. 126.
22 LC p. 141, cf. 133.
23 MB p. 33.
24 EH p. 104.
25 LC p. 134.
26 LR p. 65.
27 EH p. 51.

Redemptive God as Plotinian Fountainhead or General Soul

Colet's metaphorical application of God as an Architect or Limit moulding intractable matter sometimes shifts to a more definitely Plotinian concept, that of God as a fountainhead who flows out from himself without in the least destroying his own transcendent and exalted status; and who by this flow seeks to bring all things back to himself:

> God pours forth abundantly his sweet goodness that it may return again to him . . . who, though stationary in himself, yet marvelously extends himself to others, that by his fragrant grace he may draw them together to himself. . . . [God can] communicate bountifully . . . to others . . . his own divinity . . . without in any wise departing from himself, or lessening his own majesty.[28]

Frequently this notion of God as a fountainhead is superimposed on that of God, Christ, or Spirit as a Plotinian Soul emanating into matter. Thus the human soul "has life, growth, and strength, by means of a certain . . . spiritual light and heat, streaming down upon it from the Soul of all souls, even God. . . . From him flow all things, which are previously in himself."[29] Again, Christ is "the soul of human society." From him, "as from a fountain, there [is] diffused life"— that is, grace.[30] "There is an outpouring of the Spirit; . . . in this manifold outpouring there is a gradual decrease."[31]

---

[28] *Ibid.*, p. 86.

[29] LR pp. 61-62; CH p. 101.

[30] LR p. 70.

[31] LC p. 119. These emanationist passages seem to blur the Catholic distinction between sanctifying grace and the Holy Spirit who infuses it (cf. n. 14 of this chapter). According to Attwater, *A Catholic Dictionary*, pp. 216, 481, sanctifying grace is not (as Colet's Plotinian language would seem here to imply) a transferral of God's own divine essence, but rather the bestowal on man of a supernatural goodness that is properly the quality

Emanational Decrease Applied to Degrees of Grace

As this last quotation implies, even the Plotinian concept of emanation as decreasing in intensity as it moves out from the Fountainhead is incorporated into Colet's redemptive process: "In proportion to their apparent nearness to, or remoteness from, the head, are these [Christian] members accounted to differ from one another."[82] This gradual decrease in degrees of grace is explained on the basis of Ficino's notion, cited in Chapter 2, that some matter is more intractable than other. Thus:

> There is a spiritual and divine irradiation of mankind from God, their soul; streaming first on men of singleness—the Apostles; then on others in order; on every one, that is to say, according to his capacity. . . . For it passes from the more

of a divine personage only, and that is therefore beyond man's own nature. It is this infused supernatural goodness which provides the proper soul-atmosphere, so to speak, into which the Spirit can make its mystical entrance. Yet even after the Spirit has come to dwell in the now-sanctified soul, it and sanctifying grace are still to be distinguished. Thus Attwater notes, p. 216, that sanctifying grace "is not to be identified with the Holy Ghost indwelling in the souls of the just." On this distinction and the historical groping toward it, see Hardman, *The Christian Doctrine of Grace,* pp. 31-36.

From the standpoint of Catholic orthodoxy on this issue, Colet is on much safer ground when he frequently pictures God as a Platonic Architect imposing Plotinian "form" or grace on chaotic "matter" (i.e., the soul). Metaphorical language of this type observes the necessary distinction between the Architect himself and the grace which he infuses. Colet himself was obviously aware of this distinction, because when faced directly with the problem in the *Mystical Body* treatise, he was careful to note that "Subordinate to the Spirit's essence is spiritual being [i.e., sanctifying grace]."—See Chapter 5, p. 137. From this it would seem fair to conclude that Colet was not conscious of the implications of his Plotinian redemptive language in the passages cited.

[82] LC p. 7.

single to the more manifold, and deteriorates in its progress, in proportion as it sinks on grosser matter.[33]

In this and similar passages, however, Plotinus is by no means the lone factor. Also evident is the Dionysian adaptation of Plotinus's notion that God is a Sun beaming forth a divine ray.[34]

The God-Sun Analogy from Plato to Ficino

The concept of God as a Sun or Light originated in Plato's famous "Allegory of the Cave," where the Idea of the Good was presented as a dazzling Sun by virtue of which the Ideas cast their shadows into this world (*Republic* 7: 514-516). This Good was said to be the "universal light which lightens all things" (*Republic* 7: 540). Plotinus, having identified the Good with Beauty and the One, inevitably pictured God as a Sun pouring out light, and with light bringing unity, beauty, and goodness (e.g., *Enn.* 4:4:12, 5:1:6). To Augustine this notion was especially appealing because it had Scriptural authority. Malachi 4:2 had spoken of "the Sun of righteousness," and John 1:5 of God as "Light." Augustine therefore followed Plotinus in calling God or the Good a Sun or Light by which things are known. To reach this Sun was therefore to attain "the full enjoyment of the highest and truest Good."[35] Elsewhere Augustine noted that "God is the intel-

---

[33] LR p. 77, cf. EH p. 49, and LC p. 152—Men are "differing in brightness and perfection, according to their deserts."

[34] Lupton, *Hier.*, pp. xvi-xvii, is probably right that Colet owed to Ficino and Mirandola his preference for Dionysius, whom Ficino called "the highest of the Platonists." Lupton credits Dionysius with two main ideas in Colet— the notion of unity as good, and the emphasis on love. See LC pp. xiii, xvii.

[35] See *City of God* 8:9 and *Soliloquies* 1:3, where God is "Goodness, Beauty, Light." Consult Butler, pp. 47, 52-54, and DeWulf, 1:117.

lectual Light" (*Sol.* 1:3) who "shines like a sun in the soul" (*de Gen. c. Manich.* 1:43).

Ficino followed Augustine in calling God "infinite light."[36] In *Orphica comparatio solis ad Deum* (written in 1479 and published in the *Epistolae,* with which Colet was familiar), he further observed: "Looking at the celestial sun, we may see in it as in a mirror that supercelestial One who has pitched his tent in the sun."[37] Later Ficino elaborated the notion in *De Comparatione solis ad Deum:* "The sun can signify to you God himself."[38] Having with Plotinus identified Beauty with the God-Sun, Ficino could describe Beauty as itself

> a kind of force or light, shining from [God] through everything, first through the Angelic Mind, second through the World-Soul, and the rest of the souls, third through Nature, and fourth through corporeal matter. In much the same way ... that the single light of the sun lights up the four bodies, fire, air, water, and earth, so the single light of God illumines the Mind, Soul, Nature, and Matter.[39]

The God-Sun Analogy in the Dionysian Hierarchies

Unlike Augustine, however, Ficino appropriated Plotinian emanation with little realization of its unorthodox implicatons. In this he was preceded and no doubt influenced by Dionysius, who conceived of God as a Sun streaming forth "Divine Life" or "Divine Illumination" (*Cel. Hier.* 1:2, 12:3).[40] For Dionysius this light constitutes the being of all

---

[36] *Op. om.* pp. 98, 120, 161, 335 f., 665; see Kristeller, *Ficino,* p. 97.

[37] Kristeller, *Ficino,* p. 97.

[38] *Ibid.,* p. 98.

[39] *Com. on Symp.,* p. 140.

[40] See Lupton, LC p. xiv, and for a more detailed analysis of the Dionysian system, Charles Bigg, *Neoplatonism,* pp. 340-350. For Dionysian passages

things.[41] Since everything contains light or being in some degree, everything is in some measure an imitation of the supreme Light. However, in Plotinus there are only six major levels of imitation: Mind, Soul, man, animals, plants, and inorganic objects. Soul creates after the pattern in Mind, and everything represents an imitative diminution of the Good.

In place of these six levels Dionysius substitutes twenty-one. Eliminating the Plotinian Mind, he conceives the Platonic and Plotinian Ideas as identical with the angels, which he calls "Celestial Intelligences"—a notion suggested very probably by Plotinus's occasional designation of Ideas as "spirits" (*Enn.* 5:8:4). These angels are arranged in a descending order of Proclian triplets: seraphim, cherubim, thrones; dominions, virtues, powers; princedoms, archangels, and angels proper.[42] Beneath this Celestial or Angelic Hierarchy comes the nine orders of the Ecclesiastical Hierarchy, also organized in three triads: the three sacraments (Eucharist, baptism, extreme unction); the three ecclesiastical orders (bishops, priests, deacons); and the three lay orders (monks, communicants, non-communicants).[43] Below these is the sub-ecclesiastical hierarchy of animals, plants, and inanimate nature.

As Colet notes in his abstracts, these twenty-one levels involve a descending order of imitation: "All things . . . represent God."[44] First of all, among the angels "there is a striving with all their might to imitate . . . the very Sun of truth."[45]

---

cited in parentheses in the main text, see John Parker, *The Works of Dionysius.*

[41] Gilson, p. 83.
[42] See Colet in CH p. 18 ff.
[43] Colet, EH p. 59 ff.
[44] Colet, CH p. 14.
[45] *Ibid.,* pp. 22, 21.

The angels are in turn "the original archtypes" for earthly priests and the Ecclesiastical Hierarchy: "The Church is founded on earth by Christ after the pattern of the celestial hierarchy of angels." The nine orders of the Church are "in imitation of the angelic degrees."[46]

Dionysian Emanation Associated with Special Purification-Illumination-Perfection Triad

As in Plotinus, the Dionysian divine flow or beam is said to be characterized by unity, beauty, and goodness. However, in Dionysius these three qualities are associated respectively with purification or strength, illumination or light in the narrower sense (i.e., knowledge), and perfection or fire (i.e., love).[47] Although loving is assigned especially to the fiery Seraphim Triad, knowing to the Dominion Order, and purifying to the Princedoms, all the angels collectively may be said to pass down the purifying, illuminating, and perfecting light to the priests.[48] These in turn are imitators of the angels, because the priestly office is itself a task of purifying, illuminating, and perfecting others.[49] Through this divine emanation, mediated by angels and priests, God seeks to lure all creatures back to himself, the journey back being itself a progressive increase in deification (*Div. Names* 4:11, 2:11; *Cel. Hier.* 1:3, 2:4-5).[50]

---

[46] EH pp. 117, 114, and Lupton, *Hier.*, p. xliv. Cf. *Sac.*, p. 11, where members of the Eccles. Hier. are "models after that pattern" of the angels, and *Sac.*, p. 29—"the lower church imitates the higher church."

[47] See *The Mystical Theology and The Celestial Hierarchies of Dionysius*, ed. Shrine of Wisdom, pp. 25-26.

[48] CH p. 40 ff.

[49] *Ibid.*, pp. 33, 38 ff.

[50] See DeWulf, p. 84, and Gilson, p. 83.

The God-Sun Analogy in Colet

One of the foremost characteristics of Colet's redemptive scheme is the Plotinian-Augustinian-Dionysian concept of God as a "divine Sun" from whom "rays of grace shed forth."[51] In associating Christian grace with the divine ray, Colet was very probably influenced by Ficino's *De Amore,* where it is suggested that beauty is "a certain lively and spiritual grace, which by the divine ray is first infused into the angels, then into the souls of men, and after this . . . into . . . mundane material."[52] Here, of course, Colet takes Ficino's unorthodox emanationist concept and adapts it to Christian orthodoxy.

Most often in Colet's works the sun and its associated metaphors are applied to Christ, who with almost fanatic repetition is acclaimed "the Sun of Righteousness."[53] It is the "rays of the celestial Sun, Jesus Christ," by which the soul is "reformed."[54] This emphasis on Christ as the Sun rather than the Father is easily accounted for. First, it is Christ (through the Atonement) who is naturally central in the redemptive scheme. Second, Mirandola, on the basis of Malachi 4:2, himself frequently referred to Christ as "Sun of Right-

---

[51] LC pp. 4, 125, 152, cf. *Sac.,* p. 4—"sun-like God."

[52] From *Com. on Symp.* as quoted in Gardner, Mirandola's *Discourse on Love,* pp. xxii-xxiii. Colet must also have been impressed with the frequency of the God-Sun analogy in Ficino's *Epistolae.* See Jayne, *Colet and Ficino,* pp. 33, 151, 284, 286, 325, 331, 341, 361, 392, for examples of Colet's marginalia or underscoring of Ficinian God-Sun or God-Light passages. Typical marginal comments: "God is a never-flickering light"; "As the sun is related to the moon, [so is God to the soul]"; "The faithful human soul, bathed in the rays of the sun as though impregnated with the divine seed"; "God is to the soul like the sun to our physical eyes."

[53] CH p. 5, cf. 7; EH pp. 70, 101, 58; ExR p. 104.

[54] LC pp. 126, 152.

eousness" in his *Heptaplus*.[55] In this connection it is significant that, in Colet's Mirandolan cosmology passage cited in
Chapter 2, Christ is referred to as "our Sun," and compared
to the natural sun.[56] Third, Colet anticipated another St.
Paul's Dean, John Donne, in his fondness for word-play:
there can be no doubt that he enjoyed the implied interplay
of "Son" and "Sun." For example, in the Dionysian abstracts,
God is the "Sun of righteousness and truth. . . . At length in
his own good time the Sun himself descended."[57]

Colet's Use of Dionysian Multiple Triads

Following Dionysius, Colet's Divine Sun also performs the
functions of purification, illumination, and perfection; and
these functions are associated respectively with two other
Neoplatonic triads: unity, beauty, goodness; and strength,
light (i.e., knowledge, truth), and fire-flame-heat-warmth
(i.e., love). Thus God is

> the purification of things to unity, their illumination to what
> is beautiful, and their perfection to what is good. . . . The sun-
> like rays of Christ illumine men . . . to purification, enlighten-
> ment, and perfection. . . . This Sun, shining upon minds of
> men . . . at once unites them in strength, elevates them to the
> light, and kindles them into flame. . . . There goes forth upon
> men from Christ . . . an influence . . . that first unites the weak
> and makes them strong; then illumines them and makes them
> true; lastly warms them and makes them good. . . . The ray
> proceeding from Him, which purifies, illumines, and perfects,
> is called the Gospel.[58]

Here of course Colet has shifted Dionysian emanationism

---

[55] See Lupton, LR p. xxxiv.

[56] LC pp. 132, 127-129.

[57] EH p. 104.

[58] CH p. 15; LC p. 96; LR p. 70; LC p. 58; CH p. 31, cf. 32.

from original creation to the new creation of sanctification. Thus it is not here any natural life but rather Paul's new spiritual Life of Christ (2 Cor. 15:45, Col. 3:4) that emanates from God—a point which Colet makes indisputably clear in an early chapter heading of the Dionysian abstracts: "On the Emanation from God the Father *of all Spiritual Light and Grace.*[59] The Dionysian multiple triads are skillfully superimposed by Colet on the basic Plotinian concept of stabilizing form imposed upon darkly evil and chaotic matter:

> This Godhead ... at length shone forth in darkness, like a kindly, powerful and bright sun, and cast its rays upon darksome, earthly man. The first effect of this divine Sun ... is ... to purify them to the simplicity ... of their proper nature, by utterly dispelling all the multiplicity and unreal evil, into which men have sinfully and unhappily lapsed. Its second effect ... is to illumine them by its divine ray. ... In the third place, the same divine ray proceeds ... until it has kindled a mighty flame; that what has unmixed light in God, may have unmixed heat as well.[60]

Ficino's Reinforcement of Dionysian Light-Fire Metaphors

There can be little question that Colet's Dionysian fondness for the metaphors of light as knowledge, and especially fire as a love kindled by God, was reinforced by Ficino. In *De Amore,* for example, we are told that by "eternal love ... the soul is always drawn to God. ... The goodness of God ... always kindles this love in the soul."[61] And in the Florentine's "Theological Prayer to God" he exclaims: "What penetrates my innermost being? ... Certainly it is the admirable rays of Thy admirable goodness. ... With them reached Thou

---

[59] CH p. 2—italics added.

[60] LC pp. 58-59.

[61] *Com. on Symp.,* pp. 162-3.

me... and inflamest me."[62] Moreover, Ficino constantly compares the uniting, illuminating, and warming qualities of the natural sun to God's functions:

> Dionysius is quite justified in comparing God to the sun, because as the sun illuminates and warms the body, so God provides to our spirits the light of truth and the ardor of love. ... The divine philosopher [i.e., Plato in *Republic* 6:508] ... says that the light of the mind for understanding everything is the same God himself by whom everything was created, and he compares God and the sun with each other in that God stands in the same relation to minds as the sun to eyes.[63]

This Ficino-type comparison is easily discernable in Colet. For example:

> Various are the ways in which men are drawn from division and weakness to unity and power, by the uniting and all-powerful rays of Christ. For these, streaming as it were from the Sun of Truth, gather and draw together towards themselves and toward unity, those who are in a state of multiplicity; that they may first have light, and then warmth as it consequence. *It is as we see it to be with the powerful, luminous, and warm rays of the natural sun.* When they go forth on any object, to make it sunlit, their first effect is to render that on which they seize, wholly single, homogeneous, and so far as possible, in a state of real unity with itself—... then they illumine, and lastly warm it; that so light may spring from unity, and warmth from heat.[64]

Christ Replaces Hierarchies as Redemptive Mediator in Colet's System

As the above quotations imply, the personages of the Dio-

---

[62] Kristeller, *Ficino*, p. 268. Mirandola's "Hymn to God" also associates love with fire. See Rigg, p. 77.

[63] *Com. on Symp.*, pp. 134, 206.

[64] LC p. 57. Italics added. Cf. *Com. on Symp.*, pp. 206-7.

nysian Celestial and Ecclesiastical Hierarchies do not play any major role in Colet's redemptive process. To be sure, in the Dionysian abstracts we are told, as we would expect, that the angels "beautifully colour darksome men, and cause them in some measure to imitate and reproduce the beauty of God."[65] Colet also, working from Dionysius but not exactly duplicating him, elaborates two further triads, whereby deacons, priests, and bishops, as well as the sacraments of penitence, baptism, and the Eucharist, operate as respective media for purification, illumination, and perfection.[66] In the *Treatise on Sacraments,* for example, we are told that the priesthood in general "cleanse by penitence, illuminate in baptism . . . and perfect through the eucharist."[67]

But it is simply a fact that in works other than the Dionysian trilogy, it is Christ who very largely supplants sacraments, priests, and even angels as the mediator of God to man. Colet at times goes to some effort to emphasize this point: "Jesus Christ came into the world to support the angels, for its purification, illumination, and perfection.[68] Even more strongly, in the Celestial Hierarchy treatise itself, we are told that when the angels "were wearied out" in their attempts to reform men, Christ "did . . . come to their aid."[69] This emphasis on the redemptive role of Christ, which was almost wholly ignored by Dionysius, is another interesting sign of Colet's Clementine approach to the philosophies of the Platonic Tradition.[70]

---

[65] CH p. 31.

[66] See EH pp. 130, 76; *Sac.,* p. 33.

[67] *Sac.,* p. 27.

[68] LC p. 125.

[69] CH p. 15, cf. p. 17.

[70] On this point see Lupton, *Hier.,* pp. xiv-xlvi.

*Colet's Intermeshing of Pauline Triad
with Dionysian Triplets*

An adaptation of Dionysius to Christianity is also manifest
in Colet's association of purification, illumination, and perfection with the three infused graces or "gifts" so exalted in
St. Paul: hope, faith, and charity (1 Cor. 13:13).[71] Thus
"our unity, which is the object aimed at by our purification,
is hope. . . . Our truth is faith in the all-embracing truth
which was in Jesus Christ. Our goodness and perfection is a
love of the good." Christians are "those who hope . . . , believe, and . . . love."[72]

This theme, like a magnificent symphony, reverberates
through the Pauline commentaries. Hope is constantly associated with unity and "existence"—that is, being. "By the
uniting ray of grace, the soul is born again and has a new
existence—for nothing can have existence, save unity."[73]
Faith is constantly associated with light and knowledge.
Christ is the "Sun of Faith" who "kindles the lamp of understanding."[74] Similarly, charity is usually mentioned with
perfection: "Charity inflames to perfection. . . . In charity
consists your perfection."[75] "In these three," hope, faith and
charity, "consist the life and growth of the soul, whereby it
has being, knowledge, and love of God."[76]

Colet's intermeshing of the Pauline gifts with the multiple
Dionysian triads was apparently inspired by Ficino's *Epis-*

---

[71] For an excellent and detailed discussion of this point, see Hunt, *Dean
Colet and His Theology,* p. 103 ff.

[72] EH p. 115.

[73] LR p. 62, cf. *Sac.,* p. 36.

[74] LR pp. 101, 102.

[75] LC pp. 137, 138.

[76] LR p. 63.

tolae. In an imaginary dialogue between St. Paul and himself, Ficino had associated the three Pauline virtues respectively with the purification of the Dionysian angelic Princedoms, the illuminating function of the Dominions, and the perfecting power of the fiery Seraphim. In his marginalia to this passage Colet annotated in detail, reproducing in tabular form the correspondence between the Pauline gifts and the angelic levels of Dionysius's Celestial Hierarchy. However, as later marginalia show, Colet eventually rejected Ficino's conventional order of faith-hope-charity, and instead placed hope first in the triad because it fitted in better with his scheme of a gradual rise through faith-knowledge to love-union.[77]

There are some passages where Colet restricts Pauline sanctification to those who enjoy the "fire of love." In this context, it is only "the righteous flame-born ones," those "who are sprung from the flame of the Holy Spirit," who "will come forth happily deified."[78] Again, it is not faith alone which "is sufficient for righteousness, since that consists of something above faith, even of love. . . . By love we are begotten again to a new and spiritual being in God."[79] The most beautiful statement of this idea, stressing as it does Colet's belief in Christ as mediator and the notion of reciprocal love initiated by God, is found in the Dionysian abstracts:

> Fire is . . . the holy love of God. . . . Being born anew by the love of God, [men] may live in God. . . . For [God's] love is the source of begetting; holy love, of begetting holiness; and the love of God, of godliness. Now the messenger of this . . . love . . . of God was his lovely Son . . . , who . . . brought down love

---

[77] See Jayne, *Colet and Ficino*, pp. 102-109, 162, 332, 333.

[78] CH p. 51; ExR p. 121.

[79] LC p. 56; CH p. 60.

to men, that they, being born anew by love, might in turn love their heavenly Father.[80]

Interpenetration of Love-Faith in Romans Commentary

However, Colet seems to have had second thoughts on this theme. Even in the Dionysian treatises he qualified it by noting that "purity and light and likeness to God [i.e., perfection] are inseparably connected."[81] More explicitly, in the Romans commentary, he conceded that "no doubt these three things, faith, hope, and charity, are infused into the soul at the same moment by the one, good, and beautiful Spirit of God. But . . . there is nothing to forbid precedence being imagined in things instantaneous."[82] Again:

> This infused light is Faith, by which the mystery of the incarnation is discerned . . . whilst Love, which takes possession of the soul along with Faith, . . . is that whereby . . . God and his Christ are . . . worshipped. These two . . . thus differ, not in reality, but in a kind of interchangeableness: namely, in faith being a less united and . . . a more diffused love; love . . . a more condensed and united faith.[83]

It follows therefore that the terms can be combined: it is loving faith and "faithful love" which are "the soul's vigour."[84] The virtues of hope, faith, and charity can also be expressed by combinations of the Plotinian triad of unity, beauty, and goodness: "Such a one and beautiful goodness, and good and beautiful oneness, and one and good beautifulness, is the very life of the soul, rendering it strong, beautiful,

---

80 EH p. 62.
81 CH p. 15.
82 LR p. 68.
83 LR p. 28.
84 LR p. 111, cf. p. 122.

and active for good."[85] In this concept of the interpenetration of the three theological virtues, it is not difficult to discern the influence of Augustine, who noted that faith is "that by which we love God not yet seen" (*Epistle of St. John,* Homily 7:8).

The impact of Neoplatonic and Florentine speculation on Colet's redemptive system is summarized in the chart below:

QUALITIES OF NEOPLATONIC EMANATION
(= SUN'S RAY, BEING, FORM)

Plotinus	*Added by Dionysius*	
unity	Princedoms-purification-strength	
beauty	Dominions-illumination-light-knowledge	
goodness	Seraphim-perfection-heat-love	

Stressed by Ficino	*Added by Ficino*	*Altered by Colet to:*
strength	faith	hope
light (for knowledge)	hope	faith
heat (for love)	charity or love	charity or love

Adapted by Colet from Dionysius
(but not stressed in the
Pauline commentaries)

penitence	deacons
baptism	priests
Eucharist	bishops

Pauline-Platonic Notion of Freedom in Colet

Colet's Neoplatonic concept of grace as infused form is combined in many places with the Pauline and Platonic notion

---

[85] LR p. 68.

of freedom as release from the body's domination. Plato had spoken in *Republic* 4: 431 (cf. 4: 442 and *Phaedrus* 258) of the intemperate man as a "slave." Building on this idea, Paul had described non-believers as "enslaved to sin" (Rom. 6:6), and to his Christian colleagues had exclaimed: "You were called to freedom, brethren.... For freedom Christ has set us free.... Where the Spirit of the Lord is, there is freedom."[86]

Similarly, Colet describes the non-believer as "too truly the slave of his body."[87] Such men are "enslave[d] ... to those evil spirits" and to the "tyranny of the sensual body."[88] In expressing this idea, Colet often resorts to Platonic chain and prison metaphor: "There is in man that which is ... simple; by an evil and diverse principle, this is carried off and enchained ... ; hence it is necessary that ... all weights which had dragged him down [be] taken way."[89] As Colet sees it, the Old Law could not give the soul strength "whereby it might have released itself from bondage, and escaped from the prison of the body."[90] Only through infused grace can man be "set free from the dominion of the animal and sensual."[91] It is hope, faith, and charity whereby the soul "reins in the body and binds it in obedience to itself."[92] Christians are "slaves set free.... Christ freed us from bondage."[93] Such men enjoy a state of "joyful liberty," because they "have

---

[86] Gal. 5:13-14, 5:1; 2 Cor. 3:17.

[87] ExR p. 133.

[88] LC pp. 69, 22.

[89] *Sac.* p. 35.

[90] LR p. 24. Cf. ExR p. 128, *Sac.,* pp. 39, 43 ("chains of sin").

[91] LR p. 20. Cf. MB pp. 40, 42.

[92] LR p. 63.

[93] ExR pp. 94, 161, cf. pp. 114, 127.

rendered the body a light burden, and obedient to reason." Their "bodily faculties" are now "concentrated in obedience to the soul."[94]

Colet's Pauline-Platonic Concept that Good Works Spring from Internal Holiness

Following Augustine, Colet argues that the only genuine freedom is a "freedom towards good.... Without grace there is no liberty."[95] Conversely, freedom to do evil is really slavery to the body and its lusts."[96] It follows that the soul which is characterized by Platonic "temperance" and "good health," by Neoplatonic "form," and by Christian faith-hope -charity, will necessarily perform noble deeds.[97] Hence Colet argues that Christians are those

> who have been made righteous in Christ that they may in turn bring forth righteousness. ... Righteousness consists in a true and pure ... goodness, which cannot do otherwise than act in the best way... [He who is] truly good in himself, acts well. ... Good works are the fruit of charity. ... Love for God is manifested by love for our neighbor. If you take no dutiful thought for your neighbor, you show yourself to have no love for God. St. John ... shows us that [infused] faith without works is not only vain, but an absolute non-entity; and that all such men as say that they know Christ, without keeping his commandments, are nothing short of liars. ... True faith ... cannot by any means exist, unless accompanied by well doing.[98]

Much of this is reminiscent of Augustine's *Epistle to St.*

---

[94] LC pp. 70, 93; LR p. 25.

[95] CH pp. 29-30, cf. LC p. 89.

[96] Cf. Oates, *Basic Writings of Aug.,* p. xxvii.

[97] See LR pp. 83, 103, and LC p. 81 for the Platonic terms "temperance" and "health."

[98] LR p. 103; MB p. 36; ExR pp. 107-8; LC p. 136, 99, 57.

John, Homily 7:8—"Love and do what thou wilt. . . . Let the root of love be within, of this root nothing can spring but what is good." Such a notion has an ultimately Platonic and Pauline basis. Plato frequently remarks that virtuous conduct necessarily must follow from internal holiness: "Can he who is harmoniously constituted . . . ever be unjust or hard in his dealings? Impossible."[99] For the good or educated soul will automatically "govern" and "care for" its body (*Phaedo* 80, 94; *Republic* 3:403). Similarly, Paul argued that "a base mind and . . . improper conduct" are inseparable (Rom. 1:28), while the Christian is he who is "consecrated and . . . ready for any good work."[100] This compares to Colet's assertion that before Christ men were "without goodness, incapable of working righteousness," whereas Christians are characterized by "beauty and right action."[101] The same view had been expressed by Ficino: "Virtue of the soul . . . manifests itself in a most noble kind of beauty in words, actions, and deeds. . . . It is an internal perfection which produces the external."[102]

Platonic Governing Soul Applied to Clerical Reform

The ultimately Platonic concept that the holy soul automatically governs the body is sometimes used by Colet for purposes of church reform and moral exhortation. In the *Convocation Sermon,* for example, we are told that laymen are the body and priests the soul of the church: If therefore priests will lead blessed lives, the laity will automatically follow suit. "For the bodye foloweth the soule; and, such

---

[99] *Republic* 6:485, cf. 4:443-4.
[100] 2 Tim. 2:21, cf. 3:17.
[101] MB pp. 33, 34.
[102] *Com. on Symp.,* p. 164.

rulers as are in the cite, like dwellers be in hit. Wherfore if pristes that haue the charge of soules be good, streyghte the people wyll be good."[103]

Here the notion of harmonized governing soul is combined with two other Platonic ideas: human imitation of divine goodness, and man as a little republic analogous to the larger state where rulers properly control workers. In the *Sacraments* treatise Colet again refers to the "priestly soul" and the "people's body," and notes elsewhere that "by returning to primitive goodness" the priesthood can "recall the laity to primitive obedience."[104]

Colet's Platonic "Blessings in Disguise" Doctrine

Another related idea in Colet is that not only does a holy soul guarantee good deeds by him who is sanctified; it also guarantees that all acts done *to* such a person will be for the good, no matter how evilly they might have been intended. Conversely, "to evil men everything seems evil."[105] "To the bad all things are bad." For evil men the Law "was evil, according to their evil nature. For all things are received in

---

[103] Colet, "The Sermon of Doctor Colete, Made to the Convocacion at Paulis," in Lupton, *Life of Colet,* Appendix C, p. 302. Hereafter *Convocation Sermon* or CS.

[104] *Sac.,* p. 48; ExR p. 90.

[105] Colet's marginal comment in Ficino's *Epistolae*—Jayne, *Colet and Ficino,* p. 142. For similar and fairly independent marginal comments, see *ibid.,* pp. 79, 348, 349, 350. Samples from last two passages: "The good man, because of his goodness, repays evil with good, and thus his own good makes evils seem goods. Everything which he does will turn out well for him, in imitation of God, for whom all good things turn out well. . . . The wise man . . . learns to distinguish between good and evil; he returns good for the evils which he cannot escape; the result will be that no evil can befall him because of his goodness—not even those evils which because of his goodness are turned to good."

each case according to the measure of the receiver.... It is wonderful to observe how to the good all things—even evils themselves—are good; and how, in keeping with God's goodness, good springs up out of the very midst of evil."[106] Colet suggests that this applies even to unhappy marriages! "If thou haue an euyll wyfe, take pacience, and thanke God; for all is for the best, well taken."[107]

The idea is of course grounded in Paul's Rom. 8:28 and 1 Cor. 2:9. But Paul was by no means the only factor in Colet's thinking. Building on Boethius's notion that to good men misfortunes are blessings in disguise, Ficino had argued that supposed blessings are noxious for the bad man, because he makes wrong use of them: "For perverse souls all things are unfortunate. . . . All blessings of the world are evils for him who lives impurely in the world. . . . For bad men good fortune is bad; for good men bad fortune is good."[108] Back of this view lies surely the inspiration of Plato's *Gorgias* 470ff: "Virtuous men possess beatitude despite pain and misfortune, while vicious men are really miserable because of the condition of their souls, no matter how much wealth, sensual pleasure, or fame they enjoy."

Infused "Form" (Grace) as Source of Right Action in Colet

The almost incredible way in which the Neoplatonic notion of form was imprinted on Colet's brain is indicated not only by his use of it to explain the nature of grace, but also by his application of it to the works which follow grace. In the *Mystical Body* treatise the view is expressed that the

---

106 ExR p. 98; LR p. 22; LC p. 115.
107 RFM p. 308.
108 Kristeller, *Ficino,* p. 352.

Holy Spirit not only infuses form or "spiritual being" into the soul, but "spiritual working" as well:

> So, from the Spirit . . . , there is infused at once into those who are called . . . , both spiritual being and spiritual working. This gift is bestowed on their minds and wills, in order that they may first *be* spiritual . . . , and then *do* all things spiritually."[109]

Again: "The Agent [God] predisposes an object to the proper form; and then the object formed acts of itself. All right action of a perfect object is by the form derived from the source of action."[110]

Neoplatonic Explanations for Christian as God's Fellow-Worker

Corollary to this is Colet's use of Neoplatonism to explain the intricate doctrine that the performance of good works must "be assigned, not to the Spirit alone, but also [to] the man in the Spirit." For the sanctified man is a "fellow-worker"—that is, one who works "along with Him," the two together being "the parent of good works."[111] To explain this, the Dean falls back on Ficino's *Theologia Platonica* 2:

> The Platonists hold that . . . the causes we term natural agents, appear to us of themselves alone to act upon, transmute, and form . . . external matter; yet in truth they are not the primary cause of the changes that take place, but rather instruments of a divine skill. . . . So in like manner, when a man has been beloved by God's spirit to such a degree as to return that love, . . . although he may then be the agent and doer of numberless works in the Church in his own proper form, which is charity; yet for all that he himself is not the primary cause of the

---

[109] MB p. 37-38.
[110] LC p. 138.
[111] LC pp. 123, 143.

> works done by him, but is now a living and perfect instrument; a fellow-agent in and with that Prime Agent, the Spirit of God.[112]

Similarly, this fellow-working is clarified by reference to the Platonic concept of God as Craftsman, creating after an ideal pattern; and to the Augustinian view (prominent also in Ficino) that these Ideas are in God's mind:

> In this joint-building, all must follow the plan in the mind of the Architect, who is the Spirit of Christ. . . . In building a house it is undoubtedly the hands and eyes of the workman that . . . arrange the materials. . . . But still, though they may appear to be the sole agents at work, the construction of the house is not to be wholly set down to them. For they are but working instruments, in subservience to the design laid down in the mind of the architect. In like manner, spiritual men . . . may work at the erection of the temple of God. But the work done by them must be set down to the account of Christ's Spirit, as the first and greatest and exemplary cause; according to whose pattern all things are done.[113]

Plato's Doctrine of Godly Imitation

The concept of imitation plays a large role for both Colet and Plato. In the *Dialogues* it is not only used to explain the relation of becoming to being, but is also suggested as one method for achieving internal holiness. In *Theaetetus* 176, the principle is advanced that "God is . . . perfect righteousness." "To become like God, so far as this is possible," is therefore "to become holy, just, and wise." Similarly, in *Laws* 4:717—"God ought to be to us the measure of all things, and not man. . . . And he who would be dear to God must . . . be like him and such as he is. Wherefore the temperate

---

112 LC p. 140; see Lupton, n. 1, and Mirandola's *Heptaplus* 1: 204-6.
113 LC pp. 141-2.

man is the friend of God, for he is like Him."[114] Most often, such Platonic imitation is directed not toward Demiurge but toward World-Soul. This Soul is tripartite, but unlike human souls, it always "partakes of . . . harmony" (*Timaeus* 35, 37). Thus World-Soul is the "principle of wisdom and virtue" which, if imitated, can "discipline all things rightly to their happiness" (*Laws* 10:896-7).[115]

Colet's Adaptation of Platonic Imitation to "Increased Grace"

This Platonic imitation of God as a method of achieving holiness is shifted in Colet to that imitation of Christ which (1) constitutes the initial state of grace; and (2) provides the means for "increased grace," whereby man, once sanctified, moves on in Paul's words from "glory to glory" and from "perfection to perfection" (2 Cor. 3:18, cf. Phil. 3:12, 1 Cor. 13:10). This idea of degrees of perfection or imitation of Christ is frequent in Colet's writings. Thus we are told that the gift of grace is "instilled by God into the mind of man. And if man hold fast to this instilling, the degrees of grace are intensified."[116] Christians are those who are "formed by" God and "carried on from glory to glory until they are wholly transformed after his likeness."[117] Such men make "steady progress" toward "our ideal righteousness, Jesus Christ."[118] Christ's "whole life, deeds, and words, are

---

[114] Cf. *Laws* 10: 900, where the Gods are "temperate" and "possess virtue"; and *Phaedrus* 248, where only the soul that "follows God best and is likest to him" will be saved.

[115] Note Cornford, *Plato's Cosmology*, p. 66: "Soul must contain the harmonious order which individual souls ought to learn and reproduce in themselves."

[116] CH p. 96.

[117] *Ibid.*, p. 55, cf. 8-9, 64, 70; ExR p. 8; LC pp. 70, 75, 81.

[118] LC p. 66.

nothing else than a pattern, modelled and placed before men for their imitation, if they would follow whither he has ascended."[119] Christ is the Platonic "measure and standard . . . which all who follow him must strive to attain, and the nearer your approach to it, the more perfect you will become."[120]

Sanctified men should therefore not be satisfied with their initial state of imitative perfection; in order that they might retain and increase the Platonic governorship of soul over body, they should model their lives on Christ, the "pattern of human life," who "had his body in complete obedience and subjection to his blessed soul."[121] The presence of the Spirit is retained only so long as man's "soul keeps his body in check. . . . But if the soul has neglected this, and suffered the body to run to waste in lusts, then will it itself also be neglected . . . by the sustaining Spirit."[122] Here the Platonic concept of the soul's "watchfulness" or indolence (Laws 10: 903-6) is incorporated into the Christian context of salvation.

Summary

To recapitulate, Colet's redemptive scheme begins with an insistence on original sin—a doctrine apparently denied by Ficino. In accordance with the Augustinian-Dionysian privative theory of evil, Colet describes this inborn wickedness as a falling away from one's divinely-created good nature. To emphasize fallen man's degraded ignorance and hatefulness, Colet appropriates the Meno idea that no man knowingly seeks evil. Colet excludes man not only from the

---

[119] LR p. 115.

[120] LC p. 52.

[121] LC pp. 71, 72, cf. p. 51.

[122] LR p. 59.

innate love proclaimed by Dionysius and Ficino to exist in all creatures, but also from the inherent spirit of friendship built into the world-body of *Timaeus* through the harmonization of the four elements.

The major feature of the Dean's redemptive scheme is a highly imaginative application of Plotinian emanation, whereby the non-believer's soul is metaphorically described as evil chaotic resistant matter, and Spirit-bestowed infused grace as stabilizing form—a notion which Colet might have appropriated from Mirandola's *Heptaplus*. In this "second creation" of the Christian world, the Spirit is essentially the Platonic Architect or Limit who imposes order (grace) on disordered matter (the soul). As in Plotinus and Ficino, this order or form is identified with beauty. Sometimes the phenomenon of sanctifying grace is explained via the Plotinian Fountainhead idea: like the Plotinian One, God is said to communicate his own divinity to man without leaving his own station or lessening his own nature, in an effort to bring things back full circle to himself. Again, Christ or Spirit is sometimes described as a Plotinian General Soul emanating into matter (i.e., the human soul). The Neoplatonic notion of emanational decrease is ingeniously applied to degrees of grace, through Ficino's idea that some matter is more intractable than other: hence some souls, which are metaphorical matter, will be more fully ordered by grace-form than will other souls.

Another prominent feature in Colet's redemptive scheme is the famous God-Sun analogy, derived ultimately from Plato's *Republic,* and later applied to God (identified with Plato's Good) by Plotinus, Augustine, Dionysius, and Ficino. However, following Mirandola, Colet makes a special point of applying the Sun-metaphor to Christ, partly because of his love of word-play ("Sun," "Son"). As in Dionysius, Colet's God-Sun, via intermediary celestial and ecclesiastical hierarchies, performs the functions of purification, illumination, and perfection, these being associated respectively with two other Neoplatonic triads: unity-beauty-goodness; and strength-light (knowledge)-fire (love). Ficino's works apparently reenforced Colet's fondness for the Dionysian metaphors of light for knowledge and fire for love. However, Colet's cautious Clementine approach to Dionysius results in two fundamental changes: (1) the shifting of Dionysian emanative Life from perpetual creation to the "second creation" involving sanctifying grace; (2) the emphasis on the Spirit of Christ rather than priests, sacraments, and angels as the major agent in redemption.

In Colet's system the Pauline triad of hope, faith, and charity is skillfully intermeshed with the various Dionysian triplets, a procedure inspired by Ficino's *Epistolae*. The Pauline gifts are sometimes expressed by combinations of the Plotinian (also Dionysian) triplet of unity, beauty, goodness. Moreover, these gifts are said to be infused simultaneously but with an order of precedence—this an application of Plotinian causal rather than conventional time-sequence. The Pauline triad is also combined with Colet's Pauline-Platonic notion of freedom as release from the body's domination, the contrasting slavery being described by Colet in Platonic chain and prison metaphor. According to the Dean, only infused grace (i.e., hope-faith-charity) can harmonize the soul so that the soul can in turn govern the body. This Pauline-Platonic notion that internal virtue automatically guarantees noble acts is also explained Neoplatonically: right action follows infused form.

The Platonic doctrine of harmonized governing soul is

combined with the *Republic's* notion that workers should imitate guardians, this for the purpose of appealing for clerical reform: if priests are good, the laity will automatically be so. Colet also expresses the dictum that to the good man all fortune is good—a doctrine originating in Plato and Paul but elaborated by Boethius and Ficino. To explain how the sanctified man, in his performance of good works, is a fellow-worker with God, Colet appeals to (1) the idea in Ficino's *Theologia Platonica* that God always lies behind the "natural agents" which seem alone to form matter; and (2) to the Augustinian-Ficinian comparison of a worker directed by a master architect. Finally, Plato's doctrine of Godly imitation is appropriated by Colet as the basic method of achieving increased grace via imitation of Christ's ideal life and deeds.

It is now time to focus on two special segments of Colet's redemptive scheme, namely, light-knowledge and heat-love as the ascending way to mystical union.

K

CHAPTER 5

KNOWLEDGE AND
MYSTICAL UNION

Degrees of Knowledge in Colet

As in Neoplatonism generally, Colet recognized degrees
of knowledge, beginning with the sensory. "Men are taught
by God in three ways . . . : by his sensible creation, by his
spiritual and angelic creation; and by His Son."[1] Colet concedes that through the visible universe man "can to a certain
degree understand the things of God, which are beyond
sight and sense."[2] It is indeed in this way that the ancient
philosophers came to recognize God's existence and certain
of his attributes, such as that he is one, unchanging, and
eternal; good, beautiful, mighty. For such men realized that

---

[1] ExR p. 68.
[2] *Ibid.,* p. 65.

"no weak and mortal creature could have planned and constructed the vast mechanism of the universe."[8]

The view here expressed is of course inspired by Romans
1:20— "The invisible things of Him from the creation
of the world are clearly seen, being understood by the things
that are made." But Colet's concern with philosophers who
accrued some knowledge from a God-revealing world owes
much to *Laws* 12:967-8, in which Plato anticipated the
Pauline view:

> There are two things which lead men to believe in the Gods. . . .
> One is . . . an argument from the order of the motion of the
> stars, and of all things under the dominion of the mind which
> ordered the universe. If a man look upon the world not lightly
> or ignorantly, there was never anyone so godless who did not
> . . . see . . . an intelligent will accomplishing good.[4]

But "besides the knowledge that we can obtain from
created things," and the "knowledge drawn from Scripture,
ministered to us by angels," Colet insists that "we Christians
have a far more exalted knowledge and wisdom of God
through the . . . Son."[5] Knowledge in its highest and most
genuine sense is therefore religious knowledge, a comprehension of that which "pertains to God and things divine."[6]
This was of course the position of St. Paul as expressed
in 1 Cor. 15:34.[7]

---

[8] *Ibid.*, pp. 65-66.

[4] Though in general recognizing the validity of sensory perception as the
origin of the knowing process, Colet in one instance, LR p. 41, impugns it as
unreliable even in that limited sense: "The soul is so hoodwinked as not
. . . even to ⌈be able to⌉ behold without error all that is present and set
before the eyes."

[5] ExR p. 69.

[6] LC p. 61.

[7] See *IB* 11:216.

Highest Knowledge Asserted to be Beyond Reason

However, this comprehension of God and the Ideas in His Mind is far beyond the power of the natural reason, Colet would hold. Man should beware of ever thinking that "by the strength of reason you can attain aught of truth." Indeed, "by no human resources, by no faculty of reason even in its highest vigor, . . . by no supports of human learning and eloquence, . . . is man enabled to soar to the designs and acts of God, placed as they are above all human reason, in His own absolute reason and will."[8] If man endeavors to draw the divine mysteries to himself" and examine them by the natural powers of his own mind, it cannot fail but that they will certainly degenerate at once, from their truth and sweetness, in keeping with the fickleness and incapacity of the human mind."[9]

Purification or "Collection" in St. Augustine

It follows that the only way man can know God and the "truths of the intelligible world" is through God's aid. "The truth . . . is understood by grace."[10] The first infused grace or gift that man needs is hope or purification—a fact dictated by both the Bible and Plato, both of whom insisted that only the pure in heart shall see.[11] Thus Augustine urged that "all diligence ought to be given to . . . purification," in order that man, "delivered from the depressing weight of lusts," might "contemplate that . . . unchangeable Light" (*City of God* 8:3, cf. *Coll.* 14:1-2).

---

[8] LC p. 26.

[9] LR p. 42. Cf. LR p. 83, where natural reason is a "distempered state," and LR p. 86, where it is natural reason which produces wars.

[10] LC p. 110.

[11] E.g., Matt. 5:8, *Phaedo* 67, 82.

For Augustine this purification involved a "collection" of the soul—that is, a contraction away from all distracting elements, including thoughts as well as external phenomena and desires. This notion had been prominent in Plotinus, Porphyry, and Proclus, the latter urging that for higher knowledge "we must avoid the manifold desires which distract," shunning "multiplicity" and striving toward "unity."[12] Thus in *Confessions* 7:23 Augustine's soul, rising toward a vision of God, "abstracted itself from the contradictory throng of sense images" and "withdrew its thoughts from experience." To put it another way, the reasoning process must be wholly silenced, so that the soul exists in a state of serene "Quiet" and is "hushed to herself" (*Conf.* 9:25). This state of silence is necessary for "introversion," by which the soul turns in upon itself and absorbs itself into its own "eye" (*Conf.* 7:16), corresponding to Plotinus's "apex" (*Enn.* 5:1:1-3). The vision of God follows.

Dionysius and the Darkness of Unknowing

This Augustinian process undergirds much Dionysian thought. The Areopagite argued that God dwells in "the Darkness of Unknowing," that is, a "Darkness which is beyond the intellect."[13] This concept of God as "beyond knowing" had its germinal basis in *Timaeus* 28-29—"The father and maker of all this universe is past finding out." To know this God, to "plunge" into this Darkness, one must therefore take leave not only of senses but even of reason. One must render inactive all his intellectual powers, and place himself in a quietistic Augustinian state of *agnostia* or "wise ignorance.": "the divine knowledge of God . . . takes place

---

12 See Lupton, *Hier.*, p. xl-xli.

13 Shrine of Wisdom, *Mystical Theology of Dionysius*, pp. 11, 16.

through ignorance when the intellect quit[s] . . . all things that are" (*Div. Names* 7:3). Thus in the *Mystical Theology* Dionysius directs "dear Timothy" to

> leave behind the senses and the operations of the intellect, and all things sensible and intellectual, . . . that thou mayest arise, by unknowing towards . . . Him Who transcends all . . . knowledge. . . . Thus by knowing nothing [one] knows That Which is beyond his knowledge."[14]

Ficino's Purification as Platonic Separation of Soul from Body

Like Augustine and Dionysius, Ficino also emphasized purification or "collection" as the necessary prelude to knowledge of God. "The soul collects itself . . . and is not occupied either in perceiving corporeal qualities or in guiding and moving the members of its own body, or in performing external affairs. . . . Each soul may retire from the pestilence of the body and collect itself into its mind."[15]

Most often Ficino describes this purification in terms of Platonic separation of soul from body. In *Phaedo* 64-68, Plato had asserted that "we make the nearest approach to knowledge when we have the least possible intercourse . . . with the body, and are not surfeited with the bodily nature, but keep ourselves pure." Since "separation and release of the soul from the body is termed death," it follows (argued Plato) that "true philosophers . . . are ever seeking" to die. Ficino was fond of this concept: "This whole effort of philosophy, as Plato says, is a meditation on death. For death is the liberation of the soul from the body."[16] However, Ficino

---

14 *Ibid.*, pp. 9, 11, cf. p. 13.

15 Kristeller, *Ficino*, pp. 216, 215, 298.

16 *Ibid.*, p. 302, cf. *Phaedo* 64. In the Pauline Epistles there is of course a similar "discipline of dying," but in Paul the emphasis is on "dying unto sin" in order that we might "rise with Christ," rather than a dying unto

believed in the possibility of such "death" even in this life, sometimes expressing the notion through the metaphor of stripping or nakedness:

> The mind will then be most perfect . . . when it flies away entirely from the body. . . . [This] will prove in fact Socrates' opinion . . . that there is but one way not only to reach but also to possess incorporeal things, namely to make oneself incorporeal. . . . [Philosophers] should conduct an intellectual life separated from the body, and being themselves separated, they will at once attain the separated forms. . . . Plato commends us to flee . . . from the love of the body . . . . Strip thyself, I beseech thee, in so far as thou canst; nay more, with thine utmost endeavor separate the soul from the body. Then straight-way thou shalt see the pure gold free from the defilements of earth.[17]

The "pure gold" here refers to Ideas, but since Ideas are part of God's substance, to see Ideas is for Ficino also to see God.[18]

Colet: Purification as Prelude to Knowledge

Colet was well aware of the epistemological tradition just described: "St. Paul . . . [and] Dionysius . . . deemed it an unworthy thing that the human reason should be mixed up with divine revelation."[19] No doubt he was also aware of Mirandola's approval of Dionysius's view: "God is . . . unspeakably exalted," proclaimed Pico, "above all Intellect and Knowledge."[20]

---

the body so that we might live with the soul alone and attain knowledge.

[17] *Ibid.*, pp. 214, 217, 291; *Epistolae* I in Nesca Robb, *Neoplatonism of the Italian Renaissance, p.* 87.

[18] See Kristeller, *Ficino,* pp. 246, 117, 330, 116, 251.

[19] LC p. 18.

[20] Pico's *Discourse on Love,* p. 3.

It is against a Neoplatonic background, therefore, that we can more readily appreciate Colet's emphasis on purification as the prelude to knowledge, and his interpretation of that purification (corresponding to Pauline hope) as an Augustinian-Dionysian-Ficinian "collection" of the soul away from "scattered thoughts" as well as from passions, desires, and everything associated with "this fluctuating world."[21] The concept of collection is combined in Colet with three other elements: (1) the Ficinian metaphor of nakedness; (2) Platonic separation; (3) Augustinian introversion, whereby the soul returns to its own deepest "unity" or "center."

Collection, Introversion, Quietism, "Nakedness," and Soul-Body Separation in Colet

For example: Would anyone see truth?

> Then he must wholly strip and lay bare himself, laying aside all the thoughts of his mind . . . by which he deemed that he had learnt something. Just as primal matter, in order to be formed, is naked, that there may be nothing in it to counteract the formation; so it is needful that man should strip off his powers . . . if he would be enlightened by inspiration to understand things divine. . . . For those truths of the intelligible world, and unalloyed reasons, divine and spiritual, . . . none are qualified, but those of the very highest spiritual power, those who are wholly concentrated on the One, and who, despising the body and the world, stand unshaken on the loftiest mental pinnacle; on the one, indivisible center.[22]

Again: "This hope is the beginning of man's journey towards God, a collecting of the soul, and a uniting . . . of it."[23] The

---

[21] LC p. 21.

[22] LR p. 45, LC pp. 42-43, 32.

[23] LR p. 68.

Christian's effort is "to collect and re-unite through hope."[24]
The collected soul is "calm," corresponding to Augustine's
"Quiet."[25] For Colet collection involves Platonic withdrawal
or separation: "Christians should stand before God . . . with
no impediment either of passion or reason interposing between us. . . . Each one of us is bound to withdraw into the
stronghold of his own mind."[26] Man should retire, says the
Dean, into his own deepest unity, the "needle's eye" (cf. Matt.
19:24) of his soul.[27] For Christianity is "a profession of sin-
gleness; and men are drawn to it, as from multiplicity to
simplicity."[28]

Colet's most characteristic description of purification is by
all means that of stripping and nakedness: "Who wishes to
change his raiment must strip. . . . If you would be in his
wedding garment, [you must] come to him naked."[29] Circumcision is a symbol of "that laying bare the soul, by stripping it of all vain and superfluous imaginations."[30] He who
would know God must undergo

> every kind of separation from the flesh, to the end that [he] . . .
> may have no dealings therewith. . . . The mind . . . is clogged
> as with a covering of foreskin. By this I mean carnal affections,
> gross imagination, and loose and unbridled reason. . . . It must
> have these wrappings removed, and stand forth in singleness,

---

[24] *Sac.*, p. 37, cf. p. 38, where hope is associated with purity, nakedness,
unity.

[25] LR p. 83. The notion of Quietism is also in Ficino's *Epistolae*. See
Jayne, *Colet and Ficino,* pp. 144, 315, where Colet paraphrases: "Avoid
multiplicity, uproar, and confusion; seek simplicity, tranquility, and quiet."

[26] ExR p. 85.

[27] LC p. 87.

[28] EH p. 72. Cf. Mirandola's *Heptaplus* as discussed in C. Meiners,
Lebensbeschreibungen beruhmter Manner, pp. 48-49.

[29] EH pp. 64, 72.

[30] ExR pp. 79-80.

even as God is single. . . ; that so the mind may be inwardly free and unencumbered.[31]

Purification Followed by Illumination in Colet's System

Purification or hope is followed by illumination or faith, that knowledge of God which is beyond the natural reason. "This faith is a kind of light infused into the soul of man from the divine sun, by which the heavenly verities are known to be revealed without uncertainty or doubt; and it as far excels the light of reason, as certainty does uncertainty."[32] "The wisdom of the intellect is faith. . . . The illumination, and infused light, by which the soul may . . . see . . . perfect truth, is faith. . . . [Man] may look upon Him in the Sun by the spiritual eye of faith."[33] This faith is a new "spiritual reason," a

> faith which is above reason, a light full surely given us in Christ, and capable of the highest reason. . . . Let us ascribe to our own perverseness our want of power to comprehend the things of God, rather than disdainfully spurn what our puny reason comprehends not; yea and let us seek to become something that is above reason, namely great in faith.[34]

The reason must be "subject . . . to God . . . to the end that he [man] may be raised through grace out of blindness into light, and out of folly into wisdom . . . to the discovery of reality and truth."[35]

Accordingly, Colet prays at the outset of the Radulphian

---

[31] *Ibid.*, p. 84.

[32] LR p. 44.

[33] LC p. 12; LR p. 46; MB p. 43.

[34] EH p. 156, LR p. 79.

[35] LR p. 41. Cf. ExR p. 139, where "human reason is the enemy and opponent of grace."

Letters that God "bestow upon us some illumination from his own Intelligence."[86] For only by infused faith can man have "clear knowledge and right action."[87] We have in this last idea the Platonic notion (*Republic* 4:443-4) that wisdom is the knowledge which "presides over . . . just and good action."[88] However, Colet explicitly denies this higher wisdom to pre-Atonement philosophers. It was for the very reason that they lacked grace that in wisdom they were "not good, in light not warm, and . . . brought forth no fruit from the root of knowledge."[89]

Influence of Augustine on Colet's Illumination Theory

Evident in Colet's system of knowledge is the illuminative theory of Augustine, who stressed that as the result of infused grace God "shines like a sun in the soul," so that "the soul sees all truly intellectual objects" in God's mind (*de Gen. c. Manich.* 1:43, and *de Gen. ad Litt.* 12)[40] Thus for Augustine as for Colet, "God is the intellectual Light in Whom and from Whom and by Whom shine intellectually all things that do intellectually shine" (*Sol.* 1:3). This view, of course, springs ultimately from *Republic* 6:508-9 and 7:514 ff., where the Idea of the Good "which imparts truth" or Ideas "to the knower" is likened to "the sun" which "shines" on physical objects and makes them visible to "the eyes." For Augustine this illuminated knowledge was "sapientia" or Christian wis-

---

[86] MA p. 3.

[87] LC p. 21.

[88] Cf. *Meno* 88, where "virtue must be a sort of wisdom"; and *Protagora.* 359-60, where the virtue which assures courageous deeds is knowledge of a scale of values.

[89] ExR p. 64.

[40] See Butler, pp. 52, 54.

dom, as distinguished from "scentia" or secular learning—a distinction reflected in Colet.[41]

Colet's Knowing-Uniting Distinction a Divergence from Neoplatonism

Although purification enables the soul "to unite . . . fruitfully with God, its spouse,"[42] it is obvious that for Colet such mystical union takes place only through the intermediary step of faith or illumined knowledge. This is so because Colet held that even to know God is not to unite with him. This was not an idea common to Augustine, Dionysius, or even the mature Ficino. Dionysius had assumed the identity of knowing and uniting: "Divine knowledge of God . . . takes place . . . in the union which is above intelligence" (*Div. Names* 7:3).

Ficino also came ultimately to the position that the soul becomes what it knows, and knows what it becomes. Therefore perception of Ideas which are parts of God's substance, involves union with those Ideas and with God.[43] Thus the Florentine came to speak alternately of "the knowledge or possession of God. . . . Speculation is fully achieved when . . . the primal True or Good is loved and thought with the greatest ardor."[44] Indeed, in Ficino's later complex psychology it is the intellect that loves God, so that Cassirer is probably right that in the end Ficino worked out a synthesis between knowledge and uniting love.[45] Cassirer's conclusion

---

[41] See Eugene Rice, "John Colet and the Annihilation of the Natural," *HTR*, 45:143-4. Rice, pp. 141-163, is an excellent discussion of Colet's epistemology.

[42] ExR pp. 79-80, cf. p. 84.

[43] Consult Kristeller, *Ficino*, pp. 250-252, 117, 116, 330.

[44] *Ibid.*, pp. 176, 243.

[45] See "Ficino's Place in Intellectual History," *JHI*, 6:491-2.

is further supported by the newly discovered Colet-Ficino correspondence, in which Colet had asked the Florentine, "What is the relation between love and knowledge?" In a highly complicated reply Ficino had suggested a synthesis of the two.[46]

To Colet, obsessed as he was with the ascending Christian triad of hope-faith-love, such a synthesis was obviously unacceptable. Colet's desire was to stress above all else that it is love for God, not knowledge of him, which accomplishes mystical union. Only through "the most burning love" can man "cleave . . . to God himself."[47] It follows that "love surpasses faith" or illumined knowledge.[48] "It comes to pass that love in force and power far surpasses faith, and is far more effectual to raise man on high, and join him to God."[49]

Colet Cites Early Ficino on Mystical Power of Love

To support this view, Colet seized upon an early and uncharacteristic passage from Ficino's *Platonic Theology* 14, quoting it almost verbatim as from "the Platonist Marsilius Ficinus touching the love of God." In the cited passage Ficino had written:

> Love unites the mind with God more quickly, more closely, and more firmly than does knowledge, because the force of knowledge consists more in distinction; that of love more in union. . . . We are united more closely with God through the joy of love, which transforms us into the beloved God, than through knowledge. . . . Furthermore, recognizing God, we con-

---

[46] See Jayne, *Colet and Ficino,* pp. 277-8. For another examination of Ficino's vacillation on love (or will) versus intellect (or knowledge), consult *ibid.,* pp. 138-140.

[47] LR p. 26.

[48] LC p. 56.

[49] LR p. 28.

tract His amplitude to the capacity and concept of our mind; but loving Him, we enlarge the mind to the immense amplitude of divine goodness. There, so to speak, we lower God to our level; here, we lift ourselves to God. For we know as far as we can comprehend; but we love both what we see clearly and what we expect as the remainder of the divine goodness beyond our clear sight.[50]

Building on this passage, Colet eulogized "this exalted, expansive, God-embracing love, holding fast by Him, and linking man closely to Him" as the culmination of "true religion." "Love is not confined within the limits of knowledge [i.e., illumined faith], but advances farther, in keeping with its transcendent power, and takes a wider sweep, not satisfied till it has attained that first boundless and infinite good, wherein alone it can repose."[51]

It should not be thought, however, that Colet's emphasis on the mystic power of love was grounded solely in an early isolated passage of Ficino's. On the contrary, the emphasis had authority in both Scripture and the *Dialogues*. St. Paul had in at least one passage (1 Cor. 13:13) exalted love over hope and faith. Further, in *Symposium* 202 Plato had described love as an intermediary spirit through which God and man make contact with one another—a notion which Colet incorporated into his doctrine of the Christ-Spirit as the loving mediator between the Father and his creatures.[52]

Reciprocal Love and Exchange of Souls in Ficino and Colet

The germs of Platonic reciprocal love were elaborated by Ficino into a complex system whereby God is the "father" of love who "runs to meet us before we seek him," and who

---

[50] *Op. Om.* pp. 663-4 in Kristeller, *Ficino*, p. 273.

[51] LR pp. 29-32.

[52] See *supra.*, pp. 107-8.

through his emanated beauty or "spiritual grace" "kindles this love in the soul."[53] Thus man is filled with "a desire for the supreme divine beauty" which drives him up to God. Moreover, just as the love for a person transforms the lover into the beloved, so also the loving desire for God "transforms [man] through love into the Good itself."[54] For "it often happens that the lover wishes to transform himself into . . . the loved one. . . . Plato said about a certain lover: 'That lover is a soul dead in its own body and living in that of another.' "[55]

The Ficinian concept of reciprocal love undergirds Colet's basic interpretation of Pauline justification, despite the fact that Paul himself rarely speaks of love for God.[56] Thus in the Romans lectures we are told that by justification "we signify nothing else than that men return the love of a loving God. In this love and return of love consists the justification of man. And this reciprocal love in us is joined with hope."[57] Moreover, Ficino's notion of love as transforming man into the beloved is obviously reflected in Colet's *Right Fruitful Monition*: "Remember, as a man loveth, so he is, for the lover is in the thing loved more properly than in himself."[58] Elsewhere the idea is applied to the Eucharist: "At the table of the Lord . . . the communicants of Christ are transformed into Him."[59]

---

[53] *Com. on Symp.*, pp. 198-9, 162-3, 194, 235.

[54] Kristeller, *Ficino*, pp. 264, 282.

[55] *Com. on Symp.*, pp. 141, 143. Cf. Colet's paraphrase of Ficino's *Epistolae* passage entitled, "That a Friend Is in His Friend"—Jayne, *Colet and Ficino*, p. 307.

[56] *IB* 10:166.

[57] LR pp. 11-12.

[58] RFM p. 309.

[59] LC p. 108. Cf. *Sac.*, p. 46.

Influence of Dionysius and Mirandola on Colet's
Emphasis on Mystic Love

Another important factor in Colet's emphasis on the mystic power of love was Dionysius.[60] In the Celestial Hierarchy love is associated with the highest order of angels, the Seraphs—a fact which Colet was quick to note in his own abstract: "Seraphim signifies fire. They are the loving beings of the highest order, reposing most sweetly in the divine beauty, being associated in happiness with the most loving Jesus. . . . These most blessed loving ones are filled with unutterable delight in cleaving to the divine beauty."[61] It follows therefore that if man wishes to cleave to God, he must imitate the highest order of angels by being perfected through love: "Those who are perfected dwell in the region of fire," asserts the Dean; such folk are "heated with love so as readily to be inflamed." They are "now inflamed with love, so as, like fire, to cling to the heavenly orbs."[62]

Here Colet combines the way of love with Platonic imitation in words which seem drawn almost verbatim from Mirandola's *Oration on Man*: "The Seraph burns with the fire of love. . . . If we long with love for the Creator . . . , we shall speedily flame up with His consuming fire into a Seraphic likeness. . . . Who so is a Seraph, that is, a lover, is in God and God in him, nay rather, God and himself are one."[63]

---

[60] See Lupton, LC p. 56, n. 1.

[61] CH p. 20.

[62] EH pp. 132-3.

[63] Elizabeth Forbes (trans.), "The Dignity of Man," in *Renaissance Philosophy of Man*, pp. 227-8. Another possible inspiration is Pico's *Discourse on Love*. See Lupton, *Hier.*, p. 133, n. 2.

Likeness to God Stressed by Colet as Pre-Requisite for Union

As this implies, for Colet a certain imitative perfection must exist between man and God before the two can mystically unite. Just as oil and water cannot merge, neither can a sinner merge with the deity.

> It is necessary that those who are joined together be of some similarity. Truly the flesh is far away from God; hence it is impossible that the carnal man be joined to God. . . . If we wish to be joined and united to God who is spirit, it is necessary that we be wholly spiritual beings. . . . The marriage to God is consummated only with a virgin made young in spirit, . . . made chaste with the Holy Spirit.[64]

Note here how Colet insists on sanctification before union. He does likewise in the *Mystical Body* treatise, where he explains that "subordinate to the Spirit's essence is spiritual being"—i.e., the infused form of grace.[65]

This necessary state of likeness to God is assigned especially to the perfective grace of love: "Love makes perfect. . . . Charity is a direct imitation of God, and a being made like unto Him. . . . Christian love is the daughter of Likeness and Equality."[66] This notion is often elaborated into the doctrine that man must himself be a god before he can merge with God. In Christ "we are born to newness of being . . . that we may be holy, wise, and good, and being made like unto God, may become gods" (cf. man's imitation of the "holy, just, and wise" God in *Theaetetus* 176). Again Colet insists that "God, made man, was the means whereby men were to be gods. By His Godhead all are made godlike."[67]

---

[64] *Sac.*, p. 17.

[65] MB p. 43.

[66] CH p. 22; LC pp. 146, 136.

[67] MB p. 40, cf. EH pp. 61, 54.

L

The result of infused love is therefore that men are "rendered gods"; "there exists upon the earth a being that is plainly a god."[68] Although Paul refers to sanctified men as "saints" and "perfect,"[69] he nowhere calls Christians "gods." Here once again we can discern the probable influence of Ficino, who in his *Theologia Platonica* 13:3 had celebrated man as "a kind of God" because of his control of animals and the arts.[70]

Ficino's "Vacatio" Not Stressed by Colet

Both Augustine and Ficino had seriously accepted the notion that in mystical union the soul actually leaves the body.[71] For both men this posed the problem of keeping the soulless body alive. Like Augustine, Ficino solved the problem by stressing that few attain union, and they only briefly.[72] Colet himself makes occasional references to the "unfettered" soul's "withdrawal from this world," and of men as "passing beyond themselves" or "going out of themselves."[73]

However, there are several reasons for contending that Colet did not believe in a literal or complete separation of soul from body. First, it is not required in his Pauline

---

[68] LR pp. 63, 60.

[69] E.g., 1 Cor. 2:6, Phil. 3:15, Col. 1:4.

[70] Josephine Burroughs (trans.), Ficino's *Platonic Theology*, *JHI* (Apr. 44), 233-4.

[71] See Augustine's comment on 2 Cor. 12:2 in *De. Gen. ad litt.* 12:5:14 in Butler, p. 72. That a "vacatio" of the soul was no mere metaphor for Ficino is indicated by Kristeller, *Ficino*, p. 215; and by James Wadsworth, "Lorenzo de Medici and Marsilio Ficino," *Romanic Review*, 46 (Apr. 55), 100.

[72] Kristeller, *Ficino*, pp. 224, 226.

[73] E.g., LR p. 61; LC p. 27. Cf. 2 Cor. 12:2-3—"I know a man in Christ who . . . was caught up to the third heaven—whether in the body or out of the body I do not know."

mysticism, in which the Spirit comes to dwell in the sanctified soul. Second, Colet explicitly states in at least one instance that during this life man should not be "disobedient to God, or seem in weariness, to have thrown off that burden of the . . . body."[74] Third, the Dean's frequent Aristotelian view of the soul as the form of the body[75] precludes any literal separation in this life. Indeed, it was for this very reason that Ficino, in advocating a "vacatio," denied the Aristotelian concept: "For such a [soul], which would . . . be inseparably in the underlying body like a corporeal form, could not attempt to turn itself away from that same body."[76]

Pagan Ecstasy in Colet's Mystical Union

However, among Augustine, Ficino, and Colet, there is a common view that union is characterized by joyous rapture: "I shudder and kindle," exclaimed Augustine; "I thrilled with love and awe" (*Conf.* 9:25, 7:16). In the same spirit Colet exclaims: "Jesus . . . sates with every pleasure our spiritual senses; and through excess of pleasures transports to ecstasy his bride, the soul, which unites with him."[77] Such ecstasy is essentially foreign to Pauline mysticism, and recalls the wild delight of mystical union which, according to Porphyry, Plotinus sometimes experienced.[78]

---

[74] LC p. 73.

[75] See LR p. 28.

[76] Kristeller, *Ficino,* p. 214.

[77] EH p. 98.

[78] See Moffatt, *Paul and Paulinism,* pp. 36-41, and Underhill, p. 544. For a consideration of the various definitions of mysticism, consult Inge, *Christian Mysticism,* p. 335 ff. The definition used in this book is that of Underhill, p. 544, that "union with God" is "the central mystic doctrine." By such union is meant "the fusion of personalities"—Inge, pp. 5, 29-30. The variables of ecstasy and absorption are generally characteristic of pagan

Colet's mystical ascent can therefore be diagrammed as follows:

Pauline Triad	Dionysian Triad	Elaborations by Dionysius, Augustine, Ficino, Mirandola
hope	purification	"collection," withdrawal to "center" or "eye," "unity," nakedness
faith	illumination	knowledge (Christian wisdom, sapientia)
love	perfection	"likeness to God," making man a "god"
mystical union	ecstasy	

Why Has Colet Been Ignored as a Mystic?

In view of the evidence in this chapter, it is surprising that the significance of Colet as a mystic has been largely ignored. In her historical account of mysticism, Miss Underhill makes no mention of Colet, stating that before his time the mystical scene had shifted entirely to Italy.[79] Greene argued that Colet returned from his European trip "un-

---

mysticism; the variables of physical merging and sacramental intermediaries, of the Catholic tradition. The presence of mystical ecstasy in Origen and St. Bernard very probably derives not from St. Paul but from (1) rabbinical commentaries on the Song of Solomon, and/or (2) Plotinus and other Neoplatonic sources.

[79] Underhill, *Mysticism*, p. 555. Colet also goes unmentioned in Gerald Bullett, *The English Mystics* (London, 1950).

touched by the Platonic mysticism."[80] Such statements sound strange in light of Colet's repeated assertions that the "heavenly sun" draws men up and "makes them one with itself," so that "between God and the Church is the true marriage and the most fruitful union of the feminine man with the masculine God."[81]

Only very recently has any attempt been made to analyze the unmistakable mysticism in Colet's works.[82] Also much ignored has been the startling parallels between Colet and the writings of the 14th century mystics. The association of nakedness with purification, for example, is probably not as prominent in Ficino and St. Paul (2 Cor. 5:1-8) as in Meister Eckhart, who argued that the soul must "denude" itself to a status of "unknowing": "Into the Naked Godhead none may get except he himself be Naked."[83] Similarly, the *Theologia Germanica* (called by Underhill "the literary jewel" of the Friends of God movement) argued that he who wishes to "cast a glance into eternity . . . must be quite pure, and wholly stripped and bare of all images, and be entirely separate from all creatures."[84]

Parallels between Colet and 14th Century Mystics

The similarity of this to Colet, both in language and concept, necessarily raises the question of the extent to which he might have been familiar with the thought of the German Friends of God, and the Dutch Devotio Moderna (or Breth-

---

[80] For a protest to this, see Lupton, *Life*, p. 86, n. 2.

[81] CH p. 3; *Sac.*, p. 26.

[82] In Hunt, *Dean Colet and His Theology*, p. 104 ff.

[83] Jones, p. 77; Clark, p. 63.

[84] Shrine of Wisdom, *Dionysius*, p. 22.

ren of the Common Life).[85] Colet has frequently been linked with both these movements, but seldom with any precise documentation. Both Rice and Duhamel have however provocatively observed a similarity between Colet's views on scholasticism and those of the Dutch Brethren.[86]

Gerard Groote (d. 1384), founder of the Brethren, explicitly disapproved of scholastic philosophy.[87] Gansfort shared this view, condemning empty words and arguments for argument's sake, and criticizing the doctors at Cologne and Paris for debating at length questions of no practical value.[88] Indeed, Gansfort went so far as to say that "there is a strong and weighty argument against universities to be drawn from the fact that Paul secured but little fruit at Athens."[89] This antipathy toward the schoolmen is reflected in much of Thomas á Kempis, who puts these words into Christ's mouth in a passage against secular knowledge:

> I it am that in a point lift up the meek soul so that he shall understand my reasons of everlasting truth more than though he had studied ten years in schools. So I teach without noise of words, without confusions of opinions, without desire of honor, without fighting of arguments. . . . I am the teacher of truth within.[90]

Again: "The human reason may lightly err and be deceived,

---

[85] The first of these groups is the subject of Rufus Jones's *Flowering of Mysticism and the Friends of God in the 14th Century;* the second is treated in Albert Hyma, *The Christian Renaissance: A History of the Devotio Moderna.*

[86] Rice, p. 55; Duhamel, pp. 494, 498. See also Lupton, *Life,* p. 266.

[87] Hyma, p. 17. Groote's antipathy stands in great contrast to Mirandola's special praise of Aquinas. Note Edward Surtz, "The Oxford Reformers and Scholasticism," *SP,* 47 (Oct. 50), 551.

[88] Hyma, p. 204.

[89] Hughes, 3:221.

[90] Irwin Edman, Thomas á Kempis's (?) *Imitation of Christ,* p. 248.

but the true faith may never deceive or fail. All reason and natural enquiry ought to follow the true faith without further reasoning. Fast faith . . . surmounteth all curious enquiry."[91]

Colet's Affinity with Devotio Moderna's Scorn of Scholastic Philosophy and Secular Learning

These thoughts are remarkably close to Colet's, who also impugned the natural reason, and exalted faith as the true knowledge. Moreover, Colet's dislike for the scholastics has the same basis as that of Gansfort and á Kempis: the Scotists lacked humility, said the Dean, and they "argue[d] about the opinions of others and about words, sometimes gnawing at this, sometimes at that . . . , dissect[ing] everything minutely."[92] Indeed, almost any member of the Devotio Moderna might have written Colet's veiled attack on the schoolmen as "an intellectual race, with leisure and literature in abundance, confiding at the same time in an elaborate kind of rhetoric; they had no scruple at pleading either side, whether for or against, whatever was the subject of the debate." For such "subtleties of the versatile human intellect," Colet expresses snorting contempt.[93]

In Colet too we find the Devotio Moderna point that genuine wisdom is not possessed by kings or professors, but

---

91 *Ibid.*, p. 317.

92 Erasmus on Colet in Hunt, p. 9. Colet's dislike of the scholastics contrasts sharply with the attitude of both Ficino and Mirandola. Note particularly the latter's letter to Barbaro, in which Pico strenuously objects to his correspondent's implication that Mirandola has wasted six years studying Aquinas, Scotus, and Albertus. See Kristeller, *Ficino*, p. 13; Dulles, pp. 36-37; Pearl Kibre, *Library of Mirandola*, p. 61; and esp. Breen, "Mirandola on Philosophy and Rhetoric," *JHI*, 8 (June 52), 392 ff.

93 LC p. 26. The description is ostensibly of the Corinthians.

by those who make themselves humble "fools" in order to receive the illumination of the divine Sun:

> How unacceptable and hateful to God is the power and wisdom of this world, how opposite and contrary to the divine wisdom, ... may be perceived even from this: that it was not the will of God that the mysteries of his wisdom... should... be chiefly heard... by the wise and powerful; but should be received and delivered by those who were utterly devoid of the dark wisdom that consists in human reason.[94]

Colet's Affinity to Devotio Moderna's Redemption Scheme

An even more striking parallel between Colet and the Dutch Brethren can be found in the area of redemption. In the Devotio Moderna, as in Colet, a central teaching is original sin. This fallen state is described in terms of Platonic-Pauline slavery, unhappiness, and disharmony, whereby the soul fights unsuccessfully against the flesh and its lusts.[95] The internal disharmony of man is described by Zerbolt in words almost identical to those of Colet's:

> We have been contaminated by original sin, and wounded in all the powers... of the soul. These powers and feelings, having fallen from their proper status, have become deranged and diminished, though not completely destroyed. Hence it happens that these powers... are prone to evil.... Our reason, rendered vacillating and obtuse, often accepts falsehood for truth. . . . Our desires . . . have degenerated in carnal lusts.[96]

This woeful condition can be repaired, and "the liberty of the inner man" achieved (say the Brethren) only by the infusion of sanctifying grace. Thus á Kempis notes that he

---

[94] LC p. 18. In this connection it is interesting that Colet shows no enthusiasm for Ficino's exhortations to philosophy and learning. Note Jayne, *Colet and Ficino*, pp. 146-7.

[95] *Imitation*, p. 256.

[96] *Hyma*, p. 318.

cannot "withstand" the "passions" "unless thy most holy grace passed into mine heart . . . be assistant to me. Needful it is to have thy Grace . . . that nature may be overcome."[97] This grace, achieved through prayer, initially brings purification and consequent "holy discipline" whereby reason now commands the passions.[98] Such purification is associated with Platonic "separation" and "death" in the *Phaedo* sense.[99] From this new internal ordering good deeds automatically follow: "Of a pure heart proceedeth fruit of a good life."[100]

In the thinking of the Dutch Brethren, as in Colet, love follows from purification, and is the power which promotes mystical union. Note Zerbolt's *Spiritual Ascensions,* where "one learns to love, after having purified the heart."[101] Love is metaphorically characterized by fire and flame: Make me "inwardly united to thee by grace and burning love," exclaims á Kempis.[102] "Love is the greatest thing," proclaims Groote, because it is "born of God and cannot rest except in God."[103] Love is the "undepartable bond" which produces the "jubilant excess" of mystical union.[104] Running riot in marital metaphor, á Kempis refers to Christ as "my most sweet spouse, most pure lover."[105]

This brief summary is not intended to suggest that at every point the redemptive scheme of the Dutch Brethren

---

[97] *Imitation,* pp. 265, 270.

[98] *Ibid.,* pp. 158, 228, 198, 271; Hyma, pp. 211-212.

[99] *Ibid.,* pp. 236, 191, 265.

[100] *Ibid.,* p. 236.

[101] Hyma, pp. 80-81, cf. p. 159.

[102] *Imitation,* p. 313, cf. 314 ff.

[103] Jones, p. 247.

[104] Hyma, p. 226; *Imi.,* p. 237.

[105] *Imitation,* p. 170. St. Bernard has ninety sermons on the same theme.

agrees with that of Colet. On the other hand, it is impossible here to do justice to the many parallels. Like the Dean, for example, Groote discouraged marriage, and Zerbolt argued in favor of a communal society, supporting his position with appeals not only to Scripture but also to the Stoics and to Plato.[106]

Socratic Self-Knowledge as Starting-Point for Dutch Brethren and Colet

Even the Brethren emphasis on Socratic self-knowledge as the beginning of redemption is implied throughout Colet's works, in his insistence that man realize the extent of his baseness. Moreover, the doctrine is cited explicitly by Colet at the outset of the *Right Fruitful Monition:* "It is hygh wysedome and great perfection to knowe thy selfe, and than to dispise thy selfe; as, to know thou hast nothing that is good of thy selfe, but . . . by the infinite goodness and grace of God."[107] Compare this with Groote and especially Zerbolt: "The more we realize our own imperfections, the nearer we approach perfection. . . . Explore your sinful nature, strive to realize the extent of your fall."[108]

Did Colet Read the 14th Century Mystics?

It is possible that such parallels can be explained on the basis of the common inspiration of Dionysius. John Ruysbroeck, a disciple of Eckhart, was acclaimed "another Dionysius," and Eckhart himself was much under the influence of

---

[106] Hyma, pp. 32, 57. For Colet's views on communal living, see Chapter 6; and for his antipathy to marriage, Lupton, *Life,* pp. 77, 35, 263.

[107] RFM pp. 305-6.

[108] Hyma, pp. 35-39. Cf. the views of Radewijns in Hyma, p. 56.

the Areopagite.[109] However, certain works of Ruysbroeck and another Friend of God, Henry Suso, were available to Colet in early 15th century manuscripts.[110] Indeed, late 14th century England was inundated with mystical treatises— so much so that one old writer tells us that they "walked up and down at deer rates."[111] Among these was probably the Dutch *Imitation of Christ,* and definitely the English *Cloud of Unknowing.* This latter, as its title suggests, reflects the influence of the Dionysian German school.[112]

. Such facts indicate that further exploration of the relation of Colet to German-Dutch mysticism might very well clarify the influence of medieval on early Renaissance religious thought.

---

[109] See Underhill, p. 554; and on Eckhart's Neoplatonic sources: Clark, *Meister Eckhart,* pp. 101-103.

[110] There were about 500 Suso manuscripts in England during Colet's lifetime, some of them at Oxford. See Clark, *The Great German Mystics,* p. 63 ff; and Wichgraf, "Suso's Horologium Sapientia in England," *Archiv fur das Studium der Neueren Sprachen,* 91 (1936), pp. 176-181.

[111] Quoted by P. M. M'Intyre, *The Expositor,* Oct. 1907.

[112] See Underhill, Intro. to *Cloud of Unknowing,* pp. 6-7. It is tempting to speculate that Erasmus was the link between Colet and the 14th century mystics. As a youth Erasmus spent twelve years with the Brethren of the Common Life, and later visited Colet in England. Working against such a theory, however, is the fact that Erasmus probably did not arrive at Oxford until October 1499, and had left for London on his way back to the continent by December of that year. If our dating of the composition of Colet's works is correct, then Colet would already have finished all but two or three of his ten major works by the time Erasmus arrived. In any event, it is doubtful if a stay of such short duration could have had much mystical impact on Colet, particularly since Erasmus seems to have been hostile to the mystical tendencies of the Devotio Moderna. The philosophical relationships between Colet and Erasmus will however be more fully explored in Vol. 3 of the projected *Fishers with Platonic Nets* series. Meanwhile, consult Hyma, *The Christian Renaissance,* p. 226; and "Erasmus and the Oxford Reformers," pp. 70, 106.

Summary

To crystallize Colet's epistemological mysticism, then, we should note first his Platonic insistence on purification as the prelude to knowledge. Following Augustine, Dionysius, and Ficino, Colet discusses this purification in its various aspects of collection, introversion, quietism, and Platonic separation of soul from body. This latter is described in terms of Ficino's nakedness metaphor.

Purification, associated with Pauline hope, is followed by the illumination of infused faith. This faith is Christian wisdom or sapientia—that is, direct perception of God and the Ideas in God's Mind. This wisdom or highest knowledge is beyond the power of the natural reason, can be achieved only by grace, and is therefore to be distinguished from lesser degrees of knowledge, such as the secular learning of professors, or the knowledge derived by pagan philosophers from examining the visible universe. This epistemology owes much to the illumination theory of St. Augustine, whereby God is the supreme Light or Sun who infuses the light of knowledge into man. Combined with this theory is the view of Plato in the *Republic,* that wisdom is the basis of right action.

Colet was forced by the very nature of his ascending hope-faith-love triad to deny the common Neoplatonic idea that knowing involves union. The Dean therefore seized on an early and uncharacteristic position taken by Ficino in *Theologia Platonica,* and used this position to support the contention that mystical union comes only through love. This exaltation of love over faith (or knowledge) as the basic mystical agent was inspired not so much by Paul's isolated statement in 1 Cor. 13:13, as by four other factors: (1) Ficino's argument, on Platonic authority, that love—whether romantic or divine—transforms the lover into the object loved. (2) Dionysius's association of love with the Seraphs, the angelic order closest to God; (3) Mirandola's contention that he who wants union must himself become a Seraph—that is, must imitate the fiery love of these highest angels; (4) Colet's own conviction that love brings the goodness or perfection prerequisite to union—this on the assumption that union requires a similarity between the two objects involved. In describing this imitative perfection Colet's language is almost identical with the dictum of *Theaetetus* that men should imitate the "holy, just, and wise" God. Moreover, Colet supports his point by using the Ficinian term "gods" rather than the conventional Pauline term "saints": men must become gods before they can merge with God.

The Dean also appropriates Ficino's doctrine of reciprocal love between God and man as his own definition of justifica-tion. However, Colet's intermittent Aristotelian notion of the soul as the form of the body prompts him to deny the Augustinian and Ficinian view that at the moment of union the soul actually vacates the body. The only possible hetero-doxy in Colet's mysticism is his description of actual union in terms of a Plotinian ecstasy foreign to Pauline mysticism, though such rapture is found also in Augustine.

To the sources already mentioned for Colet's interrelated redemptive, epistemological, and mystical systems must prob-ably be added the corresponding systems espoused by such 14th century mystics as the German Friends of God and the Dutch Brethren of the Common Life. Views common to Colet and these mystics include a contempt for scholastic philosophy and secular knowledge, the fanatic insistence on original sin, Socratic self-knowledge as the starting point of the redemptive process, freedom from the body's domination through infused grace, holy soul as the Platonically automatic governor of the body, purification described in terms of Platonic separation and death in the *Phaedo* sense, purification as the prelude to knowledge and union, love as the flaming faculty which promotes mystical merging, and the description of union via the metaphor of marriage.

Another parallel, the Brethren teaching of communal living, will be treated in the next chapter.

CHAPTER 6

CHURCH SOUL AND BODY:
COLET'S NEOPLATONIC CONCEPT
OF REFORM

This chapter attempts (1) to analyze the rationale behind
Colet's advocacy of a Christian communal society, and (2)
to explore the complicated problem of Colet's multitudinous
sources in the light of preceding chapters.

Church Soul Proclaimed on Analogy with Human Soul

Colet's Neoplatonic concept of form and matter is applied
not only to individual redemption, but also to the nature of
the Christian Church. The starting point for this application
is "the case of the human body," which Colet regards in
Aristotelian terms as composed of contrary and conflicting
principles "ever striving to part asunder."[1]

---

[1] See Marriott, pp. 108-9, and Lupton, MB pp. xxx, 31.

Were there not a common force, called soul, to unite and bring into order the conflicting natures whereof the body consists, these elements would part asunder of their own natural properties. Even so it is with mankind. Of their own nature they are disorganized, deformed, and lost. Were there not some higher power, to restore, reform, reunite, and retain them constantly in beauty and good action, and in a mutual association of natures it must needs be that . . . they would of themselves be divided . . . like . . . an army deprived of its leader, or a body deserted by its soul.[2]

It follows that the Church-Body must itself have a Soul, comparable in power and function to the human soul: "This power will bear the same relation to the human commonwealth that the soul does to the body."[3] The Church's Soul is obviously God himself, and particularly the Holy Spirit:

The soul of this [Church] body, and, if I may use the Greek term of Aristotle, the entelechy [i.e., principle of energy] . . . is God Himself, the Holy Trinity . . . [From men] there is fashioned a something that is altogether one and animated, as it were, by a common soul. Now in St. Paul's philosophy, the soul which forms the connecting link between men thus joined together like members, is the Divine Spirit . . . The whole Church . . . is nothing else than an organ and instrument of the Spirit of God, as the body is of the soul . . . The Spirit of God [is] the soul of this divinely-complex and mystic body.[4]

Colet's Debt to Platonic World-Soul

With one possible exception (Phil. 1:27-30), Paul nowhere refers to Spirit as a "Soul." As this suggests, Colet's notion of a Church Soul represents an engrafting of the

---

[2] MB p. 34.

[3] *Ibid.,* p. 35.

[4] LC pp. 123, 6, 134, 135. Cf. EH pp. 128, 129, 122; LC pp. 140, 141.

Platonic World-Soul upon the Pauline concept of Spirit. Plato's World Soul had been presented as an immanent principle (*Timaeus* 36, 54), the origin of life and the effecter of some degree of order, regularity, and discipline—the governor and guide, in short, of the World Body.[5] Origen, attracted to this idea, ventured that the whole world, "as though it were a living being,' is ruled by "God's excellence and reason, as it were by one Soul."[6]

The Florentines were less cautious. Mirandola accepted the Platonic Soul without qualifications, ranking it ontologically between the angels and the heavens, and followed Ficino in advocating twelve sub-World Souls: "Next that of the World, Platonists assign many other rational souls. The eight principal are those of the heavenly spheres."[7] Following Platonic logic, Ficino himself argued that

it would be absurd for an imperfect [i.e., human] body to have a soul, and a perfect one neither to have a soul nor to live. For who is so distracted as to say that the part lives but the whole does not? Therefore the whole body of the world lives, since the bodies of animals, which are its parts, live.[8]

Considering this Platonic background, in which Colet was well versed, it is not surprising that he should have detected

---

[5] Plato's *Laws* 10: 893-8; see Solmsen, p. 90.

[6] Origen seems to have identified the World-Soul of *Timaeus* with the Christ-Logos, and to have held that this Logos-Soul orders and supports the world as the human soul does the body. See Jean Danielou, *Origen*, pp. 96-98.

[7] Pico's *Discourse on Love*, pp. 8, 14. Cf. Ficino's *Com. on Symp.*, p. 184, and Kristeller, *Ficino*, pp. 183, 385.

[8] Kristeller, *Ficino*, p. 86. Cf. *Philebus* 30. According to Colet's marginalia, Ficino frequently discussed the World-Soul in his *Epistolae*. See Jayne, Marginalia No. 61, for such Coletian paraphrases as: "Things within the World-Soul are composed of bodies and of souls, with light, life, and strength flowing through them from the World-Soul."

M

similarities between the Platonic Soul popularized by the Florentines and the Pauline Spirit. Both are immanent, unifying, governing, and life-giving principles (note Eph. 4:3, 2 Cor. 15:45). There are of course crucial differences: World-Soul is a regularizing immanent principle for the entire universe, not just for some special group of humans; and the life which it instills is natural life, not the supernatural Life in Christ of St. Paul (Col. 3:4).

These distinctions also apply of course to Plotinian emanation, five elements of which Colet uses in his concept of the Church: (1) the notion of God as an overflowing Fountainhead; (2) the introduction of form or flow as a stabilizing and unifying influence; (3) the identification of form and beauty; (4) Plotinus's transcendent General Soul which, as the third divine principle in the Plotinian system, itself overflows and emanates into this world; (5) the belief that withdrawal of divine flow produces disintegration of visible phenomena. All of these Plotinian elements, together with the major features of the Platonic World-Soul, are adapted to the Pauline Spirit. Colet maintains, for example, that the spiritual power of the Church "is present in full measure in the Head," that is, in Christ.[9]

> For as the diffused life of the body is brought back to the soul, as to the fountain-head, so too all the life of men, whereby they hold and unite themselves together (I mean, wisdom and goodness) must be referred to God from whom it came. For God is the soul of men, no otherwise than is the soul of each body: and every society has life and health in God, as the body has in the soul.[10]

Again, "When the Spirit is taken away, there is a change

---

[9] LC p. 123.
[10] LR pp. 74-75.

of form in all things . . . ; and beauty is turned to deformity."[11] "The Church . . . without its Soul, that is, the Holy Spirit, is dismembered and dispersed."[12] For the Church's

> life-giving, united, connecting power is the Holy Spirit . . . By that Spirit it is governed, moved, and sustained in a wonderful order . . . The harmony and mutual agreement of the parts is caused by that one and same Spirit, who cements them all into one . . . If the Spirit departs, the fabric falls to pieces by its natural tendency. For, when that secret link and connected essence is wanting—the Soul, as I may call it, that quickens the Church—it is inevitable that the Church, which is God's Body, being deprived of its Spirit, should fall to pieces, like a dead corpse, in dismemberment and dissolution.[13]

Other Platonic Sources for Colet's Church Soul Doctrine

The specific influence of the *Timaeus* on Colet's concept of a Church Soul and "Mystical Body" ought not to be overlooked, especially in view of the fact that Colet elsewhere quotes directly from that dialogue.[14] At one point the relation of the Church to its Soul or Spirit is described in terms which combine Neoplatonic emanation with *Timaeus* 50, where creation is described as the imposing of the Father on the Mother or Receptacle. Thus Colet notes that "the subject-matter of the Church, the female, [is] united to the masculine element, that it may be perfected in the male."[15]

Moreover, Colet's constant use of the human body and soul as philosophical justification for a Church Soul within the Church Body reflects the same argument constantly im-

---

[11] MB p. 37.
[12] *Ibid.*, p. 31.
[13] *Ibid.*, p. 36.
[14] LR p. 74.
[15] EH p. 127.

plied and often expressed not only in *Timaeus* but in other passages like *Philebus* 30: May our body be said to have a soul? . . . And whence comes that soul, . . . unless the Body of the universe, which contains elements like those in our bodies, had also a Soul?"[16] The influence of the microcosm-macrocosm concept in the *Republic* (e.g., 4:434-5) should also not be underestimated, particularly since Colet frequently refers to the Church and the human body as similar "commonwealths."[17]

Colet's Attitude toward Church Reformation

Colet's understanding of Church Reformation, in the historical sense, is closely related to his notion of a Church Soul. Involved also in the Dean's attitude on this subject are the Neoplatonic notion of form as a stabilizing agent, Aristotle's belief in the soul as the form or shape of the body, Plato's devotion to the soul as the body's governor, and Plato's concept of form or Idea as that which is or should be imitated. Thus Colet argues:

> Nor is unsoundness and disease anything else than a member's deviation from the life and form bestowed upon it by the soul, and a bursting the bonds, as it were, of the confining form. . . . The death of the whole body is nothing else than a declining and becoming detached from the sustaining form. It is from form, and from being well strung together, that the body's strength and health proceed. So too in like manner is

---

16 See LR pp. 61-62, 77, for examples not cited in this chapter of Colet's use of this analogy.

17 See for instance MB pp. 34-35. The Augustinian expression "City of God" is another frequent designation for the Church. See ExR p. 86, and MB p. 38. An obvious non-Platonic factor in Colet's Church Soul concept was Paul's use of the body-metaphor to describe the Christian community. This Pauline metaphor would easily have recalled to Colet's philosophic mind the World-Body of *Timaeus*, and thence by association the World-Soul.

it in the Christian Church, in which the souls of men live by
a spiritual life diffused by God.... This life is loving faith.
... Now if ... this faith be ... the life of the body, that is,
the church; then assuredly it must needs be, that the Church
will have and be in health so long a time as it is held together
in one faith by its soul, that is, by God.[18]

The Church Body must therefore adhere to its Soul or
"governing principle" if it is to remain in "health and
beauty." When "the Spirit keeps all things in itself, preserving every member in its own proper order . . . ; then
does the Church exhibit a fair beauty and form in God."[19]
"Moulded" by the grace of the Spirit-Soul, "the entire church
[is] . . . fixed and set firmly in place.[20] This notion is applied
not only to the conduct of Church members, but also to
heretical opinions: "Ever remember that, since you are a
member of the body ecclesiastical, it is your duty not to
break loose into some opinion of your own, but to accord with
the other members; that the health, soundness, and vigour
of the whole body may be preserved."[21]

Church Reformation a Return to Spirit-Form

It follows that Church corruption, whether of behavior or
belief, strikes Colet as disorder which can be rectified only
by returning to the basic "form" of loving faith.[22] This
Neoplatonic interpretation of historical reform is constantly
emphasized by Colet:

> All things are in such shameful disorder [in] ... our most dis-
> ordered Church.... All order is being overthrown.... I be-

---

[18] LR pp. 81-82.

[19] LC p. 124.

[20] *Sac.*, p. 36.

[21] LR p. 108.

[22] On this point note Lupton, LR pp. xxxviii, xl; also Hunt, pp. 70-71.

seech thee, merciful Jesu, of thy almighty power, speedily scatter the darkness in thy Church, and restore order. . . . I pray God . . . to reform . . . what has become deformed in us."[23] When therefore Colet, working from Romans 12:2 at the outset of his *Convocation Sermon,* pleads with the assembled bishops to be "reformed in the spyrte of God," he has in mind his own special Neoplatonic concept of metaphorically chaotic matter returning to its governing form.[24]

Colet's Brotherhood of the Spirit

The presence of Spirit in all members of the Church leads Colet, as it did St. Paul, to a profession of the brotherhood of all believers. The Spirit makes for a common bond of sympathy. If anyone is hurt, all the Church members "feel the shock simultaneously." Where "the Spirit is in pain, it is in pain everywhere; where it rejoices, it rejoices everywhere alike." For the Spirit "is present in all its fullness to every single" member.

> And the intent thereof is that, whatever happens in any part of the Church, should be instantly felt by all; that all members should feel a common sympathy and concord; and that all men, through the secret control of the Spirit, should at once apply a remedy to the injured part.[25]

Brotherhood therefore means that "each brother must take heed to deal brotherly and kindly with his brother, whoever he may be; to have compassion on his weakness."[26] One means of achieving this goal is the Eucharist, through which men are "bound together in a union of charity, . . . concord,

---

23 EH pp. 124, 126, 151, 155, 162.
24 See CS pp. 294-5.
25 MB pp. 44-45.
26 LR p. 115.

and brotherly agreement."[27] Accordingly, every Christian should work for

> the common good; ever mindful that he is a member of the body of Christ, and called to live not to himself alone; but to the body; aye even to die, if need be, for the safety of the body. For all the parts of his holy society ... must imitate a whole and sound body and its members, [where] ... all the parts have such coherence and sympathy, and do so assiduously render mutual help to one another that in the whole body there is presented, not a plurality of parts, but a united whole composed of several parts; with no private interest among them ... but everywhere ... a singular desire for ... the welfare of the whole body. This pattern of nature ... must be closely copied by that Christian body.[28]

Indeed, "the ruin of the Church consists in each one's seeking his own private advantage," rather than the advantage of the whole.[29] Each Christian should therefore remember the example of his ear or eye, which "cannot seek life and strength for itself by any better method ... than by doing all it can for the growth and strength of the whole body."[30]

Colet's Use of Plato's Doctrine of the Whole

Here the Platonic ideal of working for the Whole rather than for the parts is recommended to the believer. Elsewhere Colet applies it to God's own action and attitude: "God turned the wicked deeds of the Jews to good ends; good, not indeed for themselves, ... but good for the whole universe and ... general commonwealth."[31] "What is most

---

[27] EH p. 85.
[28] LR p. 71. Cf. LR p. 84.
[29] LC p. 111.
[30] LR p. 71.
[31] Ibid., p. 36.

pleasing to God is not what most pleases us, but what tends to the common welfare . . . of the Church."[32] Compare this with *Laws* 10:903—"The ruler of the universe has ordered all things with a view to the preservation . . . of the whole."

Communal Society Advocated by Colet

Colet's view of brotherhood leads him logically into an espousal of a communal society as the distinctively Christian way of life. Contrariwise, he regards capitalism or the system of private property as clearly grounded in man's graceless and fallen nature:

> This law of a corrupter nature is the same as that Law of Nations, resorted to by nations all over the world; a law which brought in ideas of *meum* and *tuum*—or property . . . ; ideas clean contrary to a good and unsophisticated nature; for all that would have a community in all things. . . . [It] may . . . be said with the greatest truth about money, possessions, tithes, oblations, and whatever else is of an earthly nature; . . . that they are *not* the kingdom of God. . . . Nothing that has befallen the Church [has] done more mischief than . . . titles of *meum* and *tuum,* and power of claiming property. Hence have sprung avarice and greed of money.[33]

These views are carried to a surprising yet logical extreme, namely, the assertion that in Christian communal fellowship there can be no recognition of families or mates, only of "brothers" in the Spirit:

> For the one who is born again in Christ recognizes Him alone as his true Father; and, if a son in Him, you have no brethren but those who along with you are born again the sons of God. There is now no other relationship than brotherhood in God.

---

[32] *Ibid.,* p. 107.

[33] ExR p. 134; LR p. 118. Cf. LR p. 72, where the ideal is "all things common, and nothing whatever private." Also LC p. 43, where Colet insists that Christians ought not to worry about laws of property.

... For there never lived the man, who loved even the most indulgent father or mother so exceedingly, and with such dutiful affection, as every true son of God loves one who is truly his brother in God.[34]

Pauline and Stoic Sources of Colet's Communal Fellowship

There can be no question that, in both language and concept, Colet's doctrine of communal fellowship owes much to St. Paul's simile of the body and its members in such passages as 1 Cor. 12:12-28 and Romans 12:4-5:

> Where one member suffers, all the members suffer with it; or one member be honored, all the members rejoice with it. ... As in one body we have many members and all the members have not the same function, so we, though many, are one body in Christ, and individually members one of another (cf. Eph. 4:25).

However, it is necessary to ask where St. Paul might himself have gotten this notion. Robinson lists Stoicism as the first of six frequently mentioned sources for Paul's body-analogy and its altruistic implications.[35] The Stoics did indeed teach that men's bodies are parts of World Body and men's souls parts of an immanent Reason, so that everyone is bound into a single brotherly Whole, and should regard the happi-

---

[34] LC pp. 82, 87.

[35] Robinson, *The Body: A Study in Pauline Theology,* p. 55. See *supra,* pp. 38-39, n. 28. There can be little doubt that, however unconsciously, Paul borrowed from Stoic philosophy. Tarsus itself was a prominent center of Stoic culture: five distinguished Stoic teachers who resided there are mentioned by name in Strabo. For a provocative discussion of Paul's Stoic sources, see James Stewart, *A Man in Christ: The Vital Elements of St. Paul's Religion,* pp. 27, 49, 54-59. Colet might have gotten his infrequent Stoic ideas independently of Paul. The Dean used a reference work, Nicolas Perotti's *Cornucopia* (1489), which contained a translation of Epictetus' *Enchiridion*. For this point and the erroneous tradition that Paul corresponded with Seneca, see Jayne, *Colet and Ficino,* pp. 78-80, and pp. 118-119, ns. 13, 16, 17, and 18.

ness or suffering of one's fellows as his own. Thus Marcus Aurelius observed that all men are "akin to me, not only of the same blood or seed, but [of] . . . the same intelligence and . . . divinity . . . We are made for cooperation, like feet, like hands . . . . To act against one another is contrary to nature."[36]

Communal Brotherhood and the Body-Figure in Plato

However, we know that the Stoics retained many features of Platonic philosophy.[37] Under these circumstances it is highly probable that they did not initiate the body-figure, but themselves borrowed it from its ultimate source in the *Dialogues*. At any rate, Scott's remark that "Paul was probably the first to use this metaphor"[38] surely needs revision not only in the light of the Stoic Aurelius but also in view of *Republic* 5:462-4, where "unity of feeling" among "guardians" is "admitted to be the greatest good, as was implied in our own comparison of a well-ordered State to the relation of the body and the members."

This passage features two points shared by Plato and Paul but lacking in the quotation from Aurelius. The first is the emphasis on the high merit of concord. Paul's call for "zeal" in preserving the "unity" of the Spirit (Eph. 4:3) and his denunciation of "strife" and "dissension" as vices (Gal. 5:19 ff.) is echoed by Plato's question in *Republic* 5:462—"Can there be any greater evil than discord . . . ? Or any greater good than the bond of unity?" The second common point is

---

36 Marcus Aurelius, *Meditations* (Harvard Classics), 2:200.

37 E.g., the doctrine of philosophical retreat, as suggested by *Republic* 6:496. Aurelius' *Meditations*, p. 251, cites Plato as an authority. See Burgess, *History of Philosophy*, p. 143 ff.

38 Anderson Scott, *St. Paul, Man and Teacher*, p. 118.

the restriction of brotherhood to select groups: guardians and Christians. Plato's brotherhood is of course a social rather than religious institution: it results from the guardians' community of property and their purpose as city administrators and protectors; whereas the Christian fellowship derives from the presence of the Holy Spirit and has as its purpose the furthering of the Kingdom of God on earth.

Colet's Communal Brotherhood Result of Joint Pauline-Platonic Influence

Against this background, it becomes apparent that Colet's doctrine of brotherhood reflects joint Pauline and Platonic influence. For one thing, Colet's communal views on marriage and family life are far more radical than Paul's and approximate the arrangement outlined by Plato in *Republic* 5:463, where each guardian thinks of the other "as a brother or sister" irrespective of conventional family ties. Moreover, Colet's language is at times almost identical with that of the *Dialogues*. For example, speaking of the usual squabbles over property, Plato writes that the guardians "will not tear the city in pieces by differing about 'mine' and 'not mine' " (*Republic* 5:464, cf. 462). Again, by way of stressing fellowship as an institution of mutual happiness or suffering, Plato notes that all the guardians

> will be affected as far as may be by the same pleasure and pains. . . . Then in our city the language of harmony and concord will be more heard than in any other. . . . When any one is more well or ill, the universal word will be "with me it is well" or "it is ill" (*Republic* 5:463).

Even more striking is Plato's elaboration of the body-figure, which is closer to Colet than the corresponding passage in St. Paul. Compare the *Mystical Body* treatise, pages 44-45, and the *Lectures on Romans*, page 71, with this section of *Republic* 5:462:

> Is not the best ordered State . . . that . . . which most nearly approaches to the condition of the individual?—as in the body, when but a finger of one of us is hurt, the whole frame, drawn towards the soul as a center and forming one kingdom under the ruling power therein, feels the hurt and sympathizes all together with the part affected, and we say that the man has a pain in his finger; and the same expression is used about any other part of the body, which has a sensation of pain at suffering or of pleasure at the alleviation of suffering.[39]

Summary

We have noted, then, that Colet's doctrine of a Church Soul represents an engrafting of the Platonic World-Soul on the Pauline Spirit. The popularization of the World-Soul by the Florentines no doubt prompted Colet to examine and utilize certain similarities between Soul and Spirit: for example, both are immanent, governing, and life-giving principles, though in different senses. Also prominent in Colet's Church Soul

---

[39] Such evidence would seem to belie Father Surtz's contention, in *The Praise of Pleasure*, pp. 160-165, that Colet's communal brotherhood derived more from the Bible than from Plato. Colet's brotherhood doctrine might also owe something to Ficino's discussions of friendship in the *Epistolae*. Among Colet's paraphrases of such passages are these: "So great is the power of friendship, that men who love each other mutually may somehow, even when they are apart, mutually see each other . . . ; for each holds the image of the other in his own mind." Again: "Joined together, Ficino and his friend are able to unite by virtue of their souls, which are loftier than the mountains separating them, and lovers are always joined because of the greatness and union of their souls." However, Colet transforms Ficino's secular doctrine into a religious one. Thus in an independent marginal comment the Dean insists that "From true piety comes friendship. From love of God comes love of man. Men who are joined by God are bound to each other by strong and holy bonds."—See Marginalia Nos. 23, 52, and 48 in Jayne, *Colet and Ficino*.

doctrine are many now-familiar notions drawn from Plotinian emanation, plus Plotinus's contention, here used in Colet for the first time, that withdrawal of the Divine Flow would bring utter disintegration of visible phenomena: thus by analogy, if the Spirit were to depart, the Church would fall to pieces. The fusion of Spirit-form and Church-matter is at one point described in terms of the Father-Mother symbolism in *Timaeus*. Moreover, Colet's contention that the existence of a human soul-body necessarily implies a larger Soul-Body was probably suggested by similar arguments in the *Timaeus, Philebus*, and *Republic*.

Colet's attitude toward Church Reformation is Neoplatonic: the moral corruption of the Church is conceived in terms of chaotic matter which has broken loose from its proper form—that is, from Spirit or the principle of "loving faith." (Combined here, among other things, are Aristotle's belief in the soul as the body's form, and Plotinus's position that form is the stabilizing agent of matter.) Hence Reformation means a return to the form of loving faith, which is Neoplatonically identified with beauty.

Colet advocates a communal brotherhood where each man realizes that he is a metaphorical ear or eye which can best seek strength by Platonically working for the Whole Body; and where all are so bound together by the common bond of Spirit-Soul that when anyone is hurt, all are hurt simultaneously. Accordingly, private property is denounced as sprung from avarice. Colet even goes so far as to denounce devotion to conventional family ties, arguing that Christians should recognize only their fellow "brothers in the Spirit." One obvious source of these views is the Pauline body-figure in 1 Corinthians 12 and elsewhere. However, Paul probably imbibed the doctrine from the Stoics, and the Stoics in turn from Plato's *Republic*, where altruistic guardians are compared to the cooperating members of a human body. In fact, Colet's extreme language is closer to Plato's than Paul's, and in some instances (e.g., their mutual reference to the capitalistic heresy of "mine" and "not mine") is virtually identical with Plato's. Thus we undoubtedly have here another example of joint Pauline-Platonic influence on Colet.

The Problem of Colet's Sources

Looking back over Chapters 2 to 6, we should now observe that Colet uses certain ideas which can be distinctly traced to specific Platonic dialogues—e.g., to *Theaetetus* (imitation of God) ; *Meno* (no man willingly seeks evil) ; *Phaedo* (chain and prison metaphors for body, separation of soul from body to approach truth) ; *Laws* (World-Soul, emphasis on prayer as way to holiness) ; and *Philebus* (analogy between human soul-body and World Soul-Body, Limited-Unlimited jargon). Even more prominent in Colet's thought are ideas found in the *Republic* (man as a little state, propriety of workers imitating guardians, wisdom as basis of right action), and especially in the *Timaeus* (World-Soul, God as good Architect creating after Ideas, God as father impregnating mother). Since we know from Erasmus that Colet carefully studied at least some of the *Dialogues* while at Oxford, and since indeed we have noted in Colet's works a number of obvious allusions to both the *Timaeus* and the *Republic,* there is no reason to suppose that Colet did not derive these ideas directly from Plato.

From the *Timaeus* also, reinforced by Neoplatonism, come certain heterodoxical notions in Colet: intractable matter not wholly controllable by God, matter and the body as evil, and eternity as timelessness. If to these we add Colet's other deviation from St. Paul, namely, the assigning of pagan ecstasy to mystical union, we can then say that (with the exception of the first-named) Augustine himself advanced all these views. Hence we should now more readily appreciate that, from the standpoint of Christian doctrine, Colet usually went wrong only when steered wrong by his otherwise infallible guide Augustine.

Indeed, Chapters 2 to 6 have demonstrated that the extent of Augustine's role (not to mention the probable role of the 14th century mystics) in Colet's thought has perhaps not previously been sufficiently appreciated. Not only is Augustine Colet's Clementine guide through the dangerous labyrinths of the Platonic Tradition, but in addition, Augustine supplies almost every major item in Colet's Creation scheme, as well as certain key items in his redemptive and mystical systems, particularly the privative theory of evil; the illumination doctrine of knowledge; and the mystical procedures of collection, introversion, and quietism.

Without question, however, Colet's greatest philosophical debt is to Plotinus. The key to Colet's entire body of thought —the key which deciphers it into some measure of coherence —is the fact that it is built around four parallel adaptations of Plotinian emanation. These adaptations are used to describe: (1) the emanation of natural life from the soul into the body; (2) the original creation as an instantaneous fusion of form and matter; (3) the redemptive "second creation" of man as a metaphorical infusion of form-grace into matter-soul; (4) the Reformation of the Church as a return to the proper form of loving faith. Since the first of these is relatively minor, we might say that the essence of Colet's thought is the shrewd employment of Neoplatonic emanation to explain God's relation to the universe, to man, and to the Church.

Past chapters have also indicated that Colet's obvious debt to the Pauline Epistles is characterized by: (1) an occasional violation of Paul as the result of Platonic pressure— e.g., Colet's intermittent assertion of the body's evil. (2) The superimposing of Platonic language on Pauline concepts— e.g., Colet's preference for the Platonic terms "soul" and "body" rather than Paul's "spirit" and "flesh"; likewise Colet's retention of Plato's soul faculties (reason, passion, appetite), but his reassignment of appetite to body in accordance with Paul. (3) The amalgamation of Pauline ideas with similar views in Plato—e.g., the civil war between soul and body, the advocacy of communal brotherhood, the association of time with sensibilia which are imitations of invisibilia, and the harmonized soul as automatic governor of the body.

We now have the evidence also to estimate the impact of Florentine Platonism on John Colet. Mirandola's chief contribution appears to have been the suggested analogy (in *Heptaplus*) between form-matter and grace-soul. Variously in his *Heptaplus* or *Discourse on Love,* Pico also impressed upon Colet the mystical importance of love, supplied the notion of man as a microcosm of the universal hierarchy, bolstered Colet's fondness for Origen's interpretation of Mosaic "waters," and showed the Dean how to combine the Dionysian angelic orders with Platonic cosmology.

Much more interesting, however, is the much vexed issue of Ficino's philosophical relation to Colet. First of all, we have noted how Colet's reading of Ficino's *Epistolae* and other works (1) persuaded him to study (or re-study) Dionysius—with results analyzed in previous chapters; (2) revealed to him the interconnections between the Pauline triad of hope-faith-love and the Dionysian triad of purification-illumination-perfection; and (3) suggested to him the possibility of exploiting other parallels between the Platonic Tradition and the Pauline Epistles.

Marsilio also seems responsible for other significant features of Colet's thought—e.g., the designation of sanctified men as "gods" rather than Pauline "saints"; the notion of "vital spirits" between body and soul; the interpretation of justification in terms of reciprocal love between God and man; the doctrine (from *Theologia Platonica*) that love has greater mystical power than faith; and the theory (from Marsilio's *Symposium* commentary) that love, whether romantic or divine, transforms the lover into the object loved.

Ficino also obviously reenforced ideas which Colet had borrowed initially or primarily from other writers, such as Plotinus's God-Sun analogy and identification of being-form-good-unity-beauty-rest; the Augustinian concept of Ideas in God's Mind; the Dionysian presentation of knowledge and love in terms of light and fire imagery; the Pauline conviction that the good man can suffer no misfortune; the Platonic doctrine of World-Soul; and the Pauline teaching that God is a fellow-agent in the Christian's performance of good works—a teaching for which the support of Ficino's *Theologia Platonica* is cited. None of this means that Colet accepted Ficino wholesale. On the contrary, as we have noted, the Dean rejected Ficino's Platonic concept of the soul as the "real man" and other heresies, including the Florentine's careless application of Plotinian emanation to the original creation. But the evidence unquestionably shows that the influence of Ficino on the bulk of Colet's writings was more extensive than recent commentators have been willing to concede.[40]

As the above paragraphs indicate, we have up until this point used Augustine (and to a lesser extent Aquinas) as a convenient measure of orthodoxy. When this measure has infrequently wavered, we have fallen back upon the ultimate

---

[40] E.g., Jayne in *Colet and Ficino*, p. 132 ff. and *passim*.

N

measure, St. Paul himself. Against these standards Colet's Clementine approach to pagan philosophy has been found largely successful in bolstering without distorting the Christian system. The time has now come, however, to consider Colet's thought from the more restricted perspective of 16th century Catholicism. In this consideration, two new measures of orthodoxy will be used: (a) the decrees of the Council of Trent (1545-63); and especially (b) the recorded statements of the recently canonized Sir Thomas More (1478-1535), officially appointed lay spokesman for the Catholic position. The final question which we will examine in Chapter 7, therefore, is whether Colet's Clementine approach to the Platonic Tradition was as successful in adhering to specifically Catholic dogma as it was in avoiding infringements on doctrine common to all wings of Christian thought.

CHAPTER 7 DEAN COLET AND
PROTESTANT HERESY

*Partisan Arguments on Colet's "Protestantism" or
"Catholicism"*

Unfortunately, the subject of Dean Colet's precise place
in the English Reformation has been marred by considerable
partisan spirit. Smith has called Colet a "Puritan," and Green,
Jourdan, and Seebohm have even more emphatically cham-
pioned the Dean's Protestantism.[1] The *Catholic Encyclopedia,*
on the other hand, holds that "there can be no doubt as to
his own orthodoxy"—a position with which Marriott agrees:
"On the ground of doctrinal heterodoxy no charge could
possibly have been sustained against him."[2]

---

[1] See Smith, *Pre-Reformation England,* p. 452; and W. E. Campbell,
"John Colet, Dean of St. Paul's," *Dublin Review,* 218 (Apr. 46), 97-98.

[2] Marriott, p. 165; *CE* 4:98.

Even more explicitly, Campbell argues that Colet "was a good Catholic man, and not, as some would have us believe, a forerunner of Protestantism." However, the evidence which Campbell offers to support this thesis is surprisingly vague and unsatisfactory, namely, that "Dean Colet had a real longing to end his days on earth in a monastery"; and that he translated Dionysius, "not at all the kind of spiritual literature to be translated by a man so often held . . . to be a herald of a new and Protestant dawn."[3] These arguments astonishingly neglect the fact that monastic life has always been compatible with Anglican and Lutheran belief, and that the heretic Eckhart was much addicted to Dionysian thought![4] Indeed, the only writer who has sought to approach the subject with any objectivity and documentative detail has been the British scholar Hunt, who concludes that with one exception (the exaltation of Scripture over Church) Colet belongs to the orthodox Catholic tradition.[5]

Difficulties in Determining Colet's Position: His Semantic Carelessness and Distaste for Publication

The difficulty in determining accurately Colet's true position in the English Reformation lies partly in the Dean's own inaccuracy and carelessness of diction.[6] Even more crucial, only one of his works, the *Convocation Sermon* (1512), was published in his own lifetime; and only one other, the *Right Fruitful Monition* pamphlet (1534), during the entire course

---

[3] Campbell, "John Colet," pp. 102, 106-7.

[4] See Clark, *Meister Eckhart*, pp. 101-103, 118-119.

[5] See Hunt, "Colet as Reformer," in *Dean Colet and His Theology*, p. 18 ff.

[6] On this point note Lupton, *Hier.*, p. xiii; and especially Jayne, *Colet and Ficino*, pp. 17-19, who excoriates Colet's Latin as "awkward, ungrammatical, and obscure," condemns the Dean as "a slovenly grammarian," and analyzes in detail Colet's various semantic and linguistic deficiencies.

of the Reformation.[7] It is therefore difficult to measure his thought in terms of the historical reaction to it.

Colet was not only cautious of publication, but even of oral expression. Erasmus tells us that "from numbers of the tenets most generally received" in the universities, Colet "widely dissented, and would at times discuss them among his private friends. When with others, he would keep his opinions to himself."[8] One wonders whether Colet finally regretted this policy and came ultimately to realize that his own era did not really know his beliefs. Writing to the Abbot of Winchcombe, at any rate, he wistfully remarks: "If there are any letters which contain matters of doctrine, I should not like them to be altogether lost. . . . If left behind they might help to keep alive some recollection of me."[9]

Pro-Catholic Evidence

With such difficulties in mind, let us first consider the evidence on the Catholic side of the argument. First of all, there can be no question that Colet's Neoplatonic notion of reform as an ordering of the Church's chaotic "matter" differed considerably from the revolutionary tendencies of Luther.[10] Second, Colet never questioned the authority of the Pope.[11] Third, his English translations of certain prayers and his denunciation of ecclesiastical corruption and abuses (as expressed most typically in the *Convocation Sermon*),

---

[7] Small wonder therefore that a generation after Colet's death Thomas Harding (1516-1572) should mistakenly assert: "As for John Colet, he hath never a word to shew, for he wrote no workes."—Quoted by John Jewell, Bishop of Salisbury (1522-1571). See *DNB* life of Colet.

[8] Lupton, *Life,* p. 264.

[9] *Ibid.,* p. 257.

[10] On this point consult Hunt, pp. 70-71.

[11] *Ibid.,* pp. 69-70.

fall wholly within the tradition of the Catholic or "internal" reformers.[12] Both More and Erasmus, themselves part of that tradition, went even further and advocated a translation of the entire Bible, More devoting a large portion of the *Dialogue on Tyndale* to this very subject. To the clerical objection that an English translation would result in misuse and "lewd disputing," More courageously replied: "If the abuse of a good thing should cause the taking away thereof from other that would use it well, Christ should himself never have been born. . . . The Bible should be in our English tongue."[13]

Colet More Severe than Sir Thomas in Condemning Corruption and Abuses

More also condemned clerical immorality, though never so violently as Colet. The fiery Dean's denunciations were wrathful and wholesale, while Sir Thomas's were, with few exceptions, mild and meant to apply only to the small evil segment of the "spirituality." Compare for example the daring remarks of Colet to his bishops with the more lenient attitude of More:

> *Colet:* The spouse of Christe, the churche, . . . is made foule and euyl fauored, as said Esaias: "The faithfull cite is made an harlotte" . . . [I] exhorte you reuerent fathers to the . . . reformation of the church's estate, bicause that nothynge hath so disfigured the face of the churche, as hath the facion of seculer and worldly lyuyinge in clerkes and prestes.[14]

> *More:* There be many [priests] very lewd and nought. [Yet] I

---

[12] See Colet's Catechism for St. Paul's School, Lupton, *Life,* Appendix B, p. 285 ff.

[13] More's *Dialogue on Tyndale* in W. E. Campbell (ed.), *The English Works of Sir Thomas More,* 2:243.

[14] CS pp. 293-4.

boldly say that the spirituality of ... the secular clergy, is in learning and honest living well able to match ... and far able to overmatch, number for number, the spirituality of any nation Christian.[15]

This distinction between severity and modified leniency is also observable in the area of church abuses. Colet bitterly attacked such malpractices. More admitted and deplored them, but noted by way of consolation that such evils were no greater than those found in other churches or countries.[16] Sometimes Colet saw an evil where More saw none. For example, both exalted canonical law, but More did not see the evils in its administration that prompted Colet to call ecclesiastical judges "atrocious race of men . . . deadliest plague . . . ; very devils transformed into angels of light."[17] This language is substantially repeated by More as a description, not of the judges, but of the "heretics" brought before them: to Sir Thomas, such heretics were "angels of Satan transfiguring themselves into the likeness of angels of light."

Counter-Evidence for Colet's Protestantism

On the Protestant side of the argument, there is first of all the historical fact that Colet was tried for heresy. Led by Bishop Fitz-James of London, Colet's enemies charged that certain extracts from his sermons revealed that he denounced the veneration of images and large episcopal revenues (two items which More staunchly supported).[18] Another charge

---

[15] *Dialogue on Tyndale,* pp. 215, 219.

[16] Compare More's attitude with Colet's bitter attack on the sale of bishoprics (EH pp. 123-4) and on the Probate Courts (LR p. 56).

[17] ExR p. 163.

[18] Defense of Church possessions is an important theme in More's *Supplication of Souls* and *Debellacion of Salem and Bizance.* It is debatable whether Colet ever openly condemned image-veneration. Erasmus distinctly states that

was that he had translated the Creed and certain prayers into English. Archbishop Warham dismissed the accusations as trivial and malicious.[19]

Nonetheless, these facts contrast with the position of More, who in 1527 was issued a license by Bishop Tunstall of London for the collection and refutation of heretical books. The toleration advocated in More's fictitious *Utopia* must be understood as the only means of introducing Catholicism into that pagan land. In Catholic England More advocated no such toleration. In 1515, for example, four years before Colet's death, he attended the trial of the already dead Richard Hunne, and approved Hunne's denunciation for heresy.[20] Moreover, it is a historical fact that as Lord Chancellor (1529-1532) he pressed the campaign against heretics with considerable vigor.[21]

---

the Dean never fought against ecclesiastical decrees on this point. But Erasmus adds that as the result of reading Dionysius and "other ancient theologians," Colet came "to look with less disfavor upon the views of those who did not approve of . . . adoring painted images."—See Hunt, pp. 58-60.

[19] The details of Colet's heresy "trial" may be found in Seebohm, pp. 249-255, and in Marriott, pp. 149-156, 161-5. See also P. S. Allen, "Dean Colet and Archbishop Warham," *EHR*, 17:303-6.

[20] See Campbell, *Dialogue on Tyndale*, pp. 6-7, 238 ff.

[21] More's role in the persecution of heretics is exhaustively analyzed in R. W. Chambers, *Thomas More*, "The Chancellor and the Heretics," p. 274 ff; and in E. M. G. Routh, *Sir Thomas More and His Friends*, pp. 193-7. Chambers effectively clears More of personally flogging heretics, and of personally ordering their burning. As Routh notes, pp. 193-4, both canon and common law specified that a person accused of heresy should be tried by the ecclesiastical courts, and if found guilty should be burned by the civil government. Thus More did not try or convict heretics. However, as chief officer of that government, he did see that the bishops' burning edicts were carried out. The result was four burnings during More's administration: Bilney, Bayfield, Tewkesbury, and Bainham— see Routh, p. 195, n. 3.

It is unfortunate that Catholic apologists have sought to exonerate More from these burnings, on the grounds that he was merely doing what he was

Protestant Flavor of Colet's Vocabulary

Further, Colet's vocabulary has far less Catholic flavor than More's. Such words as relics, images, pilgrimages, saints, pardons, and purgatory are almost never found in Colet's works. His distaste for relic-adoration as revealed by an infrequent visit to the Beckett shrine is vividly described by Erasmus's Colloquy "Peregrinatio Religionis Ergo."[22] With regard to purgatory, the only distinct reference is in the Corinthians commentary.[23] In discussing the afterlife, Colet almost wholly ignores the state of the soul between death and ultimate resurrection. This gains significance by the fact that in his Will he left no money for masses for the dead—a startling contrast to the common 16th century practice.[24]

---

required by law to do. Had More conscientiously opposed such burnings, he could have refused to carry out the bishops' sentences, and if necessary could have resigned his office. After all, this is precisely the much-praised action he took when he courageously refused to take Henry's Oath of Supremacy and thus brought about his own execution. Moreover, it is a historical fact that, though he did not flog heretics or cause them to be flogged, he nonetheless did cause them on occasion to endure indignities. When for example Tyndale's brother and an associate were brought before More in the Star Chamber, on a charge of selling copies of the forbidden New Testament, More sentenced them to be exhibited in Cheapside, seated on horses, their faces to the tails, and hung around with the prohibited volumes—Routh, p. 190.

Thus we must conclude that, in grave contrast to Colet, More persecuted heretics in the following ways: (1) he sometimes arrested them; (2) in a few cases he took them into personal custody, pending trial; (3) he sometimes assisted in their examination at ecclesiastical court; (4) he carried out the burning edicts of these courts; (5) in cases not involving heresy, over which he had jurisdiction, he sentenced and punished people aiding heretical causes.

[22] See Lupton, *Life,* pp. 206-213.

[23] LC p. 30. See Lupton, *Life,* p. 84.

[24] Lupton, *Life,* pp. 231-2. Cf. Seebohm, p. 222 ff.; and Lupton, EH p. 146, n.1.

This Will also made no reference to the Virgin Mary or saints. Indeed, as we have already noted, Colet avoided the term "saint" even in the Pauline sense of "Christian," and preferred the Ficinian term "god."

By contrast, two thirds of More's *Dialogue on Tyndale* is devoted to a condemnation of Luther for claiming that "no man should pray to saints, nor set by any holy relics or pilgrimages, nor do any reverence to any images."[25] Further, Sir Thomas vividly and frequently describes the "burning and broiling" of disembodied souls in the purgatorial state. Such souls describe their suffering as follows:

> "If ye pity any man in pain, never know ye pain comparable to ours: whose fire . . . far passeth in heat all the fires that ever burned upon the earth. . . . Our keepers are . . . cruel damned spirits, odious, envious, and hateful, [who] . . . from top to toe . . . cease not continually to tear us.[26]

Colet's and More's Contrasting Uses of "Charity" and "Heretic"

Two of the most striking examples of vocabulary contrast between Colet and More are the words "charity" and "heretic." Colet preferred the term "love," and identified it with the Christian virtue: "Charity and Love are one and the same: and . . . the love of God within us is kindled from God's love toward us."[27] This attitude very probably reflects the influence of Ficino, who in his later career identified "divine charity" with "divine love."[28] However, More at-

---

[25] See Duke microfilm of *Reply to Frith, Supplication of Souls;* and esp. *Dialogue on Tyndale,* p. 261.

[26] *Supplication of Souls* (Duke Microfilm XXI-cxxv-2670), pp. 42-b, 43. Microfilm spelling is modernized.

[27] LR p. 29.

[28] See Kristeller, *Ficino,* p. 277.

tacked Tyndale's New Testament on this very point, namely, the substitution of love for charity, arguing that Tyndale in so doing sought maliciously to disguise Catholic truth.[29]

As for the term "heretic," Colet uses it only twice in the Oxford lectures, chiefly to stress that heresy arises when men trust to their natural reason rather than to the illuminated knowledge of faith.[30] In the *Convocation Sermon*, delivered at a meeting to discuss ways of "extirpating the Lollard heresy," the term is used not doctrinally but rather to refer to the scandal of priests, which Colet avows is a far worse heresy than Lollardy![31] By contrast, the word "heretic" (in the doctrinal sense) occurs with almost obsessive repetition in the controversial works of St. Thomas More.[32]

There has been some speculation that Colet actually sympathized with the Wycliffe heretics. Such speculation is inspired in part by Erasmus's account of the famous trip to the Beckett shrine. In this account the character of Gratinus Pullus is "now quite conclusively identified with Colet."[33] When the third spokesman in the Colloquy says of Colet, "A Wycliffite, I fancy," Erasmus replies: "I do not think so,

---

[29] *Dialogue on Tyndale*, pp. 208-211.

[30] LC p. 114; LR p. 84.

[31] CS p. 298.

[32] E.g., More's *Apology* contains a defense of common law against "heretics," and argues that it is necessary to prohibit "the sowing of seditious heresies"—Chambers, *More*, p. 274. *Answer . . . to the Book named "The Supper of the Lord"* (Duke Microfilm xxi-cxxiv-2659) refers to "Luther's heresy." In *Debellacion of Salem and Bizance* (Duke Microfilm XXI-cxxv-2261), More argues: "I reckon it the part of every good man, that any zeal hath to the conservation of the Catholic faith, to . . . put . . . the scabbed heretics out of the clean flock."

[33] Marriott, p. 166. Cf. Lupton, Colet's *Treatise on Sacraments*, pp. 6-7, n. 1.

although he had read Wycliffe's works."[34] Ferguson's recently discovered letter from Colet to Christopher Urswick, dated at Rome on April 1, 1493, also indicates that the Dean was much interested in and had probably read Aeneus Sylvius's *Historia Bohemica,* an account of the Bohemian heretics during the Hussite Wars.[35] Colet's reading of Wycliffe and Sylvius does not in itself prove that he was sympathetic toward Lollard heresy. But at least this can be said: Colet never attacked the heretical works which he apparently read. This stands in considerable contrast to the campaign against heretical books conducted by More.

Lollard and Protestant Approval of Colet

That Colet was kindly disposed toward the Lollards might be debatable. But there can be no doubt that they were sympathetic toward him—in some cases, to the point of admiration. The word among Lollards during Colet's deanship was "Go and hear Dr. Colet."[36] After Colet's death a certain Thomas Geffrey was accused of heresy because he persuaded a friend on "divers Sundays to go to London to hear Dr. Colet." Another accused man, John Lambert, appreciatively alluded to Colet's courage in the 1512 Convocation address:

> Among a shrewd multitude of them gathered together did arise
> ... Gamaliel—a pitiful thing, verily, to see but one good man
> in such a convocation ... of priests, that should be the lights

---

[34] Marriott, p. 176. One of the crimes attributed to Wycliffe was his insistence on preaching in English—*Ibid.,* p. 140. Compare this with Colet's similar insistence as described in Hunt, "Colet the Preacher," p. 73 ff.

[35] See Ferguson, "An Unpublished Letter of John Colet," *AHR,* 39 (July 34), 696-7.

[36] Consult Seebohm, pp. 222, 249-255.

of virtue to all the people—...much like he was...to Dr. Colet.[87]

Even more significant, three Protestant leaders later referred to the Dean with marked affection. Latimer recalled the date of his attending a divinity lecture by its occurring "even at that time when Doctor Colet was in trouble, and should have been burnt, if God had not turned the King's heart to the contrary." John Bale testified that Colet "was not far from the same"—meaning punishment for heresy—"for reading Paul's epistles . . . had not there weighty matters been in the way."[88] And Tyndale noted that "Bishop Fitz-James would have made the old Dean Colet of St. Paul's a heretic, for translating the Paternoster into English, had not the Bishop of Canterbury helped the Dean."[39]

Colet's Protestant Attitude Toward Scripture versus Church

On the Protestant side also is Colet's doctrine that Scripture is the ultimate religious authority: "In the choice and well-stored table of Holy Scripture all things are contained that belong to truth."[40] This attitude, repeated almost verbatim in Anglican Article 6 ("Holy Scripture containeth all things necessary to salvation"), is reinforced by Colet's views as summarized by one Gaspar in Erasmus's colloquy, "The Child's Piety": "I believe firmly what I read in the Holy Scriptures, and the Creed, . . . and I don't trouble my head any farther."[41] Such a position underlies the Oxford lectures,

---

[87] Lupton, *Life*, p. 144.

[38] *Ibid.*, pp. 202-5.

[39] William Tyndale, *Answer to More* (Parker Society), p. 168.

[40] LC p. 110. Cf. EH p. 87—In the "canonical scriptures . . . is contained all wisdom . . . , all belief." See Hunt, pp. 62-63.

[41] Hunt, p. 62.

where Colet refused to quote the standard Church commentators (Augustine excepted), and relied largely on his own exploration of historical circumstances surrounding Scriptural texts. This spirit of free enquiry was inevitably encouraged by Plato, who constantly insisted on experimental thought and tentative conclusions.[42]

The Catholic More's position was at the opposite pole. Tyndale's *Obedience of the Christian Man* had exalted the power of personal revelation and demanded the abolition of the Church's authority in Scriptural interpretation. In reply, Sir Thomas sought to discourage independent investigation and to insist on adhering to Church commentators as the proper religious authority:

> My poor advice were in the study [of Scripture] to have a special regard to the writings and comments of the old holy fathers. . . . The reader shall be sure that no text is so to be understood as it standeth against any point of Catholic faith. . . . [If] any text yet seem unto him contrary . . . , make sure that there is some fault . . . in the translator. . . . So let him reverently [ac]knowledge his ignorance, . . . and cleave to the Church as the undoubted truth.[43]

Colet's Neoplatonic Method of Scriptural Exegesis

Plato seems to have influenced Colet not only in his free enquiry of Scripture, but also, indirectly, in the Dean's method of Scriptural exegesis. As we noted in Chapter 2, Neoplatonic thought conceives a direct relation between

---

[42] Note esp. *Euthyphro* and *Theaetetus* 210. See Kristeller, *The Classics and Renaissance Thought*, p. 49; and Shorey, *Plato Ancient and Modern*, p. 82.

[43] *Dia. on Tyndale*, p. 83. Cf. More's Preface to *Answer to Book on Lord's Supper:* "For my exposition [of John 6] ye shall not give me the thank. For I have but picked it out here and there out of the writings of divers old holy men."

unity and divine truth. The closer things approach to God, the more truth and unity they possess. Thus Aquinas had written: "Everything is stronger and more excellent the more thoroughly it is one; it follows that diversity and variety increase in things, the further they are removed from Him."[44] Accordingly, Colet's God is in the most ultimate sense "the One" and "Truth."[45] Hence Colet argued that Scriptural Truth, being the written revelation of God, cannot be other than one and undivided also.[46] The paradox is that Aquinas, accepting the same Neoplatonic belief that unity and truth are identical, came to the quite different conclusion that Scripture has many senses.

Colet versus Erasmus on the "Four Senses" Method

Colet's contention that "Scriptural Truth . . . cannot be other than one and undivided" lies at the heart of his argument with Erasmus over the medieval "Four Senses" method of exegesis, whereby any given Biblical text was said to have four levels of meaning: literal, allegorical, moral, and anagogical. In a letter to Colet, Erasmus had maintained that "nothing forbids our drawing various meanings out of the wonderful riches of the sacred text, so as to render the same passage in more than one way. . . . According to Job, 'the word of God is manifold.' "[47] Convinced that Erasmus's

---

[44] Underhill, *Mysticism,* p. 117.

[45] Note LC pp. 21, 32, 33, 57.

[46] Colet seems to have held a modified version of verbal inspiration, whereby the Holy Spirit inspired but was nonetheless moulded by the Scripture writers.—Seebohm, p. 125, and Hunt, p. 101.

[47] For an analysis of the scholastic "Four Senses" method codified by Aquinas, consult Seebohm, pp. 29-39; and *The Schaff-Herzog Encyclopedia of Religious Knowledge* (1914), 4:237 ff.

Thomistic method was "an erroneous one, . . . though you have many to keep you company in it," Colet retaliated:

> I cannot assent to your statement . . . that the Holy Scriptures, from their prolific nature, give birth to many senses. . . . I deem it to be of the essence of fertility, that it should bring forth, not a number of things, but some one thing that is perfectly genuine.

The Dean goes on to bolster this view, arguing in Neoplatonic language that the higher an animal is in the scale of creation, the less numerous are its offspring:

> But the Holy Spirit, whose offspring the Holy Scriptures are, and who is Fertility itself, bringing forth in Himself as He does by His own power the one and same simple truth, must needs produce for us, by His own truthful words, one only sense, and that the truest.[48]

On this Neoplatonic basis Colet approached Scripture from the standpoint of "accomodation," insisting on working out one strictly unified sense consistent with the "persons, places, circumstances, and times" surrounding the composition of the text in question.[49] It was for this reason that he insisted on a single allegorical interpretation of Genesis, arguing that Moses had had to function as a "popular poet" writing a "high and holy fiction" in order to accomodate the complexities of creation to the "uneducated multitudes" with which he had to deal.[50]

---

[48] See Seebohm, p. 121 ff., and Lupton, LC pp. xvi-xvii.

[49] ExR p. 60. See Cassirer, *Platonic Renaissance*, p. 13.

[50] MA pp. 8-10, 27-28. Elsewhere than his *Mosaic Account*, Colet often emphasizes the then much neglected literal meaning as the single true one. In one instance he concedes that sometimes the literal and allegorical meanings can exist together. For a detailed analysis of Colet's exegetic technique, and for a variation of certain traditional views thereon, consult Hunt, p. 88 ff. The relation of Colet's historical exegesis to Origen, Lorenzo Valla (1407-57), and Nicholas of Cusa's *De Concordantia Catholica* (1433) is

Catholic More Antagonistic to Colet's "Unity of Truth" Exegesis

Colet's Neoplatonic approach to Scripture differs considerably not only from that of Erasmus, but also from that of Thomas More, lay spokesman of the Church. Thus in one of his controversial treatises Sir Thomas argues:

> The holy scriptures of God is in such marvelous manner by the profound wisdom of his holy spirit . . . devised . . . that it hath not only that one sense true which we call the literal . . . , but also diverse other senses spiritual. And all those manifold senses may be . . . true, and all by one Spirit provided.[51]

It would seem that More, whose gradually waning hero-worship for Mirandola left him with little taste for Neoplatonism, excluded the Neoplatonic "unity of truth" concept from his exegetic technique. That such a concept was not compatible with Catholic orthodoxy is indicated by three significant facts. First, More reproved Origen for practicing a Scriptural approach similar to Colet's.[52] Second, Tyndale was himself contemptuous of the medieval Four Senses method.[53] Third and most important, More explicitly brands

---

analyzed in Albert Duhamel, "The Oxford Lectures of John Colet," *JHI*, 14 (Oct. 53), 493-510. A recent estimate of Colet's abilities in Biblical exegesis is D. J. Parsons, "John Colet's Stature as an Exegete," *Anglican Theological Review*, 40 (1958), 36-42.

[51] *Answer to Book on Lord's Supper*, pp. 4b-5. The same view is expressed in More's *History of the Passion*, ed. P. E. Hallett, pp. 7-8: "The words of holy scripture have not one sense alone, but are full of many mysteries."

[52] *Dialogue on Tyndale*, p. 90. Colet cites Origen as support for his interpretation of Genesis—MA p. 27. For a detailed treatment of Origen's exegetic technique, see Danielou, *Origen*, "Origen and the Bible," p. 133 ff.

[53] See "On the Four Senses of Scripture" in Tyndale's *Obedience of a Christian Man*, as analyzed by Seebohm, p. 31.

as heretical any Neoplatonic insistence on a single meaning
for Scriptural truth:

> Now will I not say any manner blame at all to any man that
> will expound all the whole process of Genesis by allegories and
> ... tell us that paradise is grace ..., and water the earth: or
> calling the earth mankind ... and so forth.... But mary, if he
> would teach us such a spiritual sense, to make us believe that
> those words were to be none otherwise understood beside, but
> that there were no such floods flowing forth of Paradise ... I
> would think verily he were a very heretic.[54]

This is an apparent repudiation of the kind of allegorical
interpretation of Genesis advanced by Colet. Such evidence
demonstrates that, in the area of Scriptural criticism at least,
Colet's affinity for the Platonic Tradition produced an in-
fringement on official Catholic dogma.

Colet on Calvinistic Predestination

It is however in three more crucial areas that we stand the
best chance of accurately determining Colet's position in the
Reformation: the areas of predestination, justification, and
sacraments. Let it be conceded at once that there are many
passages in Colet which are definitely expressive of Calvin-
istic predestination. For example:

> The Spirit ... does not dwell in and enlighten all, but only
> those who are predestined ... to be enlightened.... Nothing is
> of themselves, everything from God.... Man has in himself
> nothing whatever whereof to glory.... The gospel of Christ is
> received with different sensations, according as the hearer is
> elect or reprobate by the Divine will.... Those ... are the
> called, who were predestined to this grace before the foundation
> of the world.[55]

---

[54] *Answer on Lord's Supper*, p. 6.

[55] LR pp. 19-20, 80; LC p. 28; ExR p. 97; MB p. 39. Cf. LR pp. 33, 37,
56, 75; LC pp. 4-5; MB pp. 42-43; EH pp. 65, 122, 143; ExR pp. 97, 100,

Given such passages alone, it is difficult to refute Hyma's contention that Colet's pronouncements sound very similar to those of Luther in the latter's lectures on Paul's Epistle to the Romans.[56]

However, we must not overlook Lupton's observation that Colet conceived certain deterministic Pauline passages as Paul's attempt to deflate the egotism of the Jews.[57] Surely the preponderance of the Dean's remarks on the subject stress that Adam's fall corrupted but did not wholly obliterate man's free will: "Man had . . . no unclouded reason, no upright will." His "will is distorted, his understanding obscured, his fleshly appetites inflamed." God's foreknowledge does not imply determinism— man continues to sin by himself, because "his will [is] malicious, his acting an undoing."[58] Colet's basic advocacy of some degree of free will, despite certain explicit Pauline passages to the contrary, might very well have been influenced in some measure by Plato's own insistence that man is free to accept or reject the means of attaining "justice" and salvation.[59]

105; *Sac.*, pp. 30, 35. Sometimes (e.g., LR p. 37) Colet labels the problem "so great and so unsearchable."

[56] Hyma, "Erasmus and the Oxford Group," *Nederlandsch Archief voor Kerkgeschiendenis*, 25 (1932), 101-102.

[57] Lupton, LR p. xxxviii f.

[58] ExR p. 133, 130; LR pp. 5-6; LC p. 121. Jayne, *Colet and Ficino*, p. 154, takes the position that the *Epistolae* marginalia alone contradict Rice's contention that Colet denied free will altogether.

[59] Although Plato's Demiurge is described as man's "ally," this is so only in the sense that God gives man a good start by giving him the gift of reason. From this point on, man is free to accept or reject those methods which will achieve harmony—i.e., supremacy of reason over passion and appetite. These methods are prayer (*Laws* 3:687-8, *Eryxias* 398); belief in good Gods (*Laws* 10:885); imitation of God or World-Soul (*Theaetetus* 176, *Laws* 4:717); the soul's watchfulness, or influence of noble friends (*Laws* 10:903-6); and education or philosophy (*Timaeus* 44). In man's

Colet's Recognition of Limited Free Will

If there is limited free will, it follows that man can participate in the redemptive process. Thus Colet proclaims that "all who will" may be saved.[60] Salvation is offered to "all alike."[61] God "waits long for men to repent. He would not that any should be condemned."[62] "An even ray of grace is shed abroad over all, but . . . men are not evenly disposed toward it. . . . Some men are rejectors of God. . . . God rejects no one."[63] God "gently chastizes" men in the hope "they may amend."[64] He "stands at the doors of the soul, knocking that he might be admitted." But "some men refuse the light."[65] There is one type of human heart which "neither softens or melts" in the face of God's prevenient grace.[66] Some men are therefore "condemned by their own wicked will, that refuses grace."[67]

For Colet, then, man is free to respond to the light, but even in his "turn" or response he needs God's cooperating

---

choosing or rejecting of these methods, God plays no active part.

Another factor in Colet's insistence on some degree of free will might well have been Ficino, who in his complex psychological scheme insisted that the soul's "middle force" of reason is entirely free to move up to intellect or down to idolum, with consequent noble or wicked results in external behavior. See Kristeller, *Ficino,* pp. 374-5. For a historical treatment of this problem, consult Charles Trinkaus, "The Problem of Free Will in the Renaissance and Reformation," *JHI,* 10:51.

60 ExR p. 160.

61 LR p. 50.

62 ExR pp. 71, 74. Cf. *Sac.,* p. 8.

63 CH p. 30; ExR p. 75.

64 ExR p. 74.

65 EH p. 70.

66 ExR p. 74.

67 LC p. 151, cf. EH p. 88.

grace.[68] In this "submission" to God's call, the human will is "secretly accompanied" by God's will, not in any way forcibly coerced by it."[69] "When grace so draws any one, it does not hurry him violently along, but leads him naturally and gently."[70]

Platonic Prayer as Way to Holiness and Wisdom

As Colet sees it, the Christian turn to God consists of fasting, repentance, acts of contrition, and especially prayer: "Voluntary confession, grief, and compensation are necessary" to be justified.[71] If man would receive the infused light of faith, he must be "sighing for God, he must acknowledge first and foremost his own folly and worthlessness; he must own his errors, lament his sins, implore for [sanctifying] grace."[72] He that prays dutifully and constantly, the Dean assures us, "will assuredly feel that he has not pleaded with God in vain, nor sought ineffectually for the light of knowledge."[73] "The truth . . . is understood by [infused] grace: grace is procured by our prayers being heard; our prayers are heard when whetted by devotion and strengthened by fasting."[74]

In his marginalia in Ficino's *Epistolae* Colet wrote further that Christ "listens to all prayers, whether or not he is addressed in due ceremonial form. He listens to anyone who asks him for the aid we need. . . . Let us pray to him . . .

---

68 CH p. 29, ExR p. 162.

69 LR p. 38.

70 LC p. 89.

71 *Sac.*, p. 43.

72 LR p. 45.

73 LR p. 44.

74 LC pp. 110-111. Cf. CH p. 47; EH pp. 146, 151; ExR p. 85.

wisely. . . . He prays wisely who wisely . . . seeks wisdom from Wisdom itself."[75] This emphasis on prayer as the chief means to justification and illuminated knowledge recalls Plato's frequent statements in *Laws* on the same subject. For example: "Justice and temperance and wisdom are the salvation of us. . . . I pray [God] to give me knowledge, which of all medicines is the most perfect. . . . Every . . . individual ought to pray and strive for wisdom."[76]

Colet's Ambiguous Pronouncements on Pauline Justification

As in Plato, Colet conceives this prayer as bringing "justice" or justification—the ordering or harmonizing of the soul, with reason supreme.[77] But in Colet justice is of course God's infusion of supernatural goodness or beauty into man. "When sanctified" men are "beautiful in Christ Jesus, their beautifier."[78]

It is true that there are some passages in Colet which, on the surface at least, give a decidedly Protestant version of justification as a mere imputation of righteousness achieved by preparatory faith alone. Particularly in the *Exposition of Romans*, for example, we are told that Abraham was "accounted righteous" and "acceptable" to God.[79] Moreover, Colet argues that "God graciously justifies the believer. . . . If men believe the gospel, they are saved. . . . There is no

---

[75] Jayne, *Colet and Ficino*, p. 349.

[76] *Laws* 10:906, *Critias* 106, *Laws* 3:687-8.

[77] For Plato's definition of "justice" see *Republic* 4:444, 432; also *Protagoras* 333.

[78] ExR p. 54.

[79] ExR p. 147, cf. pp. 148 ("approved"), 152 ("held righteous"), 117 ff. ("counting righteous"), 124 ("esteemed righteous").

other hope of salvation, excepting the faith of Jesus Christ."[80]
By "simple faith . . . believers are to be justified."[81] One is
tempted here to argue that Colet is following the Platonic
view advocated by Ficino in *De Christiana Religione* 37, that
"by faith alone, as the Platonists show, we come to God."[82]
This notion sprang from *Laws* 10:885, where belief in good
Gods is suggested as one means of attaining "justice"—
"When we hear that [Gods are evil] . . . , the thoughts of
most of us are not set upon abstaining from unrighteous acts,
but upon doing them." Certainly it must be conceded that
the passages from Colet, taken in isolation, sound not only
Platonic but Lutheran.[83]

Surely too there can be little question that Colet recognized a juridical aspect to justification. However, it would
be well to remember that this aspect is neither ignored
nor denied by Catholic dogma. Moreover, the Dean's most
characteristic statements on justification present it primarily
as the infusion of sanctifying grace—a fact documented
exhaustively in Chapter 4. Indeed, against the background
of that documentation, many of Colet's remarks in the *Exposition of Romans* can be interpreted from a more Catholic
perspective. For example: "It is the faithful who are righteous. The faith of Christ is righteousness, and hence Christians are called a church of the faithful—of those, namely,

---

[80] ExR pp. 61-62.

[81] *Ibid.*, p. 53, cf. pp. 61, 64.

[82] See Roy Battenhouse, "The Doctrine of Man in Calvin and in Renaissance Platonism," *JHI*, 9 (1948), 467.

[83] See Hunt, pp. 64-68; and Rice, pp. 148-151. For a detailed discussion of
Protestant and Catholic views on justification, consult the *Catholic Encyclopedia*, 6:701 ff.

who are justified . . . , their past sins being freely blotted out by grace."[84] Thus when God "justifies" he "makes righteous."[85]

As this implies, faith for Colet is obviously not the means to righteousness—that is, to justification or sanctifying grace. Rather, faith *is* righteousness or grace—the terms are equivalent.[86] Thus Colet speaks of "faithful righteousness" and "righteous faith." Much of the perplexity of commentators who have sought to unravel Colet's justification views might be eliminated, therefore, if we would realize that in the Dean's system faith is *not* preparatory to justification, but is itself (along with hope and love) an ingredient of justification. Hence Colet's expression "justified by faith" is not intended in the Lutheran sense. Rather is it the equivalent of "justified by sanctifying grace"—that is to say, justified by infused faith, together with infused hope and love.

This notion—that justification is the infusion of sanctifying grace—is also prominent in the *Mystical Body* treatise, where it is laid down that justification of men involves "reforming them to an inward righteousness." Righteousness is defined as being "formed again to what is better." "By means of a life-giving principle . . . men are justified. . . . We are thus righteous when justified by grace; being made righteous by God, to the end that we should live righteously."[87]

---

[84] ExR p. 92.

[85] *Ibid.*, p. 108.

[86] *Ibid.*, pp. 94, 98. Thus when Colet says that "faith without works is . . . an absolute non-entity" (*supra.*, p. 111), he is not referring, as some commentators have thought, to pre-justification faith or works, but to infused grace, and to the works which follow justification and are involved in "increased grace."

[87] MB pp. 44, 41, 32-33.

Augustine's Influence on Colet's Justification Interpretation

There can be no question of the influence of Augustine on Colet's justification system. Colet even cites Augustine's definition of faith as "the virtue whereby we believe the things that are not seen."[88] In his early thought Augustine had conceived of faith as preparatory to justification, but later withdrew the idea, noting in his *Retractions* that he had not realized earlier that faith is really one of the infused gifts of Christians. In Augustine's final system, therefore, prayer, sorrow for sin, acts of contrition, all done with the aid of God's cooperating grace, are preparatory to infused grace, which is accompanied by the theological virtues of faith and charity. In answer to the question, "Who is just?" Augustine therefore answered that the just man is the "faithful" one. Christians are therefore a Church of the faithful.[89] In both language and concept these views are almost identical with those of Colet.[90]

In Colet, then, the four traditional divisions of grace figure in the redemptive scheme: prevenient, cooperating, sanctifying, and actual.[91] The last of these (actual grace) is the aid which the sanctified man needs to perform good works as God's "fellow-worker."[92] Man "along with" the Spirit "is the parent of good works."[93] Men are God's "assistants when quickened and perfected by charity; and serve and obey him as organic and instrumental causes," as distinguished from

---

[88] ExR pp. 92-93.

[89] Stanislaus Grabowski, *The Church: An Introduction to the Theology of St. Augustine*, pp. 324-7.

[90] On Colet's debt to Augustine's justification doctrine, see also Hunt, p. 64 ff.

[91] See Oscar Hardman, *The Christian Doctrine of Grace*, p. 67 ff.

[92] LC p. 123, cf. pp. 138, 140, 142, 144.

[93] LC p. 143.

"inanimate implements" like "a knife, or a broom."[94] As we have already noted, these good works constitute increased grace or perfection, by which man undergoes an ascending Platonic imitation of Christ.

Colet's Relation to Trent's Justification Decrees

At many points Colet's redemptive process coincides with the Decrees on Justification issued by the Council of Trent (1545-1563). Especially is there agreement on the corruption (but not obliteration) of man's will, the necessity of preparatory works or "predispositions" in advance of justification, the stress on justification as God's sanctifying or making righteous (rather than merely accounting righteous), and the importance of good works as a means of maintaining and strengthening initial sanctification.[95]

On the other hand, there are points at which Colet and Trent diverge. Among these are the Dean's intermittent and apparently unconscious identification of sanctifying grace with the Holy Spirit; his concept of infused grace as the supernatural "gifts" of hope, faith, and charity; and his occasional tendency to restrict sanctification to the third of these virtues.[96] By contrast, Trent distinguished between "grace and gifts," and between these and the Holy Spirit which bestows them.[97] However, these deviations are no doubt relatively

---

[94] *Ibid.*, pp. 141, 143.

[95] See John F. Clarkson, "Decree on Justification," in *The Church Teaches: Documents of the Church*, p. 230 ff.

[96] See for example LR pp. 10-12, 63, 68; LC p. 56; CH p. 60; and this book, Chapter 4, pp. 92, 95 and ns. 14, 31. Note also Cassirer, *Platonic Renaissance*, pp. 15-16. Jayne, *Colet and Ficino*, pp. 109-110, notes that Colet's placing of "hope" before "faith" is also contrary to Catholic dogma.

[97] Clarkson, "Decree on Justification," pp. 233-4. Consult also *CE* 6:707; Hardman, pp. 31-36; Attwater, *A Catholic Dictionary*, "Habitual Grace," p. 216; and D'Arcy, *Mind and Heart of Love*, p. 79.

minor. In any event, it is doubtful whether we should judge Colet *ex post facto* on the basis of doctrines which were in a constant state of flux until codified by Trent a generation after his death.

We can conclude, then, that Colet's views on justification made use of certain Platonic elements and yet were largely orthodox from the perspective of early 16th century Catholic thought. The relation of Colet to the justification-teachings of Plato and Trent is diagrammed below.

PLATO   prayer
         imitation   } brings
         belief in good gods

         "justice" (holiness) which brings noble deeds

COLET   prayer
         fasting   } brings
         acts of contrition

         justification
         (being declared and
           made righteous)
         sanctifying grace (identical } which brings
         with infused hope—
         faith—love)
         initial imitation

         good works
         ascending imitation

TRENT   preparatory faith,
         charity, works   } brings
         (prayer, contrition, etc.) [98]

---

[98] See More, *Answer on Lord's Supper*, p. 33b, for an excellent statement of this phase of the Catholic justification process.

justification (being
declared and made righteous)
sanctifying grace plus the   } which brings
infused gifts of faith,
hope, charity

good works
(increased
justification)

Colet's Catholic Position on Sacraments in Dionysian Treatises

Within the context of his three Dionysian treatises, Colet's position on sacraments is also quite within the Catholic tradition. The starting point for this position was the Dionysian doctrine that sacraments, like all other things in the Ecclesiastical Hierarchy, are imitative "symbols" of their counterparts in the Celestial Hierarchy. Dionysius had held that

> the mind can by no means be directed to the contemplation of the Celestial Hierarchies unless it use the material guidance suited to it, accounting those beauties which are seen to be images of the hidden beauty, the sweet incense a symbol of spiritual dispensations, and the earthly lights [i.e., candles] a figure of the immaterial enlightenments. Similarly, . . . the ranks of order on earth reflect the . . . disposition of the Heavenly Orders. . . . Everything else delivered in a supermundane manner to Celestial Natures is given to us in symbols.[99]

Following this notion, Colet observes that "sensible and carnal things are among men tokens of intelligible and spiritual things."[100] According to Colet, sensory things are not only symbolic of the Celestial Hierarchy, but also of man's spiritual condition. Thus the visible Eucharist not only symbolizes the

---

99 Shrine of Wisdom, Dionysius's *Celestial Hierarchy*, pp. 30-31 ff.
100 *Sac.* p. 22; cf. EH p. 124.

cleaving of the Seraphim to God; it also represents the Christian's similar mystical union with Christ.[101]

In his Dionysian works, Colet insists that this symbol is always accompanied by the inner condition: "As invisible things are the archtypes of sensible things, so are sensible sacraments the tokens of things invisible; and they are joined to spiritual sacraments, *as body to soul*."[102] This is quite consistent with the traditional Catholic view that sacraments are the instrumental causes of sanctifying grace.[103] Accordingly, the *Sacraments* treatise informs us that through sacraments, "as by visible cords," God strives to draw men into union with him. "All the sacraments, as Dionysius the Areopagite teaches, work our assimilation to God." "God is in Christ, Christ in the sacraments, the sacraments in men."[104] Christians are those who are "living in Christ, purified by his sacraments . . . ,illuminated by the priests with the sacraments."[105] Without sacramental signs earthbound men cannot be "imbued with the reality of the sacred rites."[106]

Is Colet's Eucharistic View Anglican?

In the Dionysian treatises, the Eucharist is presented as the consummation of all sacraments. They all purify, illuminate, and perfect, but perfection and mystical union are the special

---

[101] EH p. 77.

[102] *Ibid.*, p. 70. Italics added.

[103] See *Catholic Dictionary*, pp. 45, 216: "Baptism infuses grace. . . . Baptism produces sanctifying grace for the first time. . . . Every sacrament gives a sacramental grace, which is not distinct from sanctifying grace."

[104] EH pp. 100-101.

[105] *Ibid.*, pp. 101, 132.

[106] CH p. 6, cf. EH p. 114. Also Chapter 4 of this book, and Hunt, p. 106 ff.

attributes of the Eucharist.[107] Colet's reference elsewhere to the Lord's Supper as a "commemoration . . . and representation of the death of Christ" must not be taken out of context.[108] The evidence is clear that he rejected the Protestant view of Communion as a mere memorial service. His references to the real presence of Christ, "under the forms of bread and wine," are numerous.[109]

But a question remains as to whether Colet might have advanced the Anglican view of a spiritual real presence, as distinguished from the Catholic doctrine that Christ is present physically. In his *Treatise on the Eucharist,* More stressed this latter position, contending that through the supreme sacrament God "enter[s] with his blessed flesh and blood bodily into our bodies, [and] also with His Holy Spirit . . . into our souls." Thus are Christians "spiritually and bodily joined aknit into his here in earth."[110] There would seem to be some distinction between this position and that of Point V in Colet's Table of Sacraments: "By gracyous Eucharistye, where is the very presence of the persone of Christ vnder forme of breed, we be nourysshed *spirytually* in god."[111] Compare this with the Anglican *Book of Common Prayer:*

> What is the outward part or sign of the Lord's Supper? The outward part or sign . . . is Bread and Wine. . . . What is the

---

107 EH pp. 77-78.

108 See LC p. 116. Cf. EH p. 85.

109 Hunt, pp. 67-68.

110 Phillip Hallett (ed.), More's *English Prayers and Treatise on the Holy Eucharist,* pp. 31-35; and *Letter Impugning the Erroneous Writing of John Frith against the Blessed Sacrament*—i.e. the *Reply to Frith* (Duke Microfilm XXI-cxxv-2668), p. 82. In *Answer on the Lord's Supper,* pp. 119b-120 (cf. 84b, 93), More pictures Christ's soul as animating His body, so that Christians eat His body "animated with [Christ's] soul . . . , by which [human] flesh is itself made . . . lively."

111 Lupton, *Life,* Appendix B, p. 287. Italics added.

inward part, or thing signified? The inward part . . . is the Body and Blood of Christ, which are *spiritually* taken and received by the faithful.[112]

Colet's Protestant Position on Sacraments in the Pauline Commentaries

At any rate, no one who thoroughly studies Colet's works can fail to be struck by the sharp decrease in references to priests and sacraments as one moves from the Dionysian trilogy to the Pauline commentaries. In the former, it is sacraments which are the "visible cords" drawing men to God. But elsewhere this metaphor is reassigned to sanctifying grace itself. Speaking in the Corinthians commentary of hope, faith, and love, Colet notes that "By these three, as by a three fold cord, we are drawn out of this evil, darksome, deadly region; and are caught up by the grace of God."[113]

Similarly, the metaphor of "shadows" is reapplied. In Plato this term involved the utmost of contempt, referring to that which wholly lacks reality. It is in this sense that the word plays such a prominent role in the famous Allegory of the Cave (*Republic* 7:514-516). Combining the Platonic notion with Hebrews 10:1, which pictures Mosaic Law as foreshadowing the Christian Church, Colet had urged in the Dionysian abstracts that this Law was a mere "shadow" of the Celestial Hierarchy, while Christian sacraments were an "image" of reality.[114] By "image" Colet intended to convey the Neoplatonic view of earthly things as containing some

---

[112] "Offices of Instruction," *Common Prayer*, p. 293. Italics added.

[113] LC p. 66.

[114] CH p. 5. Cf. Hebrews 10:1—"For the law [is] a shadow of good things to come, and not the very image of the things." The distinction between "image" and "shadow" is also found in Colet's marginalia to Ficino's *Epistolae.* See Jayne, *Colet and Ficino,* pp. 335, 372.

degree of light or reality; he therefore frequently referred to sacraments as "colors" or "hues" in contrast to the absolute darkness of Mosaic Law.[115] In other works, however, it is sacraments themselves which become "but the emptiest shadows, if the reality be not existing in the soul."[116]

This is a considerable shift from the Dionysian position that the visible sacraments are "colors" containing some measure of light and reality, or the corollary assertion that "sensible sacraments . . . are joined to spiritual sacraments, as body to soul." The shift is especially marked in Colet's discussion of Abraham's circumcision, which, according to the Dean, is merely "a sign of a previous faith."[117] "First he believed; then he received the sacrament of faith, even fleshly circumcision."[118] From this Colet moves on to the logical conclusion, namely, that a man can be "circumcised in body" and yet "uncircumcised in spirit"—that is to say, holiness does not necessarily accompany its symbol. Only the person who is internally circumcised is "a Jew in reality."[119] It follows that

> True Judaism and true circumcision are reckoned not by the body but by the spirit. . . . He is a Jew . . . which is one inwardly—that is, who keeps the law in the inner depths of his mind. . . . It is the Apostle's aim . . . to convince his readers that it is not the body which is to be regarded, but the mind; not the corporeal sign, but the mental reality.[120]

---

[115] E.g., EH p. 97, which itself recalls Plato's cave-allegory where the escaped prisoner is dazzled by the sun: "They that cannot look on the sun itself, the radiance of whose powerful light blinds the vision . . . yet can endure tempered hues."

[116] ExR p. 80.

[117] *Ibid.,* p. 128, cf. 79 ff.

[118] *Ibid.,* p. 118, cf. 122.

[119] *Ibid.,* p. 80.

[120] *Ibid.,* p. 82.

In a further startling passage from the same *Exposition of Romans*, this attitude is then applied to Christian baptism:

> Baptism and the other sacraments, verily profit, if thou keep the gospel: but if thou be a breaker of the gospel, thy baptism is heathenism. Therefore if the heathen keep the righteousness of the gospel, shall not this heathenism be counted for baptism? And shall not he who is a heathen by nature, if he fulfill the gospel, judge thee, a Christian, who by the flesh and by baptism dost transgress the gospel? For he is not a Christian, which is one outwardly; neither is that baptism, which is outward in the flesh: but he is a Christian which is one inwardly; who is baptized in the heart and in the spirit, not in the flesh.[121]

The Dichotomy in Colet's Sacraments Thinking

We might be making an erroneous assumption if we called this view Colet's "mature" Protestant position, as distinguished from his "early" Catholic stand on sacraments. Such a conclusion would assume that the Dionysian treatises were written first, and the Pauline commentaries afterwards. Yet Professor Jayne has speculated that the *Exposition of Romans* 1-5, the Genesis commentary, and the *Lectures on Romans* 6-11 probably preceded Colet's Hierarchies abstracts, with the Corinthians commentary and the final portion of the *Lectures on Romans* being composed thereafter. [122] Moreover, Lupton offers reasonable evidence that Colet's *Treatise on Sacraments* (inspired by Dionysius's *Ecclesiastical Hierarchy*) was composed "not long after 1498."[123]

---

121 *Ibid.*, pp. 87-88.

122 See *supra.*, p. 21, and Table II, "Tentative Chronology of the Problem Period" in Jayne, *Colet and Ficino*, p. 50.

123 Lupton (ed.), *A Treatise on the Sacraments of the Church by John Colet*, Introduction, pp. 4-5. Documentation for Colet's own statements in the *Sacraments* treatise is from the Rowe translation, as previously indicated. Since Lupton dates the *Mystical Body* treatise at 1498, this leaves only two

P

Such chronology would invalidate any theory that Colet eventually "rejected" an earlier Catholic stand on sacraments for a more Protestant position. As already noted, the Protestant position is advanced extensively in the *Exposition of Romans,* which was probably the earliest work of the "problem period" (1496-1499) ; while the Catholic view is expressed in the *Sacraments* treatise, which was apparently composed at the very end of that period, probably in 1499. Even if the order of composition were quite different, it would seem specious to argue for "early" and "later" sacramental attitudes in works which were so obviously bunched together within a very narrow time-span. We therefore have no choice but to conclude that here as so frequently elsewhere, Colet seems to have been led by the thinker on whom he was commenting. When tied to the Dionysian text, he was compelled to stress the sacraments and priests which are so prominent as intermediaries between God and man in Dionysius's Ecclesiastical Hierarchy. When tied to the Pauline text, on the other hand, he was influenced by the deemphasis on sacraments which is frequently conceded to exist in the Pauline Epistles.[124]

---

major works—the *Right Fruitful Monition* (c. 1505-10) and the *Convocation Sermon* (1512) for Colet's later period (1500-1519). The remaining eight works were apparently composed in the early or "problem period"—i.e., 1496-99.

[124] The Pauline rite of baptism appears to be merely a visible sign of the new Christian's already achieved sanctification. Paul mentions but five of the early Church sacraments (or as he called them, "mysteries"): Baptism, the Eucharist, Confirmation, Holy Orders, and Marriage. Of these, only the first two are given substantial discussion—See Anderson Scott, *St. Paul, Man and Teacher,* pp. 123-7. For a view contrary to Scott's, however, see Ernest Colewell and Eric Titus, *The Gospel of the Spirit,* pp. 50-52, who insist that Paul was a "sacramentalist" who said that "new creation" comes only with baptism.

Quite apart from Paul's own views, the generalization that Colet hewed to the Catholic line in the Dionysian trilogy, and to the Protestant line in the

Fictitious Counterpart of Colet's "Spiritual Religion"
Condemned by Catholic More

At any rate, Colet's general position on sacraments in the
Pauline commentaries is undeniably clear: sanctification can
be had outside sacramental channels. Conversely, baptism
does not infuse grace; it is at best a token of grace already
achieved. Hence visible sacraments are invalidated: they do
not bring holiness, nor does holiness depend on them. God is
not interested in outer symbols, which might differ much
from inner condition.[125] "The good life of man, proceeding
from a holy mind, is alone pleasing to God."[126] Again:

> True righteousness in the sight of God is that which is inward,
> in the spirit. . . . God looks not at the flesh, or the body, or
> visible tokens; but at the very depths of man's inward spirit.

Pauline commentaries, is—like all generalizations—subject to some exceptions.
In the Pauline commentaries we do find infrequently the Catholic position
on sacraments as instrumental causes of grace, e.g.: Man is "born again
by grace and baptism. . . . Baptism is the divine means of expiation, whereby
God . . . cleanses and thoroughly purifies . . . souls."—ExR pp. 98, 114. Cf.
p. 116, and LC pp. 25, 38. On the other hand, there is at least one point
in the Dionysian trilogy where, in an approach to the Protestant view, the
non-necessity of sacraments for sanctification is boldly advanced: "If you
be in truth itself, you need not sensible sacraments. So did the monks in
Egypt once possess it, not having in use all the sacraments we have . . . ;
because that, being drawn to God, they needed them not."—EH p. 86. Colet's
handling of specific sacraments in the Dionysian-inspired *Treatise on Sacraments* also seems to involve an approach to Protestant heresy. In Peter Lom-
bard's *Distinctions,* the sacraments are treated in this order: Baptism, Confirmation, Eucharist, Penitence, Extreme Unction, Holy Orders, and Matrimony. This arrangement was confirmed by the Council of Trent. But Colet
places Orders and Matrimony first, and gives only cursory attention to the
others—this, according to Lupton, "under the influence of the spiritualizing
mysticism of Dionysius"—See Lupton, Intro. to Colet's *Treatise on Sacraments,* pp. 15-16.

[125] ExR p. 122.

[126] LR p. 4, cf. p. 5.

... It is true spiritual goodness that is praised by God: the law written in men's hearts. A Gentile, if a Jew in spirit, is counted for circumcised; and the circumcised, if otherwise in spirit, is counted for uncircumcised. Whatever is truly spiritually, is Christian.[127]

Such "spiritual religion" is scarcely compatible with Catholic dogma. This fact is underscored by a remarkable passage in More's *Dialogue on Tyndale,* where a fictitious "Messenger" quotes views he thinks commendable from a book called *The Image of Love*:

That book said ... all those things that were used in the old law were gross and carnal, and were as a shadow of the law of Christ; and therefore the worshiping of God with gold and silver and such other corporal things ought not to be used among Christian people; but leaving all that shadow, we should draw us to the spiritual things, and serve our Lord only in spirit. . . . For so he saith himself that God, as himself is spiritual, so seeketh he such worshippers as shall worship him in spirit and in truth, that is, in faith, hope, and charity of heart, not in the hypocrisy and ostentation of outward observance, bodily service, gay and costly ornament, fair images, goodly song, fleshly fastings, and all the rabble of such unsavoury ceremonies, all which are now gone as a shadow. And our Saviour calleth upon our soul and our good faithful mind and setteth all those carnal things at nought.[128]

This passage, both in concept and language, is virtually identical with certain statements by Colet, to wit:

The religion of the Jews was wholly carnal and corporeal; they practiced a righteousness of the body, a law of deeds done in

---

[127] ExR pp. 71-72.

[128] *Dia. on Tyndale,* p. 18. The *Image of Love* is probably a product of More's imagination. It is not listed in the Pollard-Redgrave *Short Title Catalogue of Books Printed in England, 1475-1640.*

the body ... : of the spiritual worship of God they were utterly ignorant.... God is a Spirit, making spiritual ... and they that worship him must worship him in spirit.... They who do well are acceptable and well-pleasing to God, without external signs and sacraments in the body.... By doers are not meant those who are such in the flesh, in mere bodily worship and outward observance.[129]

In considering such ideas, More is cautious not to brand the Messenger's *Image of Love* as heretical. But he asserts that its author has been "so spiritual" as to "destroy all such devotion, as ever hath hitherto showed itself":

Surely, quod I, that book have I seen, whereof who was the maker I know not, but the man might peradventure mean well and run up so high in his contemplation spiritual, that while he thought he sat in God Almighty's bosom upon high in heaven, he condemned and set at naught all earthly things, and all temporal service done to God here ... among poor silly men in earth.... For a right good man may hap at a time, in a fervent indiscreet, to say something and write it too, which when he considereth after more advisedly, he would be very fain to change.[130]

When we consider that More bitterly denounced Tyndale and Frith for arguing "that sacraments be nothing worth," we cannot help but speculate that the fictitious *Image of Love* might have been More's gentle and cautious way of replying to those of Colet's views which had persisted after the Dean's death in 1519.[131] It seems almost more than coincidence that, in concocting his imaginary title, More should have hit on two words, "image" and "love," which played such prominent roles in Colet's thinking. Such speculation is also

---

129 ExR pp. 59-76.

130 *Dia. on Tyndale*, p. 16.

131 For More's attack on the Tyndale-Frith sacrament position, see the Duke microfilm of *Reply to Frith* and *Supplication of Souls*.

prodded by the fact that Colet was obviously in More's mind during the writing of the *Tyndale* piece. This fact is demonstrated by Sir Thomas's reverent recollection of the Dean's *Convocation Sermon*:

> Undoubtedly if the clergy be nought we [laymen] must needs be worse, as I heard once master Colet the good Dean of Paul's preach. For he said that it can be none other, but that we must ever be one degree under them. . . . For surely, as he said, our Savior saith . . . that they [the clergy] be the . . . light of the world. And if the light, saith [Colet], be darked, how dark will then the darkness be [of] all the world beside?[132]

Pauline and Platonic Sources for Colet's "Spiritual Religion"

In any event, we find in Colet's doctrine of spiritual worship the decided influence of New Testament teaching as he conceived it. "The Old Testament," he says, "had regard chiefly to the body; the New to the mind and spirit. In the New, the great object is the soul."[133] Especially was Colet swayed by Paul's apparent contempt for "outward circumcision" (Rom. 2:28-29) and for "th[ose] that glory in appearance, not in the heart" (2 Cor. 5:12). A corollary factor was undoubtedly the outburst against ritual and outward observance in Hebrews 10:1-4—"The law . . . can never, by the same sacrifices which are continually offered year after year, make perfect those who draw near. . . . It is impossible that the blood of bulls and goats should take away sins."

This attitude had earlier been voiced almost verbatim in such Platonic passages as 2 *Alcibiades* 149-150, where sacrificial "altar bulls with gilded horns" are scorned as "unworthy

---

132 *Dia. on Tyndale*, p. 217.

133 ExR p. 111.

service" because "it is inconceivable that the Gods have regard, not to the justice and purity of our souls, but to costly . . . sacrifices, which men may celebrate year after year." It is difficult to believe that Colet was not influenced by this Platonic temperament. Indeed, we have already noted the Dean's frequent agreement with Plato's contempt for the body and for all earthly things external to the soul. Considering the prominence of the *Symposium* in Ficino's thought, it is also quite likely that Colet's intermittently expressed scorn of bodily worship was influenced by Plato's contention that beautiful souls rather than beautiful bodies should be reverenced: "The beauty of the mind is more honorable than the beauty of the outward form. . . . If a virtuous soul have but a little comeliness [we should be] content to love and tend him" (*Symposium* 210).

Florentine Distaste for Priestly and Sacramental Intermediary

The influence of the Florentine Platonists in this regard should certainly not be overlooked. Mirandola's nephew, in writing the young genius's life, related how Pico, "giving no great force to outward observance, cleaved to God in very fervent love." Marriott acutely notes that Pico's attitude was "precisely calculated to appeal to Colet."[134] This is amply indicated by the Dean's own frugal manner of living, as well as by his insistence in the *Convocation Sermon* that priestly candidates who have a "fear of God and love of the heavenly life" are far preferable to those who have a mastery of liturgy.[135] In this connection note also Colet's disdain for vestments (reflected in his own modest apparel): "Remember that the due execution of true religion is not in wearyng the

---

[134] Marriott, p. 80.

[135] Note Lupton, *Life,* pp. 148-150, and CS p. 300.

habyte, but with a clene mynde in very dede to execute the rules . . . of religion. For . . . to weare the habite, and not to execute the rule and order of religion, is rather to be demed ypocrysy or apostasy, than otherwyse."[136]

Mirandola's dislike for external worship and priestly or sacramental intermediaries is echoed by Ficino's *De Christiana Religione* 21: "Because God has joined himself unto man without intermediary, it behooves us to remember that our felicity consists in being turned to Him, so that without intermediary we may cleave to God." Against this background, it becomes obvious that Colet's intermittently negative position on sacraments, while retaining the Dionysian symbols-terminology,[137] is undergirded chiefly by Paul and Plato, partly through the mediation of the Florentines. It is such evidence as has been cited that lends some validity to Jones's undocumented contention that Colet was a "spiritual reformer" who advocated "spiritual religion" inspired in part by "the Platonic influence which came to England through the Humanists . . . [and] Ficino."[138]

Colet versus More on Holy Orders

The cleavage between More's Church-orientated religion and the "spiritual religion" of Colet's Pauline commentaries is most noticeable in the areas of mystical union and priesthood. In those mystical passages which fall outside the Dionysian trilogy, Colet makes little or no mention of sacramental intermediary; whereas More's only major mystical discussion features a union achieved through the Eucharist.[139]

---

136 RFM p. 307.

137 E.g., ExR p. 117—"Bodily ceremonies are symbols of the spirit."

138 See Rufus Jones, *Spiritual Reformers in the 16th and 17th Centuries*, pp. xi ff., 235.

139 See More's *Treatise on the Holy Eucharist*, pp. 31-35.

Again, More argued that "a priest, be he never so bad, in . . . his naughtiness cannot take from us the profit of his mass."[140] To the Colet of the Oxford lectures such a statement was a contradiction in terms. Carrying his doctrine of "inner sacraments" to its logical but radical extreme, Colet contended that one takes Holy Orders internally, not externally. Thus outer ordination means nothing unless ordination already exists in the heart. There can be no priest who is "bad," because if he is bad, he is not a priest. Conversely, the good man is a priest already, even without external ordination: "A layman, if he has done the work of a priest, is accounted a priest; and a priest, if he follow a layman's footsteps, is not more than a layman. He is not a priest which is one outwardly, but he which is one inwardly, in the Spirit."[141]

Colet's Anticipation of Luther's "Priesthood of All Believers"

This anticipation of Luther's "priesthood of all believers" is paradoxically most prominent in the predominately pro-Catholic *Sacraments* treatise, where priesthood is said to involve sacrifice and "marriage." Each man who is in the church "may offer himself as a . . . sacrifice to God."[142] Most important of all, priesthood involves marriage. True marriage is nothing other than union with the Spirit: "Between God and the church is the true marriage and the most fruitful union of the feminine man with the masculine God."[143] "No marriage is necessary in the church of Christ other than priesthood. Marriage and priesthood are the same."[144] It follows that

---

[140] *Dia. on Tyndale,* p. 218.

[141] ExR p. 89.

[142] *Sac.* p. 26.

[143] *Ibid.,* p. 26.

[144] *Ibid.,* p. 34, cf. 30.

"God's desire is that the entire world might be nothing but a priesthood. . . . The whole church may function as one priesthood."[145]

Colet's Changing Views on Earthly Marriage

As this implies, Colet in his early period of writing (1496-99) took a very dim view of earthly marriage, which he regarded in Platonic language as "the fleeting and empty shadow" of the ideal mystical marriage between man and Christ.[146] He maintained that no one ought to marry. If men would remain single and propagation were to cease, he argued, the result would not be tragedy but the arrival of God's kingdom on earth.[147] Yet he conceded that marriage is "a remedy for necessary evil," because it keeps men from "wantoning among many women."[148]

In the *Right Fruitful Monition*, however, written perhaps a decade after the Corinthians commentary (i.e., around 1505-10), Colet's views seem to have softened: "If thou intende to marye, or beynge maryed and haste a good wyfe, thanke our Lord therefore, for she is of his sendynge."[149] At any rate, when in 1509 Colet came to appoint a high master and governors for his St. Paul's School, he selected married

---

[145] *Ibid.*, pp. 5, 29. Colet's priesthood of all believers might very well have been inspired in part by certain passages in Ficino's *Epistolae*. Thus Colet at one point in his marginalia paraphrases Ficino as follows: "Thus the perfect priesthood, which is wisdom itself, consists in philosophy, in the desire for wisdom, in prayer, hope, and love. . . . They are truly ministers of Christ who are possessed of a unique wisdom, but try to share it with others."—See Jayne, *Colet and Ficino*, p. 350.

[146] *Sac.*, p. 6.

[147] LC pp. 91-92.

[148] *Ibid.*, p. 91.

[149] RFM p. 308.

men, alleging that "while there was nothing certain in human affairs, he yet found the least corruption in these."[150]

There is no indication that Colet, no matter how long he lived, would ever have approved anything but celibacy for the professional clergy. Yet there can be no question that he modified his earlier harsh attitude toward marriage among ordinary folk. This modification probably resulted from his increased preoccupation with practical church and school problems. Nonetheless, it is interesting to speculate how much influence the bachelor Ficino exerted on the change in his fellow-bachelor.

In one section of his *Epistolae,* Ficino had taken the Platonic view on marriage, that it is "in accord with nature," since it makes possible the perpetuation of the race. On this passage, Colet made detailed annotations, to wit: "Ficino approves of marriage . . . . Socrates [learned moral discipline] from his wife. Marriage does not prevent scholarship. . . . Man is extremely gregarious." To this latter note, Colet added a final grudging personal comment: "To this extent I agree, to this extent the laws agree. No one lives outside of society unless he is above humanity or below it."[151] It is altogether possible that Ficino's position forced upon Colet a careful re-examination of Paul and Plato, both of whom seem to have approved moderate sex in wedlock.[152] The result could only have been the kinder attitude toward marriage expressed in the *Right Fruitful Monition.*

Summary

We can now fully appreciate, perhaps, that any objective effort to place Colet in the English Reformation is severely ham-

---

150 Lupton, *Life,* p. 263, cf. pp. 75, 77, 135; and LC p. xxvii ff.

151 See Jayne, *Colet and Ficino,* pp. 162-3, 347.

152 See Scott, *St. Paul,* p. 134; and D'Arcy, *Mind and Heart of Love,* p. 196.

pered not only by partisan bias, Colet's semantic carelessness, and his distaste for publication—but also by an uncertainty as to the precise order of composition of his works, and especially by the deep contradictions which permeate his writings. These contradictions can now be presented in tabular form:

CATHOLIC VIEWS IN COLET	PROTESTANT VIEWS IN COLET
Reformation as an ordering of disorder	apparent sympathy for image-condemners
loyalty to Papacy	distaste for relics and pilgrimages
denunciation of immorality and abuses	lack of important Catholic vocabulary
English translations of prayers	Scripture exalted over Church

Tried for heresy but acquitted

original sin as corruption but not obliteration of man's will	virtual ignoring of purgatory and prayers to saints
stress on justification as God's sanctifying	sympathy wth Wycliffe and Hussites (?)
stress on works (esp. prayer) preparatory to justification, and on later works to maintain and strengthen infused grace	appreciated by Lollards and later Protestant reformers
	"unity of truth" method of Scriptural exegesis
baptism and other sacraments as instrumental causes of sanctification (in Dionysian trilogy)	deemphasis on external worship, ritual, and on priests and sacraments as intermediaries (in Pauline commentaries)
clerical celibacy	priesthood of all believers

Anglican doctrine of Eucharist
as Christ's spiritual real presence (?)

On the basis of this diagram, it is possible to draw certain conclusions. First, Colet's thought obviously does not fall wholly within either the Catholic or Protestant tradition.[153] Indeed, the accumulated evidence of this chapter surely establishes beyond all reasonable doubt that Dean Colet is best interpreted as a transition figure—though to say this is by no means to imply that he was a transition from something worse to something better. Second, if Colet had lived until the doctrinal reformation of 1534-1558, there most certainly would have existed a conflict in his mind as to which side he should join. Third, under such circumstances he would almost surely have been in difficulty with the Catholic authorities on some of his attitudes, unless he recanted them.

The undeniable Protestant segment in Colet's thought is especially noticeable when contrasted with the career or beliefs of the official lay spokesman, Sir Thomas More: Colet was tried for heresy, while More as a writer and Chancellor denounced and campaigned against heretics. Colet rarely used the term "heretic," and then only to refer to a falling away from the infused wisdom of loving faith, or to clerical corruption; while More used the term with almost obsessive repetition in the narrowest doctrinal sense. In Colet there is almost no mention of purgatory, while More specializes in long and gruesome descriptions thereof.

Especially significant is the fact that More frequently excoriated noted Protestant Reformers for holding views which turn out on investigation to be similar to or identical with views expressed in at least some of Colet's works. Thus Colet

---

[153] This conclusion represents a considerable modification of my earlier findings in "Protestant Colet and Catholic More," *ATR*, 33 (Jan. 51), 29-43.

prefers "love" for "charity," but More denounced Tyndale
for this very substitution. Colet expressed distaste for relic-
adoration and praying to Saints, yet More bitterly condemned
Luther for this very attitude. Colet (in the Pauline commentaries) denied the efficacy of sacraments, while More attacked
both Tyndale and Frith for doing likewise. Colet in the main
refused to quote Church authorities in Scriptural investigation, while More criticized Tyndale for similar independent
inquiry. Colet advocated a single meaning for any given Biblical passage, while More advocated the Four Senses approach
and condemned Origen for interpreting Scripture in a manner
similar to Colet's.

Relation of Platonic Tradition to Protestant Deviation

Colet's modified affection for pagan philosophy undoubtedly
produced some of these Protestant deviations. Ficino's identification of Christian charity with Platonic love almost surely
was the main factor in Colet's own Protestant preference for
the term "love" in discussing redemption. The Dean's spirit
of free enquiry was very probably inspired in part by Plato's
experimental approach in the *Dialogues*. Colet's Neoplatonic association of unity with truth definitely undergirded his
repudiation of the conventional Catholic Four Senses—a
repudiation in which he had been anticipated by Mirandola.
Plato's contempt for the body and outward observance as
mere "shadows", and his exaltation of inner as against outer
beauty in the *Symposum* (views also reflected in St. Paul
and the Florentines) must also have influenced Colet's sus-
picion of priestly vestments and sacramental ordination, his
consequent Lutheran assertion of a priesthood of all internally
sanctified men, and indeed his whole doctrine of "spiritual
worship" as espoused in the Pauline commentaries. Moreover, we must remember that a fictitious counterpart of this

"spiritual religion" is adversely criticized by the Catholic More in his *Dialogue on Tyndale.*

Frequent Compatibility of Platonic Tradition and Catholic Dogma

However, having said all this, it would be wise to sound one warning. The fact that certain of Colet's apparently Protestant views were influenced by the Platonic Tradition does not in any sense mean that pagan philosophy is at all points antagonistic to Catholic dogma. On the contrary, we have already noted the Platonic factors in Colet's insistence on limited free will, his emphasis on prayer as the chief method of achieving "justice," and his position (at least in his early writings) that earthly marriage between man and wife is merely a shadow of the ideal marriage between man and Christ.

All of these Platonically-tinged views are perfectly compatible with and indeed even essential ingredients of the Catholic faith. Moreover, Colet's application of the Dionysian "sacraments as symbols" concept is in the main compatible with Catholic dogma, because Colet's use of it usually involves the corollary Dionysian view that the symbol is always accompanied by its corresponding higher reality. It is true that in the Pauline commentaries the reverse (Protestant) position is taken, namely, that the symbol can exist without the corresponding inner condition. But within this latter context Colet discusses the problem chiefly in Pauline language, and the Dionysian symbols terminology is no longer prominent.

An excellent example of the frequent affinity of pagan philosophy and Catholic dogma is Thomas More's own justification of external worship on the basis of a favorite doctrine in Florentine Platonism. "Out of all doubt most true is the old said saw," notes Sir Thomas, "that the outward behavior . . . is a plain express mirror or image of the mind."[154] Thus More argues that we can tell the condition of a man's heart from the way he prays and worships.

This is almost the reverse of Colet's position in the Pauline commentaries. Yet More has based his opinion on Ficino's doctrine that beautiful souls mould bodies to their own natures: "The soul itself we do not see, therefore we cannot observe its beauty. But we see in the body a shadow of the soul, and its image, and judging from its image we conclude that there is a beautiful soul in a handsome body."[155] Such a doctrine is scarcely characteristic of Plato's *Symposium,* where Socrates himself is described as having a beautiful personality but ugly exterior. However, the germs of Ficino's Renaissance notion can be found in other dialogues. *Cratylus* 400, for example, cites as the opinion of "some" that "the body is . . . the index of the soul," and *Republic* 3:403 further hints: "The good soul, by her excellence, improves the body as far as this may be possible."

As these quotations suggest, it would seem that the pagan philosophies of the Platonic Tradition can be used to bolster Catholic as well as Protestant views, sometimes on the same issue. This fact will be further demonstrated in the next volume of this series, when we examine the major works of St. Thomas More, the second of our three "Fishers with Platonic Nets."

---

154 Hallett, More's *History of the Passion,* p. 26.

155 *Com. on Symposium,* p. 204, cf. p. 183—"The appearance of a man, . . . because of interior goodness . . . is beautiful to see."

BIBLIOGRAPHY

I. JOHN COLET

Primary Sources

Colet, John. "A Right Fruitfull Monicion concernynge the Order of a Good Christen Mannes Lyfe," in J. H. Lupton, *A Life of John Colet*, Appendix D, pp. 305-310.

_____. "The Sermon of Doctor Colete, Made to the Convocacion at Paulis," in J. H. Lupton, *A Life of John Colet*, Appendix C, pp. 293-304.

Ferguson, Wallace K. "An Unpublished Letter of John Colet, Dean of St. Paul's," *American Historical Review*, 39:696-9.

Lupton, Joseph Hirst (trans.). *An Exposition of St. Paul's [First] Epistle to the Corinthians [Delivered as Lectures in the University of Oxford], by John Colet*. London: George Bell, 1874.

_____. *An Exposition of St. Paul's Epistle to the Romans, Delivered as Lectures in the University of Oxford, 1497, by John Colet*. London: Bell and Daldy, 1873.

_____. *John Colet's Letters to Radulphus on the Mosaic Creation and Other Treatises [i.e., Christ's Mystical Body, the Church; and Exposition of Romans 1-5]* London: Bell, 1876.

Q

_____. *Two Treatises on the Hierarchies of Dionysius, by John Colet.* London: Bell and Daldy, 1869.

_____. (ed.) *A Treatise on the Sacraments of the Church by John Colet.* London: Bell and Daldy, 1867.

O'Kelly, P. Bernard. *John Colet's Enarratio in Primam S. Pauli Epistolam ad Corinthios:* A new Edition of the Text, with Translation, Notes, and Introduction. Harvard Ph.D. Thesis, 1960. Unpublished.

Rowe, John Gordon (trans.). *Colet's Treatise on the Sacraments.* Unpublished. Used by personal permission of the author.

Commentaries

Allen, P.S. "Dean Colet and Archbishop Wareham," *English Historical Review,* 17:303-6.

Battenhouse, Roy. "John Colet and Neo-Platonism." 1935. Unpublished Paper.

Campbell, W. E. "John Colet, Dean of St. Paul's," *Dublin Review,* 218 (April 46), 97-107.

Cassirer, Ernest. *Die Platonische Renaissance in England und die Schule von Cambridge.* Studien der Bibliothek Warburg, No. 24. Leipzig: B. G. Teubner, 1932.

_____. *The Platonic Renaissance in England.* Translated by James Pettegrove. Austin: University of Texas Press, 1953.

"Colet, John." *Dictionary of National Biography,* 11:321-382.

Dannenberg, Friedrich. *Das Erbe Platons in England bis zur Bildung Lylys Stufen Einer Spiegelung.* Berlin, 1932.

Dark, Sidney. *Five Deans.* New York: Harcourt Brace, 1928.

Duhamel, P. Albert. "The Oxford Lectures of John Colet: An Essay in Defining the English Renaissance," *Journal of the History of Ideas,* 14:493-510.

Hunt, Ernest William. *Dean Colet and His Theology.* London: Society for the Promotion of Christian Knowledge, 1956.

Hyma, Albert. "Erasmus and the Oxford Reformers," *Nederlandsch Archief voor Kerkgeschiendenis*, 25 (1932).

Inge, William Ralph. *The Platonic Tradition in English Religious Thought*. London: Longmans Green, 1926.

Jayne, Sears. *John Colet and Marsilio Ficino*. Oxford: Clarendon Press, ca. 1961.

——————. "John Colet and Marsilio Ficino." Paper read at Comparative Literature Section, Modern Language Association Meeting, New York, 1958.

Knight, Samuel. *The Life of Dr. John Colet*. Oxford: Clarendon Press, 1823.

Lupton, Joseph. *A Life of John Colet*. London: Bell, 1887.

MacKenzie, Kathleen C. "John Colet of Oxford," *Dalhousie Review*, 21:15-28.

Marriott, J. A. R. *The Life of John Colet*. London: Methuen, 1933.

McDonnell, M. F. *The History of St. Paul's School for Boys*. London: Chapman and Hall, 1909.

Miles, Leland. "Colet's School for Boys: Then and Now." 1953. Unpublished Paper.

——————. "Some Comments on Sears Jayne's Discovery of Colet-Ficino Correspondence." Read at Comparative Literature Section, Modern Language Association Meeting, New York, 1958.

——————. "Protestant Colet and Catholic More: A Study of Contrast in the Use of Platonism," *Anglican Theological Review*, 33 (Jan 51), 29-43.

——————. "[Review of] Ernest William Hunt's *Dean Colet and His Theology*," *Renaissance News*, 11 (Summer 58), 133-138.

Parsons, D. J. "John Colet's Stature as an Exegete," *Anglican Theological Review*, 40 (1958), 36-42.

Rice, Eugene F., Jr. "John Colet and the Annihilation of the Natural," *Harvard Theological Review*, 45:141-163.

Schröder, Kurt. *Platonismus in der Englischen Renaissance.* In *Palaestra* 83. Berlin: Mayer and Muller, 1920.

Seebohm, Frederic. *The Oxford Reformers.* 3rd Edition. London: Longmans Green, 1887.

Surtz, Edward L. "The Oxford Reformers and Scholasticism," *Studies in Philology,* 57:547-556.

II. ST. PAUL

Primary Sources

Aurelius, Marcus. *Meditations.* Edited by Charles Eliot. Harvard Classics, Vol. 2. New York: Collier, 1909. Pp. 193-306.

The Holy Bible. Authorized King James Version. Cleveland: World, (?).

The Holy Bible. Revised Standard Version. New York: Nelson, 1952.

Commentaries

Burton, Ernest de Witt. *Spirit, Soul, and Flesh.* Chicago: University of Chicago Press, 1918.

Buttrick, George A., and others. *The Interpreter's Bible.* New York: Abingdon-Cokesbury Press, 1951-6. Vols. 9, 10, 11.

Colewell, Ernest, and Eric Titus. *The Gospel of the Spirit.* New York: Harpers, 1953.

Cullman, Oscar. *Christ and Time.* Trans. by Floyd V. Filson. London: SCM Press, 1956.

D'Arcy, M. C. *The Mind and Heart of Love.* New York: Holt, 1947.

Dodd, C. H. *The Epistle of Paul to the Romans.* London: Hodder and Stoughton, 1932.

Frank, Tenny. *A History of Rome.* New York: Holt, 1923.

Griffith, G. O. *St. Paul's Gospel to the Romans.* Oxford: Basil Blackwell, 1949.

Hardman, Oscar. *The Christian Doctrine of Grace.* New York: Macmillan, 1947.

Hoyland, John S. *The Great Forerunners: Studies in the Interrelation of Platonism and Christianity.* New York: Smith, 1930.

Knox, Wilfred. *St. Paul.* New York: Appleton, 1932.

Moffatt, James. *Paul and Paulinism.* Boston: The Pilgrim Press, 1910.

Prat, Fernand. *The Theology of St. Paul.* Trans. by John L. Stoddard from 11th French Edition. London: Burns, Oates, & Washbourne, 1926. 2 vols.

Robinson, John A. T. *The Body: A Study in Pauline Theology.* Studies in Biblical Theology, No. 5. Chicago: Regnery, 1952.

Scott, Charles Anderson. *St. Paul, the Man and the Teacher.* Cambridge: Cambridge University Press, 1936.

Seltman, Charles. *Women in Antiquity.* New York: St. Martin's Press, 1957.

Stewart, James. *A Man in Christ—the Vital Elements of St. Paul's Religion.* New York: Harpers, 1935.

III. PLATO

Primary Sources

Fowler, Harold North (ed.). *Plato with an English Translation.* New York: Putnam, 1926.

Jowett, Benjamin (trans.). *The Dialogues of Plato.* New York: Random, 1937. 2 vols.

——————. *The Republic of Plato.* Oxford: Clarendon Press, 1908. 2 vols.

Commentaries

Beck, Maximilian. "Plato's Problem in the *Parmenides.*" *JHI,* 7: 232-36.

Cornford, Francis. *Plato and Parmenides.* New York: Humanities Press, 1951.

——————. *Plato's Cosmology. The Timaeus of Plato Translated with a Running Commentary.* New York: Harcourt Brace, 1937.

Demos, Raphael. *The Philosophy of Plato.* Chicago: Scribners, 1939.

Edelstein, Ludwig. "The Function of the Myth in Plato's Philosophy," *JHI,* 10:463 ff.

Freeman, Eugene, and David Appel. *The Wisdom and Ideas of Plato.* New York: Fawcett Publications, 1956.

Koyre, Alexandre. *Discovering Plato.* Trans. by Leonora Rosenfeld. New York: Columbia University Press, 1945.

Merlan, Philip. "Form and Content in Plato's Philosophy," *JHI,* 8:406-430.

More, Paul Elmer. *The Religion of Plato.* Princeton: Princeton University Press, 1921.

Shorey, Paul. *Plato, Ancient and Modern.* Berkeley: University of California Press, 1938.

——————. "The Unity of Plato's Thought," *Decennial Publications of the University of Chicago,* First Series (Chicago, 1903), 6:129-214.

——————. *What Plato Said.* Chicago: University of Chicago Press, 1933.

Solmsen, Friedrich. *Plato's Theology.* Cornell Studies in Classical Philology, Vol. 27. Ithaca: Cornell University Press, 1942.

Taylor, Alfred. *Platonism and Its Influence.* New York: Longmans Green, 1924.

——————. *Plato: The Man and His Work.* London: Methuen, 1929.

Whitchurch, Irl. G. *Philosophical Bases of Asceticism in Platonic Writings.* Cornell Studies in Philosophy. New York: Longmans Green, 1923.

IV. NEOPLATONISM: PAGAN AND CHRISTIAN

Primary Sources

Dionysius the Areopagite. *The Mystical Theology and The Celestial Hierarchies.* Translated by Editors of the Shrine of Wisdom. Godalming, England: 1949.

Edman, Irwin (ed.). Boethius's *The Consolation of Philosophy*. Modern Library. New York: Random, 1943.

Dods, Marcus (trans.). *The City of God by Saint Augustine*. New York: Hafner, 1948. 2 vols.

á Kempis, Thomas (?). *The Imitation of Christ*. Edited by Irwin Edman. Modern Library. New York: Random, 1943.

Mackenna, Stephen. *The Enneads of Plotinus*. 2nd Edition Revision by B. D. Page. New York: Pantheon Books, 1957.

Oates, Whitney J. (ed.). *Basic Writings of Saint Augustine*. New York: Random, 1948. 2 vols.

Parker, John. *The Works of Dionysius the Areopagite*. London, 1897-99.

Commentaries

Ault, Warren. *Europe in the Middle Ages*. Boston: Heath, 1932.

Battenhouse, Roy (ed.). *Companion to the Study of St. Augustine*. New York: Oxford University Press, 1955.

Bett, Henry. "The Influence of Nicholas of Cusa upon Later Thinkers," *London Quarterly Review*, 154:51-63.

——————. *Nicholas of Cusa*. London: Methuen, 1932.

Bigg, Charles. *Neoplatonism*. London: Society for Promoting Christian Knowledge, 1895.

Butler, Cuthbert. *Western Mysticism: The Teachings of Saints Augustine, Gregory, and Bernard*. 2nd Edition. London: Constable, 1927.

Clark, James. *Meister Eckhart*. New York: Nelson, 1957.

Danielou, Jean. *Origen*. Translated by Walter Mitchell. New York: Sheed & Ward, 1955.

DeWulf, Maurice. *History of Medieval Philosophy*. Translated by Ernest Messenger. London: Longmans Green, 1926.

Gilson, Etienne. *The Christian Philosophy of St. Thomas Aquinas*. New York: Random, 1956.

_____. *History of Christian Philosophy in the Middle Ages*. New York: Sheed and Ward, 1956.

Grabowski, Stanislaus. *The Church: An Introduction to the Theology of St. Augustine*. St. Louis: Herder, 1957.

Henle, R. J. *Saint Thomas and Platonism. A Study of the Plato and Platonici Texts in the Writings of Saint Thomas*. The Hague: Martinus Nijhoff, 1956.

Horst, Carl. *Vorstudien zu Einer Neuuntersuchung von Plotins Aesthetik*. Marburg, 1905.

Hughes, Philip. *A History of the Church*. New York: Sheed and Ward, 1947. 5 vols.

Hyma, Albert. *The Christian Renaissance: A History of the Devotio Moderna*. Grand Rapids: The Reformed Press, 1924.

Inge, William R. *Christian Mysticism*. London: Burns, Oates, and Washburne, 1935.

_____. "Origen." *Proceedings of the British Academy*. London: Oxford University Press, 1946. Vol. 32, pp. 123-145.

_____. *The Philosophy of Plotinus*. London: Longmans Green, 1918. 2 vols.

Jones, Rufus M. *The Flowering of Mysticism and the Friends of God in the Fourteenth Century*. New York: Macmillan, 1939.

Klibansky, Raymond. *The Continuity of the Platonic Tradition during the Middle Ages*. London, 1939.

Merlan, Philip. *From Platonism to Neoplatonism*. The Hague: Martinis Nijhoff, 1953.

Miles, Leland. "Plotinus and St. Augustine: A Study in the Beginnings of Neoplatonic Christianity," *Hanover Forum* 4 (Spring 58), 67-95.

Patch, Howard. *The Tradition of Boethius. A Study of His Importance in Medieval Culture*. New York: Oxford University Press, 1935.

Underhill, Evelyn. *Mysticism*. New York: Dutton, 1930.

Whittaker, Thomas. *Macrobius: or, Philosophy, Science, and Letters of the Year 400.* Cambridge: Cambridge University Press, 1923.

_____. *The Neo-Platonists.* Cambridge: Cambridge University Press, 1928.

Wichgraf, Wiltrud. "Suso's Horologium Sapientiae in England nach Mss des 15. Jahrhunderts," *Archiv fur das Studium der Neueren Sprachen.* 91 Jahrgang, 169 Band. Der Neuen Serie, 69 Band (1936), pp. 176-181.

Winkworth, Susanna. *The History and Life of the Reverend Doctor John Tauler, with Twenty-Five of His Sermons.* London: Smith, Elder, 1857.

V. FLORENTINE PLATONISM

Primary Sources

Burroughs, Josephine L. "Translation of Ficino's *Platonic Theology,* *JHI,* 5 (Apr 44), 227-242.

Forbes, Elizabeth (trans.). Pico della Mirandola's "The Dignity of Man" in *The Renaissance Philosophy of Man,* edited by Ernest Cassirer, Paul Kristeller, and J. H. Randall, Jr. (Chicago: University of Chicago Press, 1948), pp. 223-256.

Gardner, Edmund G. (ed.). T. Stanley's Translation of *A Platonic Discourse Upon Love by Pico della Mirandola.* Boston: Merrymount Press, 1914.

Hamm, Victor (trans.). Pico della Mirandola's *Of Being and Unity.* Milwaukee: Marquette University Press, 1943.

Jayne, Sears (trans.). Marsilio Ficino's *Commentary on Plato's Symposium.* Columbia, Mo.: University of Missouri Press, 1944.

Commentaries

Breen, Quirinus. "Melanchthon's Reply to G. Pico della Mirandola," *JHI,* 13:413-26.

_____. "Pico della Mirandola on the Conflict of Philosophy and Rhetoric," *JHI,* 13 (June 52), 384-426.

Cassirer, Ernest. "Ficino's Place in Intellectual History," *JHI,* 6: 483-501.

_____. "Giovannia Pico della Mirandola," *JHI*, 3 (Apr 42), 123-144, 319-346.

Dannenfeldt, Karl H. "The Renaissance and Pre-Classical Civilization," *JHI*, 13:435-449.

Dulles, Avery. *Princeps Concordia: Pico della Mirandola and the Scholastic Tradition.* Cambridge: Harvard University Press, 1940.

Dress, Walter. *Die Mystik des Marsilio Ficino.* Berlin: W. de Gruyter, 1929.

Jayne, Sears. "Ficino and the Platonism of the English Renaissance," *Comparative Literature*, 4:214-238.

Kibre, Pearl. *The Library of Pico della Mirandola.* New York: Columbia University Press, 1936.

Kristeller, Paul O. "Ficino and Pomponazzi on the Place of Man in the Universe, with Excerpts in Translation," *JHI*, 5 (Apr 44), 220-242.

_____. "Florentine Platonism and Its Relations with Humanism and Scholasticism," *Church History*, 8 (1939), 201 ff.

_____. *The Philosophy of Marsilio Ficino.* New York: Columbia University Press, 1944.

Meiners, C. *Lebensbeschreibungen Beruhmter Manner.* Zurich, 1796. Pp. 3-110.

Rigg, J. M. Introduction to Sir Thomas More's Translation of *Giovannia Pico della Mirandola: His Life by His Nephew Giovanni Francesco Pico.* London: David Nutt, 1890.

Robb, Nesca. *Neoplatonism of the Italian Renaissance.* London: Allen and Unwin, 1935.

Wadsworth, James B. "Landino's *Disputations,* Ficino's *De Felicitate* . . . ," *Modern Philology*, 50:23-31.

_____. "Lorenzo de Medici and Marsilio Ficino: An Experiment in Platonic Friendship," *Romanic Review*, 46 (Apr 55), 90-100.

_____. "[Review of] *Marsile Ficin, Commentaire sur le Banquet de Platon,* ed. Raymond Marcel, *Renaissance News*, 10 (Autumn 57), 143-145.

VI. RENAISSANCE AND REFORMATION

Primary Sources

Campbell, W. E. (ed.). William Rastell's 1557 Collected Edition of *The English Works of Sir Thomas More*. New York: Dial Press, 1931. 2 vols.

Clarkson, John F., and others (trans.). *The Church Teaches: Documents of the [Roman] Church in English Translation*. St. Louis: Herder, 1955.

Forstall, Josiah, and Frederic Madden (eds.). *The Holy Bible Made from the Latin Vulgate by John Wycliffe*. Oxford University Press, 1850.

Hallet, Philip E. (ed.). Mary Bassett's English Translation of Thomas More's *History of the Passion*. London: Burns, Oates Washbourne, 1941.

_____. *More's Prayers and a Treatise on the Holy Eucharist*. London: Burns, Oates, Washbourne, 1938.

More, Thomas. *Answer to . . . the Book Named "The Supper of the Lord."* London, 1534. Duke University Microfilm XXI-cxxiv-2659; Durham, N. C.

_____. *Debellacion of Salem and Bizance*. London, 1533. Duke University Microfilm XXI-cxxv-2261; Durham, N. C.

_____. *Letter Impugning the Erroneous Writing of John Frith against the Blessed Sacrament*. London, 1533. Duke University Microfilm XXI-cxxv-2668, Durham, N. C.

_____. *The Supplication of Souls*. London, 1529. Duke Microfilm XXI-cxxv-2670; Durham, N. C.

Taft, A. I. (ed.). *The Apologe of Syr Thomas More, Knyght*. Oxford University Press, 1930.

Tyndale, William. *An Answer to Sir Thomas More's Dialogue*. Edited by Henry Walters. Parker Society. Cambridge University Press, 1850.

Commentaries

Battenhouse, Roy. "The Doctrine of Man in Calvin and in Renaissance Platonism," *JHI*, 9 (1948), 447-471.

——————. *Marlowe's Tamburlaine*. Nashville: Vanderbilt University Press, 1941.

Baumer, Franklin Le Van, "The Conception of Christendom in the Renaissance," *JHI*, 6:131-156.

Baron, Hans. "Toward a More Positive Evaluation of the Fifteenth Century Renaissance," *JHI*, 4:21-48.

Beger, Lina. "Thomas Morus und Plato." *Zeitschrift f.d. Gesamten Staatswissenschaften*, 35 (1879).

Campbell, W. E. *Erasmus, Tyndale, and More*. London: Eyre & Spottiswoode, 1949.

Chambers, Raymond W. *Thomas More*. New York: Harcourt Brace, 1935.

Einstein, Lewis. *The Italian Renaissance in England*. New York: Columbia University Press, 1902.

Frye, Roland. "Symbolic Vision and Christian Faith," *The Emory University Quarterly*, 13 (Dec 57), 207-213.

Gairdner, James. *The English Church in the Sixteenth Century*. History of the English Church Series. London: Macmillan, 1904.

Harrison, J. M. *Platonism in English Poetry of the Sixteenth and Seventeenth Century*. New York: Columbia University Press, 1903.

Jones, Rufus. *Spiritual Reformers of the Sixteenth and Seventeenth Centuries*. London: Macmillan, 1914.

Kristeller, Paul O. "Augustine and the Early Renaissance," *Review of Religion*, 7 (1944), 339-358.

——————. *The Classics and Renaissance Thought*. Cambridge: Harvard University Press, 1955.

——————. "The Philosophy of Man in the Italian Rennaissance," *Italica*, 24:93-112.

——————. "The Place of Classical Humanism in Renaissance Thought," *JHI*, 4:59-63.

——————, and J. H. Randall, Jr. "The Study of the Philosophies of the Renaissance," *JHI*, 2:449-496.

Lewis, C. S. *English Literature in the Sixteenth Century*. London: Oxford University Press, 1954.

Lucas, Henry. *The Renaissance and the Reformation*. New York: Harpers, 1934.

Mazzeo, Joseph A. "Universal Analogy and the Culture of the Renaissance," *JHI*, 15:299.

O'Hagan, Thomas. "The Catholic Church and the Italian Renaissance," *Catholic World*, 108:601-610.

Powicke, Frederick. *The Reformation in England*. London: Oxford University Press, 1941.

Routh, E.M.G. *Sir Thomas More and His Friends*. Oxford University Press, 1933.

Stob, Ralph. *Platonism in English Educators and Theologians . . . of the Sixteenth and Seventeenth Century*. University of Chicago's *Abstracts of Theses*, Humanistic Series, 8 (1929-30), 335-41.

Trinkaus, Charles. "The Problem of Free Will in the Renaissance and Reformation," *JHI*, 10:51.

Wright, Louis B. "The Significance of Religious Writings in the English Renaissance," *JHI*, 1:59-68.

VII. REFERENCE WORKS

Attwater, Donald. *A Catholic Dictionary*. Second Edition, Revised. New York: Macmillan, 1949.

Brunet, Jacques-Charles (ed.). *Manuel du Libraire et de l'Amateur de Livres*. 3rd Edition. Paris: Libraire F. de Nobele, 1820. 4 vols.

Cary, M., and others. *Oxford Classical Dictionary*. Oxford: Clarendon Press, 1949.

Chevalier, Ulyssee (ed.). *Repertoire des Sources Historiques du Moyen Age*. Paris: Libraire Alphonse Picard et Fils, 1907. 2 vols.

Hastings, James, and others (eds.). *A Dictionary of the Bible*. New York: Scribner's, 1910. 4 vols.

_____. *Encyclopedia of Religion and Ethics.* New York: Scribners, 1910.

Herbermann, Charles, and others (eds.). *The Catholic Encyclopedia.* New York: Appleton, 1907 ff.

Jackson, Samuel, and others (eds.). *The New Schaff-Herzog Encyclopedia of Religious Knowledge.* New York: Funk and Wagnalls, 1908-1914.

Pollard, A. W., and G. R. Redgrave (eds.) *A Short-Title Catalogue of Books Printed in England, 1475-1640.* London: Bibliographical Society, 1926.

Societe de Gens de Lettres et de Savants, and M. Michaud (eds.). *Biographie Universelle, Ancienne et Moderne.* Paris: Chez Madame C. Desplaces, 1854.

Strong, James. *The Exhaustive Concordance of the Bible.* New York: Abingdon-Cokesbury Press, 1890.

Vacant, A., E. Mangenot, and E. Amana (eds.). *Dictionnaire de Theologic Catholique.* Paris: Libraire Letouzey et Ane, 1937.

INDEX

ance of heresy in—59, 63, 73-75, 92 n. 14, 95 n. 31, 166-7; his
view of eternity—63; psychological scheme in—83-84; original
sin in—88 ff.; C's insistence on need for grace—91-92; his use
of Neoplatonic God-Sun analogy—101 ff.; fusion of love and
faith in C's Romans commentary—108; says Christian knowledge or sapientia beyond reason—125; purification as prelude
to knowledge in—127-8; C's mystical system diagrammed—
140; why C. ignored as mystic?—140 ff.; his relation to
Devotio Moderna's scorn of scholasticism—142 ff.; C's affinity
to Devotio Moderna's redemptive scheme—144-5 ff.; rel. of
Socratic self-knowledge in *Right Fruitful Monition* to Devotio
Moderna teaching — 146; his affinity to Devotio Moderna
views on marriage and communal society—146; his Church-
Soul doctrine in *Mystical Body*—151 ff.; definition of heresy
in—157; communal brotherhood advocated by—160 ff.; C's
communal brotherhood more Platonic than Biblical—163-4;
semantic carelessness and distaste for publication as barriers to
placing C. in Reformation—172-3; C's recognition of limited
free will—188-9; his changing views on marriage—210-211;
on justification—190 ff.; dichotomy in C's sacraments thinking
—201; speculation on order of C's works—201; speculation
on C's relation to doctrinal Reformation—213.

Devotio Moderna—rel. to Colet—141 ff. (see also specific Dutch
mystics).

Dionysius, the Pseudo—called by Ficino "the supreme Platonist"—
xiii, 28, 97 n. 34; his rel. to Colet's Dionysian trilogy—28; his
relation to Colet's sermon on Wolsey—28; advocates God
beyond being—35; universal love in—80, 91; God-Sun analogy
in—98 ff.; analysis of D's imitative hierarchical system—98 ff.;
purification-illumination-perfection triad in—100; Colet's use
of D's multiple triads—102 ff.; Colet substitutes Christ for
mediating D-hierarchies—105; Colet's intermeshing of D-
triads w. Pauline hope-faith-love—106 ff.; Darkness of Unknowing in—125-6; influence on Colet's emphasis on mystic
love—136.

Eckhart, Meister—Neoplatonic heresy in—16, 58; E's soul-faculties
—83 n. 58; possible rel. to Colet—141.

R

by Colet—92; his hope-faith-love triad meshed by Colet w. Dionysian triplets—106 ff.; P's influence on Colet's notion of freedom—109-110; his rel. to Plato's doctrine that good works follow holiness—111-112; P's rel. to Boethius's and Ficino's blessings in disguise doctrine—113-114; his body-figure as one source of Colet's communal brotherhood—161; interaction between Pauline and Platonic views of soul-body in Colet—167-8; P's influence on Colet's spiritual religion—206; his view of sacraments debated—202 n. 124.

Phaedo—anticipates Paul's language on sensibilia and invisibilia—60; evil body in—67; chain and prison metaphor in—67; used by Augustine to prove immortality—77; its influence on Ficino's concept of philosophic death—126-7.

Phaedrus—prison metaphor in—67; Colet's use of prison metaphor from—75; Augustine's use of prison metaphor from—77; influence on Colet's notion of freedom—109-110.

Philebus—its Limited-Unlimited concept used in Colet's Genesis commentary—40-41, 45; its soul-body/Soul-Body analogy used by Colet—156.

Philo—his Son of God notion confused by Mirandola—13; possible use by Colet in interpreting Mosaic days—32 n. 1; on prison-house bodies—76.

Platonic Tradition, the—defined as the whole corpus of interrelated Platonic philosophies—xii ff.; relation to Protestant deviation—214; relation to Catholic dogma—215. See *Platonism, Neoplatonism, Florentine Platonism.*

Platonism—defined as original Platonism—xii ff.; Kristeller on rel. of Plato to "later Platonists"—xiv; daemons in—11 n. 34, 79; use of Platonic Ideas traced from Plotinus to Ficino—36 ff.; Platonic Ideas as used by Colet—37 ff.; Platonic intractable matter retained by Colet—48; Platonic attitude toward man (soul-body) in Colet—66-67 ff.; soul as Platonic origin of life in Colet—78; reason versus passion-appetite and soul-body conflict in—80-83; P's governing soul applied by Colet

GEORGE ALLEN & UNWIN LTD
London: 40 Museum Street, W.C.1

Auckland: 24 Wyndham Street
Bombay: 15 Graham Road, Ballard Estate, Bombay 1
Buenos Aires: Escritorio 454–459, Florida 165
Calcutta: 17 Chittaranjan Avenue, Calcutta 13
Cape Town: 109 Long Street
Hong Kong: F1/12 Mirador Mansions, Kowloon
Karachi: Karachi Chambers, McLeod Road
Madras: Mohan Mansion, 38c Mount Road, Madras 6
Mexico: Villalongin 32–10, Piso, Mexico 5, D.F.
New Delhi: 13–14 Ajmeri Gate Extension, New Delhi 1
São Paulo: Avenida 9 de Julho 1138-Ap. 51
Singapore: 36c Princep Street, Singapore 7
Sydney, N.S.W.: Bradbury House, 55 York Street
Toronto: 91 Wellington Street West